# 365
# MORE MEDITATIONS
# for TEENS

October 30, 2010

Congratulations Claire Haskin!

On your confirmation Day, we at Maple
Grove Lutheran are excited to welcome
you as a full member of the Church.
May the light of Christ Shine on you
and through you as you walk
with Him daily. "Look up verse" John 8:12.
God's Blessings,          Abound in hope!
                          Pastor Christine Chiles
                          Romans 15.13
      Dave Wall

# 365 MORE MEDITATIONS for TEENS

Sally D. Sharpe, Editor
Brian Coats
Tega Ewefada
Ryan and Ellen Gray
Leanne Ciampa Hadley
Mary Lynn Johnson
Hoon Kim
Danette Matty
Racie Helen Miller
Philip F. Newman
Brent Parker
Devin Penner
Anjelyka Shaw

*Abingdon Press*
*Nashville*

365 MORE MEDITATIONS FOR TEENS

*Copyright © 2009 by Abingdon Press*

All rights reserved.

*This book is printed on acid-free paper.*

**Library of Congress Cataloging-in-Publication Data**

365 more meditations for teens / Sally D. Sharpe, editor ; Brian Coats . . . [et al.].
    p.   cm.
    ISBN 978-1-426-70258-7 (binding: pbk./trade pbk., adhesive perfect : alk. paper)   1. Christian teenagers--Prayers and devotions.   2. Devotional calendars.   I. Sharpe, Sally D., 1964-
II. Coats, Brian.
    BV4850.A144 2009
    242'.63--dc22

                                                                                    2009022818

09 10 11 12 13 14 15 16 17 18—10 9 8 7 6 5 4 3 2 1
MANUFACTURED IN THE UNITED STATES OF AMERICA

# Contents

# Introduction: The Habit of Spending Time with God

If you are like most teens, you have a crowded schedule. Your days are crammed with school, homework, activities or hobbies, and a multitude of technological diversions. When you're not checking e-mail or IMing or texting your friends, you're likely cruising the Internet or scrolling your iPod. Slowing down for some quiet time with God may not be at the top of your list! But the truth is that just a few moments alone with God each day will enrich your life more than anything else you could ever choose to do.

Just think about it: the God of the universe *wants* to spend time with *you*! God wants a relationship with you, and as with any other relationship, the best way to develop a relationship with God is by spending time with God. God wants to talk with you and hear all about your challenges, your concerns, your frustrations, and your hurts. God wants to give you advice and direction and encouragement. And God even wants to celebrate your joys—all the things you're excited about.

Spending time with God is so important that it's virtually impossible to grow spiritually without it. So, how do you begin? First, simply decide to do it. Tell God of your desire and intention, and make a commitment. (You also might ask a friend to join you in this commitment so that you can encourage each other and help hold each other accountable.) Next, make a plan. Set aside a specific time and place where you can spend a few minutes alone with God each day. Some people like to have their quiet time in the morning to jump-start their day; others prefer to have it at bedtime as a way of reviewing their day with God. Choose a time and a place that work for you, and stick with them. As anyone who excels in a particular skill or talent knows, consistency and "practice" are the keys to success.

Once you have made a commitment and you have a plan, you are ready to begin. And that's where this book comes in!

## Introduction

*365 More Meditations for Teens* will help you develop a relationship with God and grow in your faith by guiding you through a simple, daily quiet-time routine. Whether you start in January or June, you will find a short reading for each day of the year, including a Scripture verse, a brief devotion, and one or more questions to prompt personal reflection and, if desired, discussion with other teens (such as a youth group, Sunday school class, Bible study, or online discussion group). As you make your way through the book, you will meet a diverse group of adult and teen writers who have experienced similar challenges, questions, and needs. Although their writing styles and personalities are refreshingly unique, their purpose is one and the same: to offer you encouragement and practical help for understanding God's word and living out your faith in your everyday world.

As you begin the practice of a regular quiet time, remember to give yourself grace, just as God does. There will be times when you will miss a day—or several. Don't get discouraged or throw in the towel! Just start again the next day and keep on going. The more you do it, the easier it will get; and before long you will have developed a habit that you will look forward to and even depend on. Remember, like a faithful and loving friend, God is *always* eager and delighted to spend time with you. So, why not get started now?

*Sally D. Sharpe, Editor*

# About the Writers

**Brian Coats** (DECEMBER) is currently Director of Youth Ministry at First United Methodist Church in Houston, Texas. He has been in youth ministry leadership for fourteen years, serving as a local youth minister, camp and conference director, retreat speaker, and private school chaplain. He also has served as a senior pastor. Before going into ministry he was a sportswriter in the Dallas area. Brian, Nicole, and their daughters, Kiley (5) and Cailyn (1), live in Katy, Texas. They enjoy trips to the pool; walking their golden retriever, Hattie Bear; and traveling to see extended family. Brian has two passions: Texas A&M sports and being a missionary of the gospel of Jesus Christ to young people. He also enjoys waterskiing and snow skiing.

**Tega Ewefada** (OCTOBER) is a sixteen-year-old junior in high school. During her high school career, she has been active in student council, school plays, and the National Honor Society. She has a heart for children and aspires to become a pediatric nurse. Tega dreams of traveling the world and living out God's plan for her life.

**Ryan and Ellen Gray** (FEBRUARY) are a husband-wife team who have been married for three years and currently serve at North Point Ministries, Inc. in Alpharetta, Georgia. Ryan is Multicampus Creative Director for Middle School Ministries, and Ellen is Assistant to the Executive Director of Multisite Ministries. Previously, Ryan has been on the staff of Young Life in Chattanooga, Tennessee, and has served as a high school youth director. Ellen also has been a high school youth director, as well as an administrative assistant at Buckhead Church. In his free time, Ryan enjoys fly-fishing and movies. Ellen enjoys spending time with her group of high school girls, being outside (especially when mountains are involved), hiking, biking, running, or simply reading at a park. Both love traveling and just hanging out together.

**Leanne Ciampa Hadley** (APRIL) is the president and founder of the First Steps Spirituality Center, which is dedicated to providing spiritual care to hurting children and workshops for adults who are interested in the spirituality of children and teens. Leanne also serves as an associate pastor at First United Methodist Church, Colorado Springs, where she oversees and directs the children's ministries. In addition to working at the church and center, Leanne travels nationally and internationally, leading retreats, workshops, and training events centered around the spirituality of children and teens. Leanne is the author of *Friends and Followers of the Bible I and II* and *A Walk with God for Women*; a contributing author to *365 Meditations for Mothers with Young Children, 365 Meditations for Mothers,* and *The Children's Worker's Encyclopedia of the Bible*; and the creator of two videos: *Praying with Children* and *Creative Children's Sermons.*

**Mary Lynn Johnson** (MAY), a sixteen-year-old home-schooled high school student, lives in Signal Mountain, Tennessee. At her church, she co-leads a Bible study for middle school girls. As an attorney and witness in mock trials, Mary Lynn has competed locally and at state and national competitions, placing third in the nation. She also is a member of the National Home School Honor Society. Mary Lynn is an avid volunteer, has been a student writer for a local newspaper, and has taught violin. She enjoys photography and spending time with friends at coffee shops.

**Hoon Kim** (SEPTEMBER) has served in youth ministry for thirteen years and is currently the pastor of New Covenant Church in Little Neck, New York. He is the author of *Creative Bible Lessons in Genesis* and has written for *Youthworker Journal, Journal of Student Ministries,* and other publications. He enjoys writing and speaking, fly-fishing, reading, and drinking coffee. He would also love to plant a new church if God calls him that way. Most of all, he is passionate about God; his wife, Shelly; and his two sons, Sean and Liam.

**Danette Matty** (MARCH) has been a volunteer youth leader since big hair was in. She is a wife and the mother of two teenagers who contributed four of these meditations. She is a freelance writer and speaker, contributing articles, curricula, advice, and tool reviews for numerous youth ministry magazines and Web resources. Danette is also on Group Publishing's national training team. She lives and laughs with her family in Minnesota.

**Racie Helen Miller** (AUGUST) is a seventeen-year-old junior who has been home-schooled all her life. She lives in Signal Mountain, Tennessee, with her parents and four brothers. She enjoys hiking, bicycling, walking, reading, and writing. She also enjoys co-leading a Bible study for a group of middle school girls at her church. Racie Helen loves the Lord and studying the word of God.

**Philip F. Newman** (JANUARY) is a writer, editor, and public relations specialist who runs a little one-man company called NewManifest Communications. When he's not clicking away on his laptop, Phil loves playing and coaching soccer, hiking in the Rockies or the Smokies, playing piano, and spending time with his awesome family. He and his wife, Robin, and their three children—a teenage daughter and two preteen sons—make their home in Franklin, Tennessee.

**Brent Parker** (JUNE) has served as a local youth minister, a camp and conference director, and a retreat leader. He now accompanies congregations in prayerfully discerning ministry plans for their young people through This Way Ministries (www.thiswayministries.org). Brent, his wife, Kori, and their sons, Caedmon and Kai, live in The Woodlands, Texas, and enjoy spending days together at the park, the pool, and anywhere they can find a ball field or court.

**Devin Penner** (JULY) is a writer and speaker who lives in Fairview, Tennessee. He is currently a junior in high school. Soon he will be attending college, where he plans to major in dramatic writing so that one day he may please moviegoers with outstanding scripts.

**Anjelyka Shaw** (NOVEMBER) is thirteen years old and in the eighth grade. She lives in Dumfries, Virginia, with her parents and older brother. Besides writing, Anjelyka likes drama and community service activities. Anjelyka has loved Jesus from an early age and desires to share that love with other teens.

# JANUARY

# New Days, New Ways

## PHILIP F. NEWMAN

JANUARY 1                                A FRESH START

*"Forget the former things; do not dwell on the past. See, I am doing a new thing! Now it springs up; do you not perceive it?"*
*(Isaiah 43:18-19a)*

Happy New Year! January means a fresh start; a chance to begin anew; a do-over if we need one. Sure, it's true that every day is different from the one before. We serve a loving, forgiving, faithful God whose mercies are "new every morning," as the prophet Jeremiah put it in the Old Testament (Lamentations 3:23).

Still, the beginning of the year carries a special sense of unspoiled promise. It can feel like an exciting opportunity to hit the "refresh" button as we navigate from the year that was—the great, the good, and the not so good—and enter an unexplored page in front of us.

Each day this month, we'll explore a different aspect of the *new days* ahead with some ideas for *new ways* to go deeper with God and to view ourselves, our schools, our relationships, and the culture around us. Are you ready for a fantastic year?

**What "new thing" do you sense God leading you to in the coming year?**

**What "former things" from last year are you glad to put behind you?**

JANUARY 2                    D—DEVOTIONAL BEGINNINGS

*Train yourself to be godly. (1 Timothy 4:7b)*

Hope you had a fun New Year's Day!

For the next seven days we'll spell out the acronym "Daily QT" as we focus on getting to know God better and growing stronger in our faith. "QT" is short for "quiet time," a one-on-one meeting with God—preferably in a quiet, private place—that can last anywhere from a few minutes to a half hour or more. The QT is reserved for reading the Bible, thinking about what God is saying through the word and how it applies to your life, listening for God's voice, and praying for others.

Having a regular devotional time like a QT does require discipline, but it shouldn't feel like drudgery. Think of your best friend; you don't force yourself to be with him or her, right? You can't wait to see your friend. That's a good way to approach time with God, too. God is, after all, the best friend you'll ever have. God is also gracious, meaning that if you miss a day, God will still be excited and eager when you meet together the next day.

**What do you think are some of the benefits of meeting daily with God?**

**What are some of the distractions that make setting aside a quiet time difficult, and how could you overcome them?**

JANUARY 3                              A—ATTITUDE CHECK

*Do nothing out of selfish ambition or vain conceit, but in humility consider others better than yourselves. Each of you should look not only to your own interests, but also to the interests of others. Your attitude should be the same as that of Christ Jesus. (Philippians 2:3-5)*

Philippians—the book sandwiched between Ephesians and Colossians in the New Testament—contains a power-packed message from Paul, the apostle who experienced a 180-degree life change when Jesus met him on the road to Damascus.

As you let today's verses soak in, think about the attitude that Paul is describing here: humility rather than vanity; other-centeredness rather than self-centeredness; a servant's heart rather than a selfish heart.

Now, think about your own life in light of how Paul describes Jesus and the attitude that led Jesus to the cross. Jesus could have proclaimed himself king and ruled by force, but instead he suffered and died, not only to rescue us but also to transform our attitudes as we walk with him.

*Spend a few minutes asking God to reveal any areas where your attitude might be more selfish than humble and write down what comes to mind.*

*What difference does it make to remember that Jesus, who lives within every Christian by the Holy Spirit, helps us walk in greater humility when we ask?*

## JANUARY 4                                            I—INQUIRE WITHIN

*"Ask and it will be given to you; seek and you will find; knock and the door will be opened to you." (Matthew 7:7)*

One of the keys to success in any area of life—school, friendships, career, family, and more—is the ability to ask good questions (and to listen carefully for answers; more about that tomorrow). Having an inquiring mind can be especially helpful in our spiritual growth and quiet times with God.

God loves it when we ask questions! Questions like: *What would you like to show me through the Bible today as I read? What's your purpose for the hard time I'm going through right now? How can I know you and feel your presence more than I have before? Will you give me strength and energy for tomorrow's midterm exam?*

Whatever is on your heart today, take a few minutes to pray or journal your questions to God—and trust that God will speak to you with wisdom and direction as you stay open to hear God's voice.

*What question(s) would you like to ask God today?*

*Can you think of a time when you asked a big question of God and the answer came in a way that surprised or amazed you?*

## JANUARY 5        L—THE LOST ART OF LISTENING

*"Everyone who listens to the Father and learns from him comes to me [Jesus]." (John 6:45b)*

*I will listen to what God the LORD will say; he promises peace to his people, his saints—but let them not return to folly.*
*(Psalm 85:8)*

Does it ever seem to you that our world has a lot more talkers than listeners? How often do we find ourselves in a conversation and while the other person is talking, we're thinking about the next thing we are going to say? (If you've done this, join the club; so have I and just about everyone else!)

Good friends are good listeners, and those who learn new things quickly and successfully are almost always good listeners.

In your times with God, listening is just as important as expressing your thoughts, feelings, and questions. It might feel strange or unnatural at first, but the more you sit quietly in God's presence, listening to God's voice, the more attuned your spiritual ears will become to receive the insights, inspiration, encouragement, and truth that God wants to pour into your life.

*What qualities do you think make a good listener?*

*Why do you think it's important to become a really good listener when it comes to your relationship with God?*

## JANUARY 6        Y—YIELD TO THE LORD'S LEADING

*"Father, if you are willing, take this cup from me; yet not my will, but yours be done." (Luke 22:42)*

If you've driven a car—or even just paid attention while riding in one—you're aware of how important *yielding* is on the roads. When your eyes see the red-and-white, upside-down triangle with the word *yield* in the center, they signal your brain to slow down, let other vehicles go first, and make sure the way is clear before you proceed. Failure to yield can lead to a smashed-up car or much worse.

In your life as a follower of Jesus, yielding is critically important. To yield is to give up control, to slow down and look for God's leading, to resist the urge to do whatever you feel like doing at the moment. Yielding means saying, as Jesus said to his Father, "Not my will, but yours be done."

As you yield to God, you'll discover a great truth: God will lead you into much better places than you could ever take yourself!

*If you were to let God take the lead in every area of your life, how do you think your life would change?*

*Is there any specific thing that you know you need to yield to God but it seems too hard or scary to give up control?*

## JANUARY 7             Q—QUIETING THE NOISE

*This is what the Sovereign LORD, the Holy One of Israel, says: "In repentance and rest is your salvation, in quietness and trust is your strength." (Isaiah 30:15a)*

Much of what our world calls "strength" today comes with a lot of sound and fury attached. Think about it: the weightlifter in the gym who pumps the most pounds—and grunts the loudest while doing so; the movie star who screams while blowing the bad guys to smithereens; the guitar hero who cranks up the band's amp until every note rings in the audience's ears; the misguided parent (or teen) who thinks yelling and slamming doors will demonstrate power.

Often, strength is loud.

But the kind of strength that God cares most about doesn't need crashes and booms. *Inner* strength holds the highest value, and it's developed in moments of solitude, in times spent with God, listening, sensing the Spirit at work within us, reading the Scriptures and letting their truth sink into our spirits and souls.

*That*'s how we grow the strongest spiritually—by making room for quiet.

*As you go about your day, listen closely to all the sounds in your home, your bedroom, and your car. What noises could be turned down or off for a while to create some quiet time and allow you to hear God more clearly?*

JANUARY 8                    T—TEACHABLE MOMENTS

*Show me your ways, O* LORD, *teach me your paths; guide me in your truth and teach me, for you are God my Savior, and my hope is in you all day long. (Psalm 25:4-5)*

When you meet one-on-one with God, you're meeting not only with the Creator of the universe and the hope of the world, but also with the greatest teacher in history.

Among its many benefits, your daily quiet time provides amazing opportunities to learn more about God, God's ways, and God's good plans for your life. The word *teach* appears a whopping 349 times in the Bible. In one place, Jesus promises his disciples that the Counselor—a.k.a. the Holy Spirit—will come from the Father to "teach you all things and...remind you of everything I have said to you" (John 14:26).

As we wrap up our focus on daily devotional times, I hope you'll keep them going and keep that promise in mind: the Spirit is with you—teaching, guiding, and reminding you with every step you take along your journey with God.

*Think about the best teacher you've ever had. What made her or him so special? What did you learn from this teacher that has stuck with you?*

*Will you make a commitment—and share it with a parent, youth pastor, or friend—to meet daily with God this year?*

JANUARY 9                    YOU ARE GOD'S HANDIWORK

*For you created my inmost being; you knit me together in my mother's womb. I praise you because I am fearfully and wonderfully made; your works are wonderful, I know that full well.*
*(Psalm 139:13-14)*

Today, we begin a series of messages focused on your identity as a Christian—*who you are* in God's sight.

In the popular book series The Clique, a few of the "in" characters refer to classmates they don't like with the phrase "loser beyond repair" (LBR). In other words: you are so not cool and you never will be.

Have you ever felt that way about yourself? Or—let's be honest—have you ever called someone else an LBR to his or her face or behind his or her back? Whatever the case, in Psalm 139 we discover that just the opposite is true.

You and every other person were carefully created, lovingly formed, wonderfully made. You bear God's imprint. Before you were born, God fashioned you with great precision and purpose.

Loser beyond repair? Don't buy it. In our Creator's eyes, each of us is a WBC—winner beyond compare.

*How aware are you of the great truth that you are "fearfully and wonderfully made" by a loving Creator?*

*Considering that this is also true about everyone else, is there anyone you need to speak to, or about, in a different way than you have been?*

JANUARY 10                    YOU ARE GOD'S BELOVED

*But when the kindness and love of God our Savior appeared, he saved us, not because of righteous things we had done, but because of his mercy. (Titus 3:4-5)*

*"Let the beloved of the Lord rest secure in him."*
*(Deuteronomy 33:12a)*

19

You don't have to earn it; you only have to receive it as a gift. "It" is God's love. It's free. God's love for you is deeper, stronger, and more lasting than any other love in the world.

If, for whatever reason, you've got the idea that God loves you more when you're "good" and less when you're "bad," today would be a great day to chuck that notion. It's simply not true. Nothing you do could make God care for you any more or any less. In Christ, you are God's beloved child!

It *is* true that if you sin or drift away from God, your *experience* of God's love will decrease. You won't enjoy the close fellowship and friendship that God wants you to enjoy until you turn back, reconnect, and receive God's forgiveness. But God's love for you will never waver.

**Do you ever think that God loves you less or more at certain times than at other times?**

**What difference could it make to remember that God's love for you never changes?**

JANUARY 11                                    YOU ARE RESCUED

*For he has rescued us from the dominion of darkness and brought us into the kingdom of the Son he loves, in whom we have redemption, the forgiveness of sins. (Colossians 1:13-14)*

Just about every day, cable news channels carry another image of a harrowing rescue: frightened people, with flood waters raging all around them, stuck on top of a car or house. Imagine how that kind of terror might turn to extreme relief as a helicopter lowered its basket and plucked you to safety, lifting you away from almost certain death.

In a similar way, all who come to God in faith have been rescued, too. It might not feel as dramatic as a last-second rooftop liberation, but being rescued *spiritually* means so much more in the long run. If you've said yes to God through Jesus Christ, then you have been freed from an empty, purposeless life. As Paul puts it in today's verse, you have been "redeemed"—purchased by God, forgiven, and set free.

And *that* is news worth shouting from the rooftops.

**What does it mean to you that God has rescued you from darkness and brought you into the Kingdom?**

**Does knowing that God has "purchased" you and set you free change your view of God in any way?**

JANUARY 12                    YOU ARE A NEW CREATION

**This means that anyone who belongs to Christ has become a new person. The old life is gone; a new life has begun!**
**(2 Corinthians 5:17 NLT)**

Having grown up at the foot of Colorado's Rocky Mountains, I remember that awesome feeling of walking outside on winter mornings and stepping into a powdery blanket of freshly fallen snow. The whole world seemed new.

It's kind of like walking on a beach after the tide has gone out and left the sand smooth and glistening. Or like washing the car, inside and out, and spraying it with a little "new car" scent. Ah . . . fresh! When things are new, they seem more special, don't they?

That's how it is to belong to God. Because of God's incredible love, mercy, and grace, we have been made new. God views us as new creations thanks to the sacrifice of Jesus on our behalf.

Being "new" doesn't make us perfect, of course; we're still prone to stumble at times, and we still need forgiveness. But it *does* mean that if you've accepted Christ's invitation to walk with him, then at the core of your being you're a whole new person!

**What images or memories cause you to think most about "newness"?**

**In what ways can you draw encouragement and strength from knowing that God sees you as a "new creation" in Christ?**

JANUARY 13                                    YOU ARE SET APART

*Look at this: look Who got picked by God! He listens the split second I call to him. (Psalm 4:3 THE MESSAGE)*

*But in your hearts set apart Christ as Lord. (1 Peter 3:15)*

If you've ever been singled out in a good way—presented with an award in front of the class or the school, taken to dinner by your mom or dad, mentioned in the newspaper, or interviewed on television—then you know how special it can feel to be "set apart" for individual recognition.

In an amazing and mysterious way, your heavenly Father has done just that for each of his children. He has set you apart for special care and consideration. He hears and responds to you when you call to him.

Today's topic doesn't end there, however. It's like a two-sided coin. "Heads" is what God has done by setting you apart as someone he created, rescued, and cares deeply about. "Tails" is what you do by setting Christ apart as Lord of your life—by opening your heart and saying, "God, you're in control; whatever you have for me, I'm ready."

*When have you felt the most "set apart" or recognized?*

*Is anything in your heart or mind competing for the "set apart" place that the Lord wants to occupy as your leader and best friend?*

JANUARY 14                          YOU ARE PART OF A ROYAL
                                                     PRIESTHOOD

*But you are a chosen people, a royal priesthood, a holy nation, a people belonging to God, that you may declare the praises of him who called you out of darkness into his wonderful light.*
*(1 Peter 2:9)*

At the same time you are "set apart" as an individual who God loves and cherishes, you're also a member of a larger group of

22

God's people—the "body of Christ," as the New Testament often puts it.

In today's verse, Peter writes to a band of followers of Jesus who were scattered out and scared for their lives. He makes a big deal of reminding them of two great truths: who they are, and what they are part of.

Peter's strong words still apply to us today. If you belong to God, you're part of a huge "family" of believers. You have been transferred from darkness to light, from the "outside" to the inner courts of the King.

You are royalty! And as royalty, you're called to bring praise, honor, and glory to the King who has welcomed you into his loving, gracious presence.

**What do you think it means to be brought from darkness into God's "wonderful light"?**

**How does it feel to think of yourself as a member of God's "royal family"?**

## JANUARY 15        SCHOOL LIFE: WHAT'S THAT SMELL?

*But thanks be to God, who always leads us in triumphal procession in Christ and through us spreads everywhere the fragrance of the knowledge of him. (2 Corinthians 2:14)*

OK, I know you might not want to think about school much more than you already do. After all, you spend most days focused on classes, books, and homework. But since your educational environment is such a central part of your life, let's take a little time to zero in on some new ways to approach it.

First, what do you smell like when you walk into school?

When you were a baby, your parents probably placed you in the church nursery or in a daycare setting at some point. When they picked you up, if one of the workers had rocked you to sleep or held you, the scent of his or her cologne or perfume would be evident to your parents.

Fast forward to today. The closer you get to Jesus, the more you will "smell" like him at school. His love, truth, grace, and compassion coming through you will be impossible for your classmates and teachers to miss. The fragrance of Jesus on you will attract others to him through your life!

**What do you think it means to "smell" like Jesus?**

**How strong is the "fragrance" of Christ on you and other believers at school?**

JANUARY 16                    SCHOOL LIFE: KEEP ME AWAKE,
                                                                    GOD

*I can do all things through Christ who strengthens me.* *(Philippians 4:13 NKJV)*

*"I will strengthen you and help you; I will uphold you with my righteous right hand." (Isaiah 41:10b)*

Some mornings—let's be honest—it's *really* hard to get out of bed. For some reason, education professionals tend to think teens should start school at sunrise. (OK, I'm exaggerating—but only a little.)

So, maybe you stayed up late last night working on a huge homework assignment. The alarm goes off, but those covers—oh, they feel so irresistibly cozy. You know what's coming: first-period drowsiness, an after-lunch lull, and heavy eyelids as you wait, forever, for the last bell to ring.

On days like this—every day, really—it's great to know that we serve a God who loves to strengthen us when we're weak or weary. Yes, we are called to steward our bodies well by eating well and getting enough sleep. But when moments of fatigue inevitably come, God is faithful to fill us with energy and endurance. So, as you lean on God today, praying for strength, know that God's "righteous right hand" will uphold you.

**When do you usually feel the weakest and most in need of strength?**

*What challenge are you facing at school that the truth of Philippians 4:13 could help you through?*

JANUARY 17        SCHOOL LIFE: IS IT HOT IN HERE?

*"If we are thrown into the blazing furnace, the God we serve is able to save us from it, and he will rescue us from your hand, O king. But even if he does not, we want you to know, O king, that we will not serve your gods or worship the image of gold you have set up." (Daniel 3:17-18)*

Shadrach, Meshach, and Abednego would not bow to King Nebuchadnezzar's golden statue, so the king prepared to toss them into the furnace—unless they caved. I love their answer: "Do what you must. Live or die, we serve the Lord, not your idol." Talk about courage!

Does the pressure to "go along" at school ever feel like that? The lure of "idols" can be intense, especially when everyone seems to be bowing to them: using this language, drinking that drink, picking on others, going this far with the opposite sex, and so on.

When the temptation to conform seems overwhelming, remember to cry out to God. As you do, God will hear you, help you, and sustain you. Your security rests in God, not in what anyone might think of you for standing out.

*In what situations do you find yourself most tempted to go along with the crowd, even though you know it might compromise your relationship with God?*

*What help do you find in today's Scriptures?*

JANUARY 18        SCHOOL LIFE: FASHION AND FADS

*"If you decide for God, living a life of God-worship, it follows that you don't fuss about what's on the table at mealtimes or whether the clothes in your closet are in fashion. There is far more to your life than the food you put in your stomach, more*

*to your outer appearance than the clothes you hang on your body." (Matthew 6:25 THE MESSAGE)*

We live in a fashion-obsessed world. At Hollywood's dozens of awards shows, the camera focuses just as tightly on "who's wearing what" down the red carpet as it does on the awards being presented. Meanwhile, New York publishers churn out thick, glossy magazines peddling the latest trends.

Closer to home, what you wear to school—and what others wear—might be seriously stressing you out. If fashion has you frazzled, remember that God looks much deeper than outward appearance, and God calls you to look beyond it, too.

How you dress and take care of yourself does matter, but it's only a small part of who you are. The truest beauty is inner beauty—the kind that begins in your heart and grows stronger as you draw near to God each day.

*How important to you is dressing and looking a certain way at school?*

*As God sees it, what do you think are the main differences between outward appearance and inner beauty?*

JANUARY 19            SCHOOL LIFE: THE COST OF COOLNESS

*Obviously, I'm not trying to win the approval of people, but of God. If pleasing people were my goal, I would not be Christ's servant. (Galatians 1:10 NLT)*

You've seen it: classmates (maybe even some of your best friends) who are so desperate to be part of the cool crowd that they undergo a bunch of radical changes to make themselves popular. The trouble is, you end up hardly recognizing them. And, if they're honest, they might not recognize themselves, either. Or maybe you've been the one thinking, *Man, if I could just be part of that; friends with them; in their circle; then I'd have it all.*

Let's face it, though: trying to win the approval of a certain group just so they'll accept you is exhausting. And if it means compromising your principles or your faith, it can be downright dangerous to your spiritual health.

A wiser approach is to focus on being who you are—who God has made you—with all of your unique talents, interests, and attractive qualities. Yes, you've got a ton of them. And whether you're considered cool at school, God thinks the world of you.

*What are the major cliques at your school? Have you ever been tempted to change who you are to fit in to one of them?*

*What's the difference between pursuing coolness and seeking to live as Christ's servant?*

JANUARY 20                      SCHOOL LIFE: JUGGLING

*"But seek his kingdom, and these things will be given to you as well. Do not be afraid, little flock, for your Father has been pleased to give you the kingdom." (Luke 12:31-32)*

Is your life busy? Do you ever feel pressed for time, with too much to do and too few hours to get it done? OK, I see your head nodding and your eyes getting big as if to say, "Uh, yeah!"

You've probably heard a lot about the idea of *balance*. The key to life is to find balance as you juggle classes, homework, sports, church, clubs, friends, family, and maybe even a part-time job. And—oh, yes—God. It all seems so overwhelming sometimes.

Here's the thing: according to Jesus, *balance* is impossible if we're talking about giving every item on our calendar equal attention. Giving God 5 percent won't help us much. The key is to seek *first* the Kingdom, with all your heart, and then trust God to lead you to a Christ-centered "balance."

When we try to squeeze Jesus into a packed calendar, we usually end up squeezing him out.

*What are some of the things that you're juggling at school and other places?*

*Could anything be adjusted in your schedule to make sure seek-ing God's Kingdom comes first?*

JANUARY 21                    RELATING: FACEBOOK AND FACE
                                                              TIME

*Let us not give up meeting together, as some are in the habit of doing, but let us encourage one another—and all the more as you see the Day approaching. (Hebrews 10:25)*

Relationships are the glue that holds life together; so, for the next few days, we'll examine some fresh ways to relate to others.

Whether you're into My Space, Facebook, Twitter, texting, IMing, chatting, or other online and mobile "connecting" tools, today's verse from Hebrews gives us a valuable reminder.

It's so easy to type or click messages to friends, upload photos, and comment on each other's "status." But while the tools we use can be fun and helpful—I love keeping in touch with faraway friends on Facebook, for example—they also lack the personal touch that helps friendships grow strong and deep.

If you want to know someone beyond a surface level, you've got to spend some actual time together—talking, laughing, encourag-ing, praying, getting to know each other—yes, face-to-face.

*How much time do you spend each day reaching friends online or on the phone?*

*What step could you take to make sure you connect with at least one close friend one-on-one this week?*

JANUARY 22              RELATING: SPIRITUAL FRIENDSHIP

*Two are better than one. (Ecclesiastes 4:9)*

*A true friend sticks by you like family.*
                              *(Proverbs 18:24b THE MESSAGE)*

*And let us consider how we may spur one another on toward love and good deeds. (Hebrews 10:24)*

At its core, the Bible is a book about relationships—between God and people; people and God; people and other people. One of the main themes throughout the Scriptures is *friendship*. Jesus surrounded himself with twelve disciples whom he called "friends" (although one eventually betrayed him). We also read about David and Jonathan, Ruth and Naomi, Paul and Timothy, and so on.

Most of these were "spiritual friendships" centered on the Lord. One of the best ways to grow stronger in your faith is to walk it out with a close friend. Spiritual friends talk openly about God; study the word and pray together; listen to each other; and wrestle with tough questions, fears, struggles, and doubts. They "sharpen" each other.

If you have a friend like that, then count your blessings! If you don't, then I would encourage you to begin by praying that God will lead you into that kind of friendship in God's perfect way and timing.

*What makes a "spiritual friendship" different from other friendships?*

*In what ways do you think your faith would grow if you shared it with a close friend?*

JANUARY 23          RELATING: PARENTAL CONTROLS

*"Honor your father and mother"—which is the first commandment with a promise—"that it may go well with you and that you may enjoy long life on the earth." (Ephesians 6:2-3)*

No doubt you've heard this phrase or seen it on a television or computer screen: "parental controls." It's a reminder that, although you're certainly not a little child anymore, you're still under the authority of adults.

If you find yourself yearning for independence and looking forward to the day when Mom and Dad won't have "the last word," that's a perfectly normal desire—a part of growing up. Even so, as you move toward adulthood, you'd be wise to keep Paul's words from Ephesians in mind. Honoring your parents is a rock-solid biblical principle that will only come back to bless you.

Does showing honor mean always agreeing? No, not at all. To honor another means to treat him or her with respect, to extend trust, to pray for the person, and to speak and act toward the individual as you would have him or her do to you—even when you don't see eye-to-eye.

*Why do you think the Bible teaches us to honor our parents and others in authority over us?*

*Can you think of any specific ways—even simple ones—that you could show honor to your parent(s) this week?*

JANUARY 24          RELATING: THE LOST AND BROKEN

*The Spirit of the Sovereign LORD is on me, because the LORD has anointed me to preach good news to the poor. He has sent me to bind up the brokenhearted, to proclaim freedom for the captives and release from darkness for the prisoners. (Isaiah 61:1)*

At the beginning of my junior year, I was going through a tough time. My family recently had moved from Colorado to Tennessee. I didn't have any friends, and everyone already seemed to have a group. I felt lost and unknown.

After I made the soccer team that fall, two older teammates—their names happened to be Steven and Steve—welcomed me and treated me as if they had known me for years. They included me and became my friends. When I eventually learned that they were Christians, the kindness they had shown played a big part in my own decision to follow Jesus.

Whether it's at school, in your neighborhood, or where you work or hang out, the world is filled with lost, hurting people who could use a kind word, a smile, a prayer, and maybe even a chance to become your friend.

*Have you ever felt out of place, lost, or otherwise hurting? Do you know anyone like that?*

*What tangible, specific step could you take to reach out to someone who is lost or hurting today?*

JANUARY 25                    RELATING: SERVANT-HEARTED

*"My command is this: Love each other as I have loved you. Greater love has no one than this, that he lay down his life for his friends." (John 15:12-13)*

A friend of mine had a brother who was very sick. He had been born with only one kidney, and it was failing. He desperately needed a transplant. My friend, David, was tested and deemed a donor match, so he gave one of his kidneys to his brother. David underwent a painful surgery and a lengthy recovery, but, several years later, both brothers are healthy and thankful.

What made David take such a servant-hearted approach, giving up part of himself and enduring so much pain? It's simple: his obedience to God and his love for his brother. David is a follower of Christ, a recipient of God's deep love, and so he was moved to obey the command of John 15:12-13.

It might not cost you a body part. In fact, it probably won't! But God calls you to have this same servant-focused, sacrificial attitude toward your friends, family, teachers, classmates, and others.

*Can you think of an example of sacrificial love in your life or the life of someone close to you?*

*What are some specific ways that you could "lay down your life" for your friends?*

JANUARY 26                    RELATING: TRUE FRIENDSHIP
                                                  TAKES GUTS

*An open rebuke is better than hidden love! Wounds from a sincere friend are better than many kisses from an enemy.*
                              *(Proverbs 27:5-6 NLT)*

Friends aren't supposed to "wound" us, are they? A friend loves at all times, right (Proverbs 17:17)? Isn't a friend one who accepts me and allows me to be myself? Yes! But true friendship doesn't end there.

Today's proverb reminds us that friends aren't afraid to confront us if they see us heading down a dangerous or unwise path. Those who really care are willing to speak the truth in love when it's necessary. An "open rebuke" isn't a rejection; it's a truthful message of loving correction, delivered gently with the recipient's best interests at heart.

Whether you're willing to receive a rebuke from a friend will depend on how secure you are. Remember our earlier messages this month about "who you are" in Christ? The more confident you are that you're a loved, accepted, forgiven child of God, the more willing you'll be to listen to a word of gentle but firm correction from a "sincere friend."

*Think of a time when a friend told you something that was hard for you to hear. Are you glad your friend did?*

*Have you had to deliver a gentle rebuke to a friend? If so, how did it go, and what did you learn from the process?*

## JANUARY 27          CULTURE: HOLLYWOOD'S ACCESS

*Guard your heart above all else, for it determines the course of your life. (Proverbs 4:23 NLT)*

*I will refuse to look at anything vile and vulgar.*
                                        *(Psalm 101:3a NLT)*

Is it just me or is January flying by? Let's wrap up the month with a few messages focused on our culture.

I'm going to sound *really* old; I remember life before cable television. In the 1970s, I noticed a strange box on top of a friend's TV. "That's our new cable box," she said. Your *what*? Suddenly, dozens of channels were available (not just three fuzzy ones). I was stunned.

Today, we have access to millions of television channels, Web pages, songs, video clips, and so on. But do we have too much access?

If you spend more time in front of a screen than you do with God or others, it's probably time to cut back. Plus, a lot of the content—violence, sexuality, and rough language—isn't healthy for us to take in.

Here's a quick movie tip: before plunking down your money at the theater, check out a faith-based review site such as plugged-inonline.com for insights about whether the film is worth your time and money.

*Do you believe it is important to limit the media you watch and listen to? If so, why?*

*Are you willing to recruit a few friends and do a "media fast," unplugging from television, the Web, music, and so on for one week?*

JANUARY 28                CULTURE: IN PURSUIT OF PURITY

*Put on the Lord Jesus Christ, and make no provision for the flesh, to gratify its desires. (Romans 13:14 ESV).*

*If we confess our sins, he is faithful and just and will forgive us our sins and purify us from all unrighteousness. (1 John 1:9)*

To be pure before God means to have a clear conscience and to be "clean." Purity goes way beyond the one area that it's often associated with. (Hint: the word begins with *s* and ends with *x*.) Purity in thought, speech, motives, and actions—all of these are important to pursue as we go deeper in faith.

If that sounds like a lot of work, keep this in mind: you've got help! Walking in purity, clean before God, doesn't happen through sheer effort. It's something that God works in your life as you draw near and stay close to him day by day.

When Paul wrote, "Put on the Lord Jesus Christ," he was talking about "wearing" the Lord like a garment. Because Jesus is pure, the more you put him on—and give him room to shape your heart and mind—the more you'll be able to walk in purity.

*As you seek to walk in purity, what things make it difficult?*

*Does it encourage you to know that God is faithful to forgive, cleanse, and purify you whenever you confess your sins?*

JANUARY 29                    CULTURE: GOTTA HAVE IT?

*Don't be obsessed with getting more material things. Be relaxed with what you have. Since God assured us, "I'll never let you down, never walk off and leave you," we can boldly quote, God is there, ready to help. (Hebrews 13:5-6 THE MESSAGE)*

Our culture tends to glorify the latest, greatest, coolest products. Commercials are slickly designed to create an urgent demand in you and make you wonder, *How on earth have I been able to live this long without owning that?*

The "gotta have it" approach runs counter to God's way, which places more emphasis on being content with what God provides. Paul wrote, "Godliness with contentment is great gain" (1 Timothy 6:6). There is peace in being thankful and satisfied with the simple gifts that God blesses us with: food, shelter, essential clothing, and friends and family who love us.

So if you find yourself obsessing over the newest music player, phone, jeans, or shoes—and who hasn't been there?—hit your internal pause button, wait a while, and ask yourself: *Do I really have to have that? Could I be content and happy without it?*

*How often do you find yourself thinking or saying, "I have GOT to get one of those"?*

*What are the benefits of being content with the way God meets our needs, rather than chasing our wants?*

JANUARY 30          CULTURE: HEROES AND VILLAINS

*So think clearly and exercise self-control. (1 Peter 1:13a NLT)*

In the old days of cowboy Westerns, it was usually easy to identi-fy the "good" guys and the "bad" guys. The hero wore white; the villain dressed in black. In the end, the villain ended up in jail or dead. The hero—and justice—prevailed.

Today, "good" and "bad" are tougher to distinguish. Real people with a worldview and an "agenda" create every movie, television show, book, Web site, and magazine. And, unfortunately, a lot of pop culture is hostile to the Christian faith. For example, when is the last time you saw a pastor portrayed on screen in a positive light, or a family praying together in Jesus' name before a meal?

That's why it's wise to think critically and carefully about what comes across the screen, asking questions such as: What's behind this message? Does it line up with God's word? What motivated the author or filmmaker to present it in this way? Is it healthy for me to be watching or listening to this?

*Think about one movie or television show that you've watched recently. What message do you think the creators were trying to get across? Did they succeed?*

*Why is it important to think critically about the media that we see and hear?*

JANUARY 31                    CULTURE: FIX YOUR EYES

*Let your eyes look straight ahead, fix your gaze directly before you. (Proverbs 4:25)*

*Let us fix our eyes on Jesus, the author and perfecter of our faith. (Hebrews 12:2a)*

These days, if someone talks about having his or her "eyes fixed," chances are the person means laser surgery. As amazing as that procedure is (trust me; I've had it done), today we're talking about fixing our eyes on God—and not necessarily our physical eyes, but our *spiritual* eyes, sometimes referred to as "the eyes of the heart."

Where are your "eyes" fixed? In other words, what excites you the most? How do you spend your time and money? Given a choice between a half hour of texting and a half hour of meditating on the Bible, does the phone always win out? How often are your thoughts directed toward God's incredible love, truth, and goodness?

Whenever our "gaze" wanders away from God, the good news is that we don't need a surgeon or a laser to correct it. It just takes a change of direction, a fresh start, a refocusing on the God of new beginnings whose love for you is crystal clear!

**What distractions make it challenging to keep your eyes focused on God?**

**Will you seek out a friend or youth pastor and ask him or her to help you stay focused in your walk with God this year?**

# FEBRUARY

# Following Jesus

## RYAN AND ELLEN GRAY

FEBRUARY 1                    ARE YOU READY?

*His divine power has given us everything we need for life and godliness through our knowledge of him who called us by his own glory and goodness. (2 Peter 1:3)*

Hello, friends! My husband, Ryan, and I are delighted to share our hearts with you this month through these devotions. (You'll hear from Ryan in days two through eleven, and then I'll take us to the end of the month.) Being involved in student ministry for more than seventeen years collectively, we understand the need for relevant, biblical truth in a world that teaches moral relativity and universalism.

The lessons we share with you this month are designed to encourage and equip you to live out your identity as God's child and disciple. This calling of God to be a disciple is a high one, but we believe God has given us all we need to live lives that honor and glorify him. Our prayer is that God would use these devotions to speak right to your heart and remind you of how much you are loved, cherished, and equipped to be a disciple of Christ. Thanks for embarking on this journey with us. To God be the glory!

*Do you feel fully equipped to be a disciple of Christ? Why or why not?*

*What do you feel you need in order to be better equipped? (We will begin this month by offering you ten essentials for spiritual growth.)*

37

FEBRUARY 2                                    TALK IT OUT

*Be joyful always; pray continually; give thanks in all circum-stances, for this is God's will for you in Christ Jesus.*
*(1 Thessalonians 5:16-18)*

Let's be honest; this is one of those verses that can be easy to recite or memorize, yet rather difficult to continually practice. I have found that many people are up for the daily challenges of being joyful and giving thanks, but continually praying is an idea that most find intimidating. Perhaps the reason so many of us are intimidated by praying regularly is that we are intimidated by prayer itself. We trick ourselves into thinking that our lives and our words need to be perfect—that our prayers need to be poetic and inspirational, even to the angels! We unnecessarily complicate this simple act of devotion.

I have always appreciated Clement of Alexandria's belief that prayer is "simply keeping company with God." It is just hanging out, talking and listening to our heavenly Father and Friend, getting to know his heart, and being peacefully reassured that he knows ours. You see, the more you talk with God, the more you know him. The more you know him, the more you want to be around him. The more you are around him, the more you love him and want to continually talk and listen to him.

*What are some obstacles that keep you from praying to God on a consistent basis?*

FEBRUARY 3                              FORMED BY THE WORD

*My son, pay attention to what I say; listen closely to my words.*
*Do not let them out of your sight, keep them within your heart.*
*(Proverbs 4:20-21)*

One of the scariest events of my childhood happened at a major league baseball game. My dad had taken me to see our favorite team play. During the sixth inning, I told him that I had to go to the restroom. He began to give me directions on how to proceed to and from the men's room. Of course, being a stubborn child, I did not listen closely. To make a long story short, I ended up getting lost, crying in a security guard's office, and having my dad's name paged over the PA system.

As you continue your journey with Christ in a fallen world, there is nothing more imperative than learning how to "pay attention" to the truth of God found in God's word. Reading the Bible and listening to the teachings of Christ can radically transform your life as well as protect you even more from getting lost in a world that attempts to distract from and disown the living truth of God.

***When was the last time you read, found comfort in, and applied a verse from the Bible?***

***What was it, and what happened?***

## FEBRUARY 4                                    A MUST READ

***That is, that you and I may be mutually encouraged by each other's faith. (Romans 1:12)***

I used to hate reading when I was growing up—seriously. I found it meaningless and absolutely boring. Of course, in school I was always forced to read old, smelly textbooks written by old, perhaps also smelly doctors and professors I did not know.

As you read the first chapter of Romans, you get a sense that Paul desires to know and be known by other believers in Rome. The great apostle humbly stresses the importance of learning from one another, listening to one another's successes and failures, in the hope that we might be encouraged in our faith.

When I was seventeen, a dozen friends and I read a book together called *Seeking the Kingdom*. I remember being in awe of how open the author was about the experiences of his life and his shortcomings, and how we all could relate.

I strongly urge you, as did Paul, to take advantage of the words written or spoken by fellow Christians, in hopes that you may be taught, strengthened, and encouraged in your faith.

*What inspirational words have inspired you to be closer to God, and how can you pass those words along to your friends and family?*

FEBRUARY 5                    THE HEART OF WORSHIP

*Therefore, I urge you, brothers, in view of God's mercy, to offer your bodies as living sacrifices, holy and pleasing to God—this is your spiritual act of worship. (Romans 12:1)*

When we think about the goodness of Jesus Christ and all that he has done for us, our hearts fill with gratitude, leading our mouths to overflow with praise. Many would call this an act of worship. Paul urges us to recognize that when we worship, it brings pleasure to our God. Even more than that, I believe this verse is trying to teach us that when we fully trust the Lord with all our fears, pride, confusion, desires, doubts, and our entire selves, we begin to "offer ourselves" to the only One worthy of our praise.

The next time you find yourself thinking that worship is merely the act of reciting words out of a hymnal or clapping your hands along with the choir, remember that worship begins when we recognize our continual need for a merciful Savior. Then we may offer all of who we are and all of what we have to Christ and Christ alone, for at the heart of worship is surrender.

*What are some things in your life that you have a hard time handing over to God?*

FEBRUARY 6                         TRUE FRIENDSHIP

*Two are better than one, because they have a good return for their work: If one falls down, his friend can help him up.*
                                        *(Ecclesiastes 4:9-10)*

Our faith journeys were never meant to be walked alone. Time and time again in the Bible, God's word makes abundantly clear the importance of a believer being in community with other believers. One of the greatest assets of being in community with others, or being in close relationships, is accountability.

Simply put, accountability is being held responsible for our actions. The truth is, we are all fallen individuals with a sinful nature. No matter how much we love God and love others, we have a tendency to make a mess of things. For this reason, we need people in our lives we trust enough to share our joy, sorrow, successes, and failures.

The truth is, accountability is scary. No one enjoys other people knowing his or her secrets and faults, but there is not a human being on this earth without them. Yet I assure you there is nothing greater than the feeling of support, comfort, and motivation found in a friend who holds you accountable to your actions for the purpose of being more like Christ.

*Are you the type of person whom people can come to for genuine accountability?*

*What characteristics do you look for in a person before confiding in him or her?*

FEBRUARY 7                                                    RETREAT

*"Are you tired? Worn out? Burned out on religion? Come to me. Get away with me and you'll recover your life."*
*(Matthew 11:28 THE MESSAGE)*

We live in a world and culture that sprints. Everyone is busy with everything under the sun. Calendars fill up, daily checklists become longer, and stress levels increase because there are "not enough hours in a day." Sure, we may busy our lives with positive things like school, jobs, sports, and friendships, but if we are not careful, those "good" things can consume our lives and schedules, leaving no room for communing with God.

How lucky are we that in the midst of filling our lives up with so much stuff, Jesus offers an open invitation to retreat and find rest in him. In today's verse, the heart of our Lord longs for us to be restored when we become tired, exhausted, or weary of our lives. We see that Jesus cares about our burdens, our worries, and our shame. He always beckons us, no matter how hectic life gets, with his arms wide open. Sure, rest is certainly a gift, but the true gift is being in the presence of the Son of God.

***When was the last time you truly rested in the presence of God?***


FEBRUARY 8                                    LEARN BY HEART

*I have hidden your word in my heart that I might not sin against you. (Psalm 119:11)*

One of the greatest ways of defending ourselves against the enemy, who so desperately wants to steal and destroy our souls, is to memorize Scripture. It is no secret that we are tempted in our minds numerous times throughout the day to turn our backs on a loving God and listen to the lies of the enemy. We can see this in the forms of lust, fear, depression, insecurity, and deception. How do we stop letting the lies of the enemy take our minds captive?

In this verse, the meaning of *word* in the Hebrew language is *'imrah*, which means "promise." The psalmist declares that he keeps the promises of God deep within his heart so that he might not sin. This is a wonderful piece of hopeful application. If we, as children of God, read and memorize the words of God, then there is a greater chance of us speaking those words in the face of temptation and claiming victory over sin.

May this encourage us to dive into the Scriptures, remember God's great promises, and find a deeper love for the Lord.

***What is one promise of God that you need to hide in your heart?***


FEBRUARY 9                                    REAL SUPERHEROES

*Remember your leaders, who spoke the word of God to you. Consider the outcome of their way of life and imitate their faith. (Hebrews 13:7)*

When we were young, we all wanted to be Superman or Superwoman. There was nothing more mind-blowing than the life of a superhero. As a child, I remember trying to run faster than a speeding bullet, trying to catch imaginary bad guys with ease, and, of course, attempting to fly. As children, we imitated our heroes, truly believing the impossible feats they committed were, in fact, possible.

As funny as it may sound, I am thirty years old and still have superheroes. There are men and women in my life who have no problem believing that "nothing is impossible with God" (Luke 1:37). Their faith in the midst of personal struggles, fears, trials, and persecution is unwavering. They seem to never allow circumstances to diminish their faith in God. To them, God is still in control, can always be trusted, and loves them unconditionally.

Beloved children of God, look for examples of how to follow Christ in the people who remind you of him. Watch how they live. Listen to their words. Imitate their faith, for it will bring you one step closer to the hope of imitating Christ.

*Who is your hero, and why do you think his or her faith is worth imitating?*


FEBRUARY 10                          GIVE YOUR LIFE AWAY

*We loved you so much that we were delighted to share with you not only the gospel of God but our lives as well, because you had become so dear to us. (1 Thessalonians 2:8)*

There were many things that Jesus talked about and did during his ministry on earth, so much in fact that not all of it could be recorded. If you study the life of Christ, it does not take you long to figure out his two main priorities: loving God and loving people.

When I was in high school, a man by the name of Joe began to spend quality time with my friends and me. He was involved with a parachurch organization and was the first person to introduce me to the gospel of Jesus. Joe invited us to go on fun trips, to come over for dinner, and to go to church with his family. There was never a doubt that Joe loved God, his wife, and his children, and he even loved giving his life to a bunch of lost and crazy teenagers.

***With whom are you purposely sharing the gospel of God?***

***How can you minister to people with both words and actions?***

FEBRUARY 11                                              DEAR DIARY

***At the Lord's command Moses recorded the stages in their journey. (Numbers 33:2)***

When I was growing up, I was the stereotypical mean older brother. My sister still informs me of the ways I terrorized her during our childhood. To be honest, I do not like remembering how I used to make her feel. Sometimes, the past is hard to live with.

Moses was given the task of recording the journey of the Israelites from Egypt to Canaan. There are memories of slavery, oppression, and heartache. Why would the Lord ask Moses to journal about this? Why would God allow Moses the chance of remembering past hardships?

I truly believe that God uses hardships in life to bring people to himself, in order to reveal God's glory. In Moses' case, and ours as well, the past has to be recognized but not dwelt upon. Moses did not forget the past but focused on the present celebration of God delivering the Israelites out of the hardships.

When I look at my old journals, I marvel at all the prayers God answered and the promises God kept. Sure, I read and remember the struggles and hardships I faced, but I am quickly reminded of 2 Corinthians 5:17: "Therefore, if anyone is in Christ, he is a new creation; the old has gone, the new has come!"

***If you had the opportunity to record a recent example of God's redemptive work in your life, what would it be?***

FEBRUARY 12                                    GOOD ENOUGH

*How great is the love the Father has lavished on us, that we should be called children of God! And that is what we are!*
*(1 John 3:1)*

The world we live in is all about appearance and performance. If you're a guy, the world says you have to be the strongest and the best at what you do to be a man. If you're a girl, the world says you have to be the skinniest or the prettiest to be the best. I can remember feeling in high school that, no matter what I did, there was always someone skinnier or prettier than me. No matter how hard I practiced, there was always someone faster than me on the track. No matter how hard I studied, there was always someone smarter.

Trying to hold myself up under all this pressure from the world was impossible. Living by the world's standards always left me feeling empty, inadequate, and insecure. One day I realized that if I simply surrendered myself to living by the Lord's standards, he would welcome me into his unconditional acceptance and love. What relief, security, and freedom I found! No longer did I have to constantly strive to reach unattainable, worldly standards. I was finally "good enough," and loved as I was for who I was. That's my kind of living!

*Are you trying to live up to the world's unattainable standards, or are you living in the freedom found in Christ?*


FEBRUARY 13                                    GOD'S MASTERPIECE

*For we are God's workmanship, created in Christ Jesus to do good works, which God prepared in advance for us to do.*
*(Ephesians 2:10)*

I don't know about you, but this verse from Ephesians is a very familiar one for me. I had read it dozens of times, but it never really stood out to me before. Seems pretty straightforward, right? We are God's workmanship, created to do good works. Makes sense to me.

It wasn't until I dug a little deeper into this verse that I was blown away by God's truth. My perspective on my life was transformed, all because of one word: *workmanship*. Yep, *workmanship*. When translated from the Greek, do you know what other word can be inserted here for *workmanship*? *Masterpiece.* And that, my friends, changes everything.

God doesn't just call you good, or even great. God calls you his *masterpiece*. God loves you for who you are—imperfections, sins, and all. As God's masterpieces, we are created to do good works. God doesn't call us his masterpieces *because* we do good works. God calls us his masterpieces so that we *want* to do good works.

***May you walk in the joyous freedom that comes with knowing the depth of the Father's love for you!***

***Do you really believe you are a masterpiece? Why or why not?***

FEBRUARY 14 THE LOVER OF YOUR SOUL

***"The LORD your God is with you, he is mighty to save. He will take great delight in you, he will quiet you with his love, he will rejoice over you with singing." (Zephaniah 3:17)***

I always dreaded Valentine's Day. For some, Valentine's Day was the best day of the year. For the rest of us, it was a way to announce to world that, yes, we were single. After surviving several lonely February 14s, I became convinced that Valentine's Day should be renamed "National Singles Awareness Day."

However you see Valentine's Day, my prayer is that you may be captivated by the mystery of the gospel—that amid your sin and ugliness, God loves you with an everlasting love and sees you, through Christ, as his flawless one. Jesus is the greatest lover of your soul. He delights in you! You are his beloved. His love for you cannot and will not be contained as he dances over you with song! Instead of dwelling on what others have in earthly relationships, remember that you have found all you could ever want in Jesus, the greatest lover of all time. He will bring more satisfaction and fulfillment to your life than any human relationship ever will. May you walk in fullness of joy!

*How does knowing how much Jesus delights in you change your perspective?*

*Will your heart ever be fully satisfied until it is satisfied in him?*

FEBRUARY 15                                    THINK ABOUT IT

*How precious to me are your thoughts, O God! And how vast the sum of them! Were I to count them, they would outnumber the grains of sand. When I awake, I am still with you.*
*(Psalm 139:17-18)*

Have you ever had a crush on someone and, no matter what you did, you could not seem to stop thinking about him or her? You think about this person in class, while you brush your teeth, during practice. You can't seem to get him or her off your mind—and you like it that way!

Our minds focus on our objects of affection. Whether we're dreaming about a certain person or the latest flat screen HDTV, our minds are almost always distracted by something we love. Unfortunately, few of us could honestly say that our minds are filled with longing for God. God may be the object of our affection on Sunday mornings, but come Monday, our thoughts are elsewhere.

Fortunately for us, God is not distracted in his love and affection for us. God says that if we were to count his thoughts towards us, they would outnumber the grains of sand on the beach! God is the greatest lover of our souls, and we are the objects of God's affection. May you delight in God's love and make him the sole object of your affection.

*What things compete for attention and affection in your life?*

FEBRUARY 16                    THE SECRET OF LIFE (PART 1)

*"Do not store up for yourselves treasures on earth, where moth and rust destroy, and where thieves break in and steal. But store up for yourselves treasures in heaven." (Matthew 6:19-20)*

For years, when we asked my grandfather what he wanted for Christmas, he would always say he didn't need anything. After he passed away, I found several of the gifts I had given him over the years: a hat from Ireland, several ties, and a sweater, to name a few. As I looked at all the things I had given him, I was struck by a very real sense of the emptiness of it all. Though he appreciated the gifts, once he passed away it all became just *stuff*. None of it went with him to heaven.

So much of our lives are spent striving to have the right stuff. But in the end, none of our earthly things matter. The only thing we take with us—the only thing we will have to cling to when we die—is our soul's relationship with Jesus.

Thankfully, my grandfather understood this. He spent his life deepening his relationship with Jesus and helping others do the same. How satisfying it must have been for him to reach the end of his life with no regret, knowing that his life was not spent in vain.

**Will what you're doing today make a difference when you die?**

FEBRUARY 17          THE SECRET OF LIFE (PART 2)

*I have learned the secret of being content in any and every situation, whether well fed or hungry, whether living in plenty or in want. (Philippians 4:12b)*

My husband, Ryan, and I love our families. One of his family's traditions is to come to Thanksgiving with a Christmas list in hand. I've learned to start making my list in June so as not to disappoint. I realized this year that what starts as an innocent Christmas list begins to look like a list of material things I don't have, staring me in the face. I notice that I become less and less content with what I do have, and more and more discontent with what I don't.

This year I decided to make a list of everything I do have and keep it next to my Christmas list. The things on this list aren't material things but things that have no price tag, such as my amazing husband, my great family, my friends, my health, and most important, my relationship with Jesus.

When we focus on all the things we don't have, we will be very unhappy. But if we can "have an attitude of gratitude" for all the blessings in our lives, we will live in contentment and peace.

*What are you thankful for? Make a list of all the blessings you have in life, and give God thanks!*

FEBRUARY 18                  WHY WAIT? (PART 1)

*Gathering them together, He [Jesus] commanded them not to leave Jerusalem, but to wait for what the Father had promised.*
*(Acts 1:4a NASB)*

I guarantee that if you were to write out your top five activities, waiting would not be on your list. Waiting in traffic, waiting for a teacher to return a graded paper, waiting for a slow Internet connection—nobody likes to wait! I find it odd, though, that this is exactly what Jesus commanded his followers to do after he ascended into heaven. Wait? Wait for what? While Jesus told his followers to wait for what his Father had promised (the Holy Spirit), I think Jesus knew waiting would produce other things that they needed in their lives .

One Hebrew word for *wait* is *qavah*, which literally means "to gather together." Jesus knew that waiting would naturally produce community among his followers. Instead of being annoyed by waiting, like we are when we wait in traffic, Jesus intended to create purposeful, fun, and expectant waiting, like the kind we watch at Times Square every New Year's Eve. Maybe waiting isn't such a bad thing after all. In fact, maybe it's exactly what God wants and exactly what we need.

*What are some things God has asked you to wait for?*

*What are some of the blessings you have found along the way?*

FEBRUARY 19                                    WHY WAIT? (PART 2)

*Gathering them together, He [Jesus] commanded them not to leave Jerusalem, but to wait for what the Father had promised.... "You will be baptized with the Holy Spirit not many days from now." (Acts 1:4-5 NASB)*

Jesus loved his followers so much that he not only promised to send the Holy Spirit as their helper, but he also cared for their hearts while he was physically away by telling them to wait.

We learned in the previous devotion about the Hebrew word *qavah*. This word is translated into two English words: *wait* and *hope*. Jesus knew that waiting would not only produce Christian community among his followers; he also knew it would naturally produce hope. This hope was initially for the promised Holy Spirit to arrive; but it was also for the time when Jesus would return to earth, just as he had left it.

Waiting creates longing, sometimes for a desired outcome, but it also creates a deep longing and hope for heaven—a time when everything will be as it should. Waiting is a gift from God. It produces in us an unquenchable desire for heaven and a deeper longing for intimacy with Jesus. With these outcomes, how can we ever again complain about waiting?

*What is your greatest hope?*

*How does this compare to your hope for heaven?*


FEBRUARY 20                                            CHOOSE LIFE

*This day I call heaven and earth as witnesses against you that I have set before you life and death, blessings and curses. Now choose life, so that you and your children may live.*
*(Deuteronomy 30:19)*

Searching for life is a journey on which we all embark. But what is the difference between those who find it and those who don't? The answer may be easier than you think. Our loving God has clearly told us in Scripture how we can find true life.

In the Old Testament, after God rescued the Israelites from the Egyptians, he began to lay out guidelines by which they were to live. Because God loved them so much, the guidelines were (and are) always meant to bring freedom and life, not restraint. God warned that not following the laws would bring curse and death. God then encouraged them to "choose life."

God always wants what's best for us, and God sent his Son so that we may have life abundantly. If we love God with all of our hearts and obey God's commands, we will find a life that is far greater than any we could have ever imagined!

You have a choice: life or death.

***Judging by your heart and your actions, are you choosing death or life?***

## FEBRUARY 21                    HOW FAR WILL YOU GO?

***They called the apostles in and had them flogged. Then they ordered them not to speak in the name of Jesus, and let them go. The apostles left the Sanhedrin, rejoicing because they had been counted worthy of suffering disgrace for the Name. Day after day, in the temple courts and from house to house, they never stopped teaching and proclaiming the good news that Jesus is the Christ. (Acts 5:40b-42)***

Every time I read this story about the apostles, I am amazed at the lengths they went to proclaim the gospel of Jesus. Their love for Jesus was so great and their passion for spreading the gospel so consuming that they let nothing get in their way. Even when they were flogged and threatened, they counted it a blessing to suffer for Jesus. These guys were truly unstoppable worshipers.

What about you? Are you so passionate about telling others about Jesus that you suffer ridicule? If not, what holds you back? Are you worried about what others will think of you? Are you worried that your social life might be over if you told your friends what you believe?

The disciples thought Jesus was worth it. Do you?

***What would it take to cause you to become an unstoppable worshiper?***

FEBRUARY 22                                                    REAL LIFE

*Not that we are adequate in ourselves to consider anything as coming from ourselves, but our adequacy is from God.*
                                            *(2 Corinthians 3:5 NASB)*

When I was in high school, I was happy and confident, and I considered myself to be a strong Christian. I would have told you that the anchor of my life was my relationship with Jesus. That was pretty easy to say, though, when everything was going my way: I was a star athlete, class officer, and homecoming court representative.

All that changed when I went to college. Suddenly, all those things that had made me feel important were gone. No one knew or cared that I used to be really popular or a star athlete. There was nothing making me stand out from the crowd, and all of a sudden my confident self became extremely insecure. Though I thought my identity was firmly planted in Jesus, I quickly learned that was not true. Without being aware of it, I had placed my identity in the fleeting things of this world, and when the rains came and the waters rose, I was left feeling alone and insecure.

If only I hadn't let false securities get in the way of my trust in Jesus when I was in high school, I never would have had to go through what I did in college.

*Does your security lie in Christ or in your accolades?*


FEBRUARY 23                                                    STAND UP

*"If you do not stand firm in your faith, you will not stand at all." (Isaiah 7:9b)*

Middle school and high school are quite possibly the hardest seasons of life. Although it was tough for older generations, it's even harder for you. We had fire drills; you have lock downs. We could bring our backpacks into class with us; you walk through metal detectors and by drug dogs. We didn't know anyone our age who was pregnant; you know someone in your grade who is. It was unthinkable for someone our age to have cancer; one of your friends may have died from it.

How are you to survive high school and come out on the other side without being broken and jaded, having given in to temptation, fallen on your face, or given up on God? I truly believe that, like the verse says, if you don't stand firm in your faith in Christ, you most certainly will fall. There is simply no way to get through life without standing firm in what you believe. Christ is the only true rock and foundation in life. Everything else will fail, but Jesus and his word will remain.

*What things do you turn to other than Jesus to help you survive high school?*

## FEBRUARY 24                                    GOD'S WILL

*For this is the will of God, your sanctification.*
*(1 Thessalonians 4:3 NASB)*

How many times have you asked what God's will is for your life? If you're anything like me, God's will is one of the most popular prayer topics in your life, and it can seem like such a mystery. How can we know what God's will is if we can't audibly hear God? Good question. Sometimes, though, we make the answer a lot more complicated than it has to be.

What is God's will for your life? God's word clearly states the answer: "This is the will of God, your sanctification." It's that simple. God desires us to be sanctified. In other words, above everything else, God desires for us to be made holy. Instead of asking God what we should do on Friday night, maybe we should ask, "What activity will set us apart and make us more like Christ?" Instead of losing sleep over a tough decision, maybe we should trust that, in the midst of our struggle, God is sanctifying us—and that in itself is God's will.

*What does the word sanctification mean?*

*How does it make you feel to know that the answer to* **What is God's will for my life?** *is your sanctification?*

FEBRUARY 25                                          REAL LOVE

*Some men came, bringing to [Jesus] a paralytic, carried by four of them. . . . When Jesus saw their faith, he said to the paralytic, "Son, your sins are forgiven." . . . He got up, took his mat and walked out in full view of them all. (Mark 2:3, 5, 12a)*

These four men loved the paralytic so much that they were willing to risk embarrassment and financial burden (having to pay for the roof they broke) in order to meet his need. What do we know about the paralytic? Nothing. We know nothing but his need. Do you think it's an accident the Bible left out what kind of personality this man had or whether he was grateful? For all we know, this man could have been bitter, angry at the world, and really annoying to be around. The paralytic could have been a nerd, a bully, or really awkward. The Bible doesn't say.

This is so significant because it does not matter! It does not matter if the paralytic was annoying or really fun to be around, a nerd or cool, bitter or grateful. The only thing that matters is that he was a human being in need. Four men saw that he had a need, and what did they do? They did whatever it took to get him to the feet of Jesus.

*When you see people in need at school, what do you do?*


FEBRUARY 26                                          TOO BUSY

*This is what the Sovereign LORD, the Holy One of Israel, says: "In repentance and rest is your salvation, in quietness and trust is your strength, but you would have none of it."*
*(Isaiah 30:15)*

We live in a culture that tells us more is better, that being busy means you are important, and that missing out on even one minute of anything means time lost. You have papers, exams, college application deadlines, tournaments, volunteering, youth group, music lessons, rehearsals, after-school activities, science projects, and the list goes on and on.

How are you possibly to find time to sit in quietness and find rest? Considering how busy you truly are and how much strength you will require to make it through each day, perhaps the better question is this: how can you possibly not find time for quietness and rest? For it is there that God promises to strengthen and to save you. Though it is seemingly counterintuitive that your busiest days are the ones you need the most time of quiet, God promises to give you the strength you will require when you take time to rest in him. May you come to God as you are, as busy as you are, and find the refreshment and renewal only he can provide.

*Do you create time and space in your life for God to act? Why or why not?*

## FEBRUARY 27                                                    LISTEN UP

*The LORD called Samuel a third time, and Samuel got up and went to Eli and said, "Here I am; you called me." Then Eli realized that the LORD was calling the boy. So Eli told Samuel, "Go and lie down, and if he calls you, say, 'Speak, LORD, for your servant is listening.'" So Samuel went and lay down in his place. (1 Samuel 3:8-9)*

I wonder if Samuel would be embarrassed if he knew that God recorded this incident in Scripture for all to read. Samuel mistook the voice of God three times in a row for the voice of another. Though we will never know how Samuel would feel, I know I feel thankful that God chose to record this human foible, for it brings great comfort to the rest of us imperfect people.

I wonder how often the voice of God has called to me and I have instinctively run to someone else; how often God has placed a longing in my heart for something more, something deeper, and yet I have run to adventure, friendships, or retail therapy in hopes of quenching the longing.

My friends, Jesus is calling. He is calling you. He is whispering your name in the still of night, beckoning you to come to him. He is the only one who can satisfy all your deepest longings. Softly, tenderly, Jesus is calling. May your answer be as Samuel's: "Speak,

LORD, for your servant is listening." If your experience is anything like Samuel's, it will change your life forever.

*What keeps you from hearing and heeding the voice of God?*

FEBRUARY 28                                        KNOW AND RELY

*And so we know and rely on the love God has for us. God is love. Whoever lives in love lives in God, and God in him.*
*(1 John 4:16)*

We rely on many things in this world: water and food for nourishment, homes for shelter, friends for companionship, family for love, accomplishments for security, and acceptance for significance. With all this world has to offer, why do we need to rely on God for anything?

The band Caedmon's Call put it well when they sang: "This world has nothing for me and this world has everything. / All that I could want and nothing that I need." They are right; the world has everything we could want. At the end of the day, though, everything the world offers will eventually let us down, run dry, or leave us empty. Don't be fooled! Stay centered on the exhortation to know and rely on the love God has for you. God's love is the only thing in the world that will never fail, never leave, and never falter. Don't just know God; *rely* on God. When everyone and everything else fails, your God remains faithful and strong—your mighty warrior, greatest lover, and truest friend.

*What in this world do you rely on that potentially could let you down?*

*Do you know God, or do you know AND rely on God?*

FEBRUARY 29            EQUIPPED TO BE A DISCIPLE

*Being confident of this, that he who began a good work in you will carry it on to completion until the day of Christ Jesus.*
*(Philippians 1:6)*

Friends, a good work has begun in you. You are equipped to be a disciple of Christ. As you follow Jesus on a daily basis, that good work God began when he created you will continue to unfold in your heart and your life. Of course, there will be some discouraging days when you may wonder if God really cares, if God really has a plan for your life, and if you will ever overcome some of your greatest sins. That is normal. But be encouraged: God's word and promises will never fail; no matter how much you mess up, God's plan for your life cannot be thwarted. God *will* carry to completion the good work he began in you. Your job is not to make your life perfect. Your job is simply to follow Jesus. Leave the rest to God. When you do, he will bring about in you the righteous life that he desires and the good work he intends for your life.

*What is one important thing you have learned this month about being a disciple of Christ?*

# MARCH

# Bringing Out the Best in Your Parents

## DANETTE MATTY

MARCH 1          INVEST IN YOUR FUTURE FRIENDSHIP
WITH YOUR PARENTS

*A man who has friends must himself be friendly.*
*(Proverbs 18:24a NKJV)*

Ever hear people say they became friends with their parents after they left home? It's funny how that works. Today's verse is usually applied to friendship building between peers. This month, think about it regarding your parents. Read it again. If you're willing to invest in your future relationship with them, one day your mom or dad will become your friends as much as they are your parents.

Of course, you can't control anyone's attitude any more than you can control the weather. But you know by now it's easier to get along with your parents when you're friendly toward them.

I posted a couple of questions on my Facebook profile for teenagers and parents to answer. Of teenagers I asked, "What question would you ask your parents, and how would you describe your parents in one word?" I asked parents, "What's one thing you wish your children knew about you?"

This month, a few responses to these questions will be braided throughout the meditations as we explore the teen-parent relationship and how to "bring out the best" in your parents.*

I also asked my thirteen-year-old son, Denver, and my seven-teen-year-old daughter, Ariana, to contribute their own meditations for this month. I, for one, am glad they said yes. They've been bringing out the best in me all their lives.

*What questions would you want to ask your parents? Do you feel you can?*

*How would you describe your mom in one word? Your dad?*

*What would your parents say they wish you knew about them? (I dare you to go ask them later. You might be surprised by their answers.)*

*All names have been changed.

## MARCH 2        PARENTS WERE TEENAGERS ONCE

*Listen, my son, to your father's instruction and do not forsake your mother's teaching. (Proverbs 1:8)*

Remember when your younger self looked up to teenagers as cool beings to be envied? Now, having arrived in teenagehood yourself, it feels great to no longer be considered a child and to have more freedom.

Still, you probably have your sights set on the next phase of life. If you're in middle school, that's sixteen, when you are eligible for a driver's license. If you're sixteen, maybe you're dreaming about graduation or turning eighteen.

It's OK to look forward to your future. But, while you're in this stage, lean on your parents for wisdom and advice, even if you think they've forgotten what hormone-ville is like. Chances are, they actually haven't.

> I wish my son knew the teenage years weren't easy for me either. If he could just see what it was like, maybe in the future he wouldn't alienate us. I want him to know he can and should keep looking to us for feedback because we've been there too. —Harry

*What's one challenge you are dealing with now?*

*Ask your mom or dad what challenged them when they were your age.*

## MARCH 3 THE COMPARISON TRAP

*We have different gifts, according to the grace given us.*
*(Romans 12:6a)*

> Do you love my brother [or sister] more than you love
> me? —John

That's the question John told me he would have liked to ask his parents when he was a teen—and still today. Knowing what his parents would say is a different story. Sometimes it feels as if parents are playing favorites because one sibling is more easygoing than another. But is that true?

Do you think you already know your parents' answer? Let me, as a parent myself, clue you in: most of us parents love all our children with the same die-for-you commitment. But each child has a different personality, temperament, and gift set, all of which influence not only his or her individual behavior but also his or her relationships—including the relationship with parents. Some days, depending on the mood of either parent or teenager, one child might be easier to get along with than another. That's not planned; it's just life in a family.

Be yourself and allow your siblings, if you have them, to be themselves. Don't get caught in the comparison trap. Don't make your parents feel bad if your sibling happens to be getting along with them at the moment. And don't get full of yourself if you're the one on their good side.

One more warning regarding the comparison trap: your mom can't always be the most beautiful and popular mom. Neither can your dad always be the funny comedian or hero. Let your parents be themselves, and don't compare them to other parents any more than you want them to compare you to other teens.

**What would you say are your siblings' and parents' gifts? List them in the margin.**

MARCH 4                                    DIVINE DAD

*Look at the birds. They don't plant or harvest or store food in*
*barns, for your* **heavenly Father** *feeds them. And aren't you far*
*more valuable to him than they are?*
                    *(Matthew 6:26 NLT, emphasis added)*

It seems unfair to compare earthly dads with God the Father.
Those are big shoes to fill. Whether your earthly father strives to
reflect the image of God, we can think of God as our heavenly
Father. Jesus' life and sacrifice make that possible. In fact, when
Jesus wasn't calling God "my heavenly Father" (Matthew 15:13;
18:35) he referred to God as "your heavenly Father" (Matthew
5:45; 6:14; 6:26; 6:32). The Savior of the world was willing to share
his divine dad with us. Cool.

   In today's verse, Jesus emphasizes the value God places on us,
as people, over all other creatures God made. Like a good and wise
dad, God may not give you all you want. But you can count on God
to provide everything you need.

*What kinds of things do you trust your earthly father for?*

*What should you trust God your Father for?*

*Write your greatest need in the margin, and ask God to meet it.*

MARCH 5      WHEN YOUR DATE DOESN'T MEASURE UP

*Listen to your father, who gave you life, and do not despise your*
*mother when she is old. (Proverbs 23:22)*

You introduced your new boyfriend or girlfriend to your parents.
You've been IMing with him or her for weeks. You feel like you've
known each other FOR-EV-ER. What's with the raised eyebrows
and "code" eye contact your parents make with each other when
you talk about how connected you feel with your sweetie?

   Finally, they confess, they think you've begun to change since
seeing your friend. "That's my boyfriend [or girlfriend]," you

emphasize. But they don't consider him or her good for you. Why not? They can't put their finger on it; they just don't feel right about him or her.

Before you scream into your pillow or your parents' faces, remember they have twice as many years' experience with people as you do. They don't know everything, but they can discern when someone may not be the best person to open your heart to. Be willing to listen to your parents. They may save you months—even years—of heartache.

*If you were a parent, what's the number one character trait that you would want your child's boyfriend or girlfriend to have?*

*What kind of boyfriend or girlfriend can you be now that you will still respect in two years?*

## MARCH 6                    FOOLPROOF YOUR LIFE

*Be very careful, then, how you live—not as unwise but as wise.*
*(Ephesians 5:15)*

Here are some questions we should ask when making decisions:
• How much time or money will it cost?
• Is it scriptural or legal?
• How will it make me look?
• How close can I get to the edge without sinning?

Pastor Andy Stanley suggests a different question has the power to foolproof our decision-making for the rest of our lives. After all, we all have chapters in our lives we wish we could go back and rewrite. Just ask your parents about it, and they'll probably roll their eyes, remembering their stupid mistakes.

According to Stanley, the best question is this: Is it wise?* An easy-to-remember definition of wisdom is this: doing what's right in the right way at the right time. Making decisions based on whether something is wise can foolproof your life. Read Ephesians 5:15-17, do what it says, and regularly ask yourself, *Is it wise?*

*In what area of your life do you need to be careful?*

*Write in the margin a challenge you're facing of which you need to ask,* **Is it wise?**

*Andy Stanley talks about this in a six-part series called *The Best Question Ever*, available on DVD at Christianbook.com or free audio download from www.northpoint.org/site/page/podcasts or iTunes.

MARCH 7                    MOMMY DEAREST OR MOMMY
                                                    CLUELESS?

*"Come and see a man who told me everything I ever did! Could he possibly be the Messiah?" (John 4:29 NLT)*

Mom—control freak. That's how Abby described her mother. She went on: "There can't be a relationship because she's too busy try-ing to control it." In her stress, Abby has given up relying on her mom for support. "She's trying to control me," Abby continued, "but little does she know she will lose this one." She told me if her mom knew she had shared this, "She might have a panic attack because then someone would know the truth of her not being per-fect."

If you have a nurturing mother, stop and thank God for her right now. But maybe your mom, like Abby's, is clueless about how her negative traits affect you. Like the woman at the well in John 4, she'd be bowled over if someone exposed the truth about her dys-function. Yet after Jesus' truth collided with the woman's self-deception, she stayed in the conversation. And he changed her.

Pray for your mom. Jesus paid an enormous price to exchange brokenness for wholeness. Praying for her wholeness will add to yours.

*How do your mom's good qualities affect you?*

*How do her negative traits influence you?*

MARCH 8 WHAT TALK SHOWS DON'T TELL YOU

*When words are many, sin is not absent. (Proverbs 10:19a)*

I used to love talk shows—Oprah, Maury, Montel, and the like. These informative and dramatic programs could be ridiculously theatrical, and often they involved childhood trauma, such as someone being someone else's "baby mama" who was cheating on the cheater—really highbrow drama.

Eventually, I stopped watching (translation: I got a life). When I think of those episodes with woeful prepubescence tales on exhibit, I'm reminded of something a mom of teens once said: "People seem to recall their childhood as being worse than it really was."

Most people who had difficult childhoods are too busy rebuilding their lives to go on talk shows. Even those of us with painful memories know that with God's help we can move past them. Those experiences have influenced us, but they do not define us.

You may not agree with everything your parents do, but before you call up the network to voice your suspicions that Mom or Dad could be the antichrist, trust me: years from now you'll see that neither your life nor your parents were as horrible as you thought.

*What about your childhood was great?*

*What parts of your childhood do you now see weren't as bad as you thought they were then?*

MARCH 9 THEY DO IT BECAUSE THEY LOVE ME?
(Written by Denver Matty, age 13)

*Don't sin by letting anger control you. Think about it overnight and remain silent. (Psalm 4:4 NLT)*

When you've gotten in trouble and are angry with your parents, it's hard to just "get over it." When lying on your bed intensely studying the muffling capabilities of the pillow, what do you think about? *They do it because they love me? Very funny.*

My parents rarely seem to understand when I get angry. "So what if I don't go to bed on time?" I ask. "I eat so much sugar, I probably couldn't sleep if I tried!" (That last bit doesn't help.)

Have you heard your parents say something like this? "You're being defensive, so you're guilty."

*Hel-lo!* you think to yourself. *I'm only raising my voice to make my point!*

Or, what about this one? "You always have an excuse."

"They're not excuses," you explain. "They're *good reasons.*"

Still in trouble.

When you're angry, you may not believe this popular saying of parents: "I do what I do because I love you." But it's true. So, eat a banana, read, take a walk, or pray through gritted teeth to help yourself get past it. Popping balloons may help, too. Like today's verse says, don't let anger control you.

**Think about fun you've had with your parents. When? Where?**

**When have your parents helped you through something difficult?**

## MARCH 10                                LISTEN UP

***Isaac said, "I am now an old man and don't know the day of my death." (Genesis 27:2)***

Here's Isaac, revered Old Testament father, about to die. He wants to give his sons his "blessing," an affirmation that says, "You'll have the skill and help from God to do whatever God requires."

Isaac instructs his oldest, Esau: get your weapons, go hunting, and prepare a meal. Why Isaac chose these specific tasks isn't important. Esau probably had listened to and obeyed countless instructions from his father throughout his life. So he didn't argue: "What the heck? I'm tired. Can't I just run down the hill and pick you up a camel burger?"

How many times have your parents told you what to do? Sometimes it feels like they're nagging. OK, sometimes they are nagging! But mostly they're helping you understand what works best in life—from maintaining a home to balancing a checkbook to taking care of your car to relating well with others.

Your parents care more about you than you do. One day, when they're gone, you'll be glad you listened.

*How does listening to your parents' instructions affect your choices and habits?*

*When have you been glad you listened to your parents?*

MARCH 11                                                    PARENT INTERVIEW

*Reflect on what I am saying, for the Lord will give you insight into all this. (2 Timothy 2:7)*

For years I carried around a folded paper called "Great Kid Questions." As the title implies, it was a list of conversation-starting questions, from silly to serious, that parents could ask their sons or daughters just for the sake of communicating. I'm always surprised, impressed, and enriched by what children—particularly my own—share.

You might experience the same effects from a spontaneous interview with your mom and dad. You're bound to learn things that will help you see them in a different light. Showing interest in your parents' opinions and life experiences will show them you care and will probably deepen your appreciation for them. Ask God to show you how to pray for them in light of their answers. Here are some suggested questions:

What was a fad when you were young?
What was popular slang when you were a teenager?
What's your idea of a hero?
What's the best part about being a parent?
What's the hardest part about being a parent?
If money, time, and age were irrelevant, what would you do?

*What is one surprising thing you learned about your parent(s)?*

*How did this interview help you see your parent(s) in a new light?*

MARCH 12                              THREE THINGS BY THIRTEEN

*The father of godly children has cause for joy. What a pleasure to have children who are wise. (Proverbs 23:24 NLT)*

I have a thing for threes. Some of the best things in life come in threes: PB&J sandwiches, the Three Musketeers (the candy bar and the movie), and a three-ring circus. In the next few days, we're going to unpack some threes that, unlike my shallow picks, are worth thinking about long after you read this.

A friend once said there are three things everyone figures out by the time he or she is thirteen:
1. The kinds of friends you choose
2. How you respond to authority
3. Whether you're a giver or a taker

Those are three significant areas that will affect how the rest of your life will go. And they're three areas in which most parents try really hard to influence their children.

In yesterday's devotion, I encouraged you to interview your parents. Today, I challenge you to ask them questions about you. Their understanding may be more insightful than you may think.

Ask them: Have I chosen friends wisely? Am I easy or hard to lead? How can I give to our family in a way that helps?

Use the answers your parents give you as you think about today's meditation and questions that follow.

*How have you shown wisdom in your choice of friends?*
*What does it mean to be humble in your response to authority?*

*Are you more of a giver or a taker in life, and why?*

MARCH 13                                           THREE BIGGIES

*Direct your children onto the right path, and when they are older, they will not leave it. (Proverbs 22:6 NLT)*

It has been said that three things come with age: wisdom, experience, and maturity (that is, mental, spiritual, and emotional growth).

Today's verse is given almost exclusively as encouragement to parents who have adult children who have turned away from God. A pat on the back, a sympathetic sigh, or a pitying look usually accompanies it, as if to say, "Oh, well, your children have strayed, but because you suffered through, they'll wander back one day."

But if God were quoting this proverb to you, he might say, "This is your parents' job: to help you apply wisdom to the experiences they provide, enabling your maturity. If they do it right and you respond well, then you will form habits that one day will beautifully influence you and your own family for the rest of your life."

**What kinds of things are you doing that the Bible would call wise?**

**What's something important you've learned from experience?**

**How have you changed (matured) in the last year?**

## MARCH 14                                   THREE EQUALS TWO

*"Do this and you will live." (Luke 10:28b)*

Boom. It's that simple. Jesus said that life is the result of following two of the most important biblical commands: love God with everything you are, and love people as much as you should love yourself. (See Luke 10:25-28 for the entire conversation.) Jesus was quoting Deuteronomy 6:5, which tells us that before Jesus walked the earth, it was important to God for his people to live by these commandments.

Do these two things, and you'll find inner and outer life in a myriad of ways. Don't do them, and true, God-honoring life will elude you, as if you were watching movie credits but had missed the movie.

So as life happens with your parents—from arguments and disappointments to laughter and embarrassing moments—three of the most important words you'll ever form into a question are these: *What matters most?* According to Jesus, it is loving God and loving people. Three words equal two life-changing to-dos.

*Why does honoring your parents show you love God?*

*How does loving your parents translate into the self-love to which Jesus referred?*

*Write in the margin three simple acts that will honor your parents.*

MARCH 15                                    THREE MORE THREES

*The right word at the right time is like precious gold set in silver. (Proverbs 25:11 CEV)*

Some of the most important words you'll ever say come in threes:
   I love you.
   I need help.
   Please forgive me.
Interesting how all three of these statements work well in conversations with parents. Whether it's easy or hard to talk this way in your family, it's this kind of communicating that makes the difference between flimsy and meaningful relationships. And the way you relate to your parents is practice for how you'll relate in your own family someday.

How often do you tell your parents you love them without them saying it first?

Is it easy or difficult for you and your parents to say, "I love you" to each other? Why?

On a scale of one to ten, how much would you say you need your parents?

10 = As independent as I'm becoming, I still lean on them a lot.

5 = I've learned to do a lot on my own because my parents are so busy. But if I really need them, they're there for me.

1 = They've let me down regularly, so I've learned not to ask them for anything. I pay for most of what I want and even things I need.

*When was the last time you asked your parents to forgive you?*

*Is there something you should ask your parents to forgive you for now?*

MARCH 16                      MAKING YOUR PARENTS SMILE
                            (Written by Ariana Matty, age 17)

*A happy heart makes the face cheerful. (Proverbs 15:13a)*

One year for Mother's Day I decided to take my mom to an Imax theater to see one of her favorite childhood cartoons come to life on the big screen: *Speed Racer.* I used birthday and babysitting money, asked my dad to help me order tickets online, and printed directions to the theater. It was worth it to watch her transform from middle-aged mother to giddy child. Crushing my ribcage with maniacal glee, she dragged me through the line and to our comfortably centered seats.

During the entire movie, I watched her laugh and gasp, her enormous smile never ceasing. Near the end, when Speed won the race, she leapt out of her seat, applauding and cheering with the actors in the stands. Despite the fact that I had slunk so far down in my chair that my neck was about to break, I was smiling underneath hands that covered my humiliated face.

I'd made my mom happy. Mission accomplished.

*What can and will you do to make your parent(s) smile?*

*What sentimental surprise might you make the effort to work into one of their next special holidays?*

MARCH 17                      EVERYBODY NEEDS A SAM

*There is a friend who sticks closer than a brother. (Proverbs 18:24b)*

One of my family's holiday traditions is to watch *The Lord of the Rings* trilogy between Christmas and New Year's Day. One element that always strikes me is Sam's loyalty to Frodo, even when Frodo is in a ring-induced stupor or a Gollum-manipulated mood. Sam's right there, prodding him to keep going—or simply keep his head. "It's me, Mr. Frodo! It's your Sam."

My seventeen-year-old daughter and I are fond of saying, "Everyone needs a Sam in their life." Even Frodo admits the real hero of the tale is Samwise Gamgee. Sam braved the elements to Mordor, fighting against poorly dressed creatures with bad hair, all the while believing in Frodo's ability to do what was right, even when it seemed he wouldn't.

We parents bark and nag when we have to, but we are your greatest advocates and biggest fans. When it comes down to it, we'll go the distance on your behalf with fight-and-die-for-you devotion. There will come a time in your life when you realize that, more often than not, your parents are your Sam.

*When has your mom or dad shown loyalty to you?*

*What are you doing to show loyalty to your parents?*

MARCH 18                    KITCHEN SLAVES UNITE!

*"In everything I did, I showed you that by this kind of hard work we must help the weak, remembering the words the Lord Jesus himself said: 'It is more blessed to give than to receive.'"* (Acts 20:35)

On my thirteen-year-old son's Facebook profile, it says:
Employer: My parents
Position: Kitchen slave

I laughed when I read that. Poor boy, those plates and utensils must weigh, minimum, three ounces each! He's exhausting himself unloading that dishwasher. Someone call Child Welfare!

I felt similarly when I was a teenager. Yet chores were part of life, like school and playing—normal, not "extra."

Strangely, that's not the case for everyone. A girl from my old youth group, who now is in her first year of college, told her mom how ridiculous it was that many students didn't know how to do the simplest tasks, such as laundry, or how to cook basic, nongourmet meals.

I promised myself I wouldn't cripple my children by helping them do things they were capable of doing for themselves. I know what your parents probably know: there's something empowering about learning new skills that lead to other new skills in life beyond the kitchen.

Reread today's verse.

*How is working around the house similar to giving?*

*How does doing household chores bless your parents?*

*How does it help you, both now and later?*

MARCH 19                                      WHY SHOULD I CARE?

*Whatever you do, work at it with all your heart, as working for the Lord, not for men, since you know that you will receive an inheritance from the Lord as a reward. It is the Lord Christ you are serving. (Colossians 3:23-24)*

Why is it easier to do work for someone whose name isn't Mom or Dad? As a teenager, I used to be amazed at how tempting it was to slog through my chores, even if I was receiving an allowance. But if the neighbor lady asked me to do light housekeeping for a few bucks, I went all Martha Stewart. OK, not that good, but you get the point.

If you relate, ask yourself: Why do I offer my best efforts for those who don't provide for or love me like my parents?

Could it be because other adults don't have the same emotional impact and psychological influence on us? We're not as comfortable being less than perfect with nonfamily. With family, we're often so comfortable that we're lazy.

No matter who you're doing work or favors for, God expects you to make the kind of effort that acknowledges him as the One you're really trying to please.

*Which chore helps your parents out most?*

*Why do you think God cares about our work ethic so much that, as today's verse says, he rewards us?*

MARCH 20       SWITCH WEAPONS ON YOUR PARENTS

*We use God's mighty weapons, not worldly weapons, to knock down the strongholds of human reasoning and to destroy false arguments. (2 Corinthians 10:4 NLT)*

When I asked Katie how her mom's job stress was affecting her, she explained:

> When she comes home from work, it's like she's still there in a way. It feels like I'm one of her employees and not her daughter. I wish she were more like the mom I had a year ago when she was more fun and less of a manager.

Katie understands, as she put it, that "being a mom is kind of like being a boss of sorts," but her mother's strain makes Katie not want to come home.

When your parents' stress affects you, what weapon do you pull out to handle it—avoidance, sulking, anger, sarcasm, or even phony compliance to keep peace?

Although that last option might seem like the nice thing to do, let me encourage you to check your motives and switch weapons—to prayer. Let compliance and kindness follow praying for your parents. They struggle, like anyone, and need those closest to them to pray for them regularly.

*What kind of stress do you see your mom or dad dealing with lately?*

*What's the best way you can respond to them right now?*

*Write a prayer for them in the margin.*

MARCH 21       GOD AND ZITS: WHAT THE BIBLE AND
       JEREMY CAN TEACH YOU ABOUT YOUR PARENTS
       (PART 1)

*"Just say 'yes' and 'no.' When you manipulate words to get your own way, you go wrong." (Matthew 5:37 THE MESSAGE)*

Zits is my favorite comic strip. Jeremy Duncan, the fifteen-year-old protagonist, struggles through homework; relating to his on-off girlfriend Sara; and giving Walt and Connie, his suburban parents, a one-guy course in adolescent psychology.

As archaic as Walt and Connie seem to Jeremy, readers can see they care about their son—even when it's overdone, as when Connie worries that something's wrong. She tells Walt, "Jeremy has been in his room for hours! He could be sick... injured... depressed." Walt calmly replies, "Or he could be sprawled on the floor texting pointless non sequiturs* to his friends." Certain that Walt is clueless, Connie threatens, "Look, if you're not going to jump to conclusions with me, I can jump alone!"

Parents sometimes jump frantically to deduce what you really mean or what's really going on, because they care about you. So, communicate clearly with them—no code words, meaningless grunts, or non sequiturs. Be straight up, and help keep your parents from jumping.

*Is it easy or difficult to communicate plainly in your family?*

*Write in the margin a polite, clear way of communicating to your parents (1) that you want to be alone; (2) that you want to talk.*

*non sequitur—a conclusion or statement that does not logically follow from the previous statement.

MARCH 22       GOD AND ZITS: WHAT THE BIBLE AND
      JEREMY CAN TEACH YOU ABOUT YOUR PARENTS
      (PART 2)

*Children are a gift from the LORD; they are a reward from him.*
*(Psalm 127:3 NLT)*

Under my desk glass, I keep an old ZITS comic in which Jeremy complains to best friend, Hector, about their parents' latest restriction.

"This bites so bad!" Jeremy yells with eyes shut tight in frustration.

"What possible justification can our folks have for not letting us go to the concert?"

Hector shares Jeremy's bewilderment. "My dad said that I'm not old enough to be exposed to the sexually suggestive stage show or the alcohol and probable drug use among the other audience members."

"Yeah! See?" Jeremy sulks. "My parents didn't have a good reason, either!"

Seems like parents are speaking a different language when they're saying no to something you want. But the biggest reason they have for guarding your purity, intellect, health, and well-being is found in today's verse: you are a gift from God to them, a blessing, a reward. That's how they see you. That's how they know you. And you don't treat a gift carelessly. You protect it.

So ease up on your parents' restrictions. They're just treating you like a gift.

*If you're really the gift from God the Bible says you are, how should you act toward your parents?*

*How are your parents a gift from God to you?*

MARCH 23        BOUNDARIES ISN'T A FOUR-LETTER WORD

*And the LORD God commanded the man, "You are free to eat from any tree in the garden; but you must not eat from the tree of the knowledge of good and evil, for when you eat of it you will surely die." (Genesis 2:16-17)*

God set the first boundary. If the limitation (or rule) were breached, there were to be consequences.

Like God, my friend Pam has good reasons for setting boundaries with her teenager:

> I wish my son understood that part of my job is to provide consequences that are meaningful now, so he can learn important life lessons before the stakes for poor choices are so high they're difficult to recover from.

It's tempting to think of boundaries as fun-murdering restrictions. But your parents give you certain freedoms too, just as God gave Adam and Eve a freedom to eat from the tree of life. Boundaries simply help you develop what Pam calls your "chooser"—the ability to choose wisely in questionable situations.

> I wish he knew my motivation for providing boundaries is not to hold him back, but to create a place of reasonable safety for him to develop his chooser.

**Which of your parents' boundaries do you dislike?**

**Which of their boundaries makes sense?**

**Which will you have for your own children?**

MARCH 24

MY PRNTS CNT RD THS!
HOW 2 REL8 2 YUR PRNTS
(Written by Denver Matty, age 13)

**Patience is better than pride. (Ecclesiastes 7:8b)**

If u shwd ths 2 yur prnts, wd they undrstnd? Mybe; mybe nt.

Parents, it seems, don't always get this generation. For example, when you buy a video game, your mom might ask, "Is that guy on the cover good or bad?"

"*Please,* Mom. Just because he's wearing an ominous cloak, has a sweet sword, and the ground around his feet is littered with skeletons doesn't necessarily mean he's evil."

When my dad tries to play *Legend of Zelda,* he says, "These fancy gadgets; how does this touch screen work?"

"It's simple," I explain. "All you do is take the force gem to the tri-base without being spotted."

"Take the whatsit where?" he asks.

Or maybe your mom only lets you wear your favorite holey jeans around the house because it makes you look "tacky." But you know it's the style.

Believe it or not, your parents likely went through the same thing with their parents, who probably said, "What the hey?" to "new" technology and fashion WAY BACK THEN.

If you swallow your pride, answer their questions patiently, and limit holey garb to indoors, they'll eventually stop pestering you—and you can game or text or whatever in peace.

***When do you find yourself being impatient with your parents?***

***Write in the margin ways you can practice patience with them.***

MARCH 25                                    PARENT PRAYERS

***As for me, far be it from me that I should sin against the LORD by failing to pray for you. (1 Samuel 12:23a)***

The respected Old Testament leader Samuel felt so strongly about praying for his people, Israel, that he considered it a sin not to do so. That's a pretty extreme thought. What would it be like if you were that compelled to pray for people in your life? What if you took praying for those you care about so seriously that your day seemed incomplete if you didn't?

Well, even though God's word tells us to "pray continually" (1 Thessalonians 5:17), there's no indication in Scripture that we'll fry eternally if we don't. But imagine if you prayed like it mattered more than you think. How might your parents' job situation change? How might their marriage be blessed?

Imagine. Then pray with the attitude that your prayers will touch God's heart and move God's hand. Here are some suggested prayer areas:
- Your parents' spiritual growth
- Their wisdom
- Your relationship with them
- Their marriage, if married
- Challenging situations they're facing

Pray that God develops in your parents the things these verses mention:

- 1 Corinthians 13:4-7
- Galatians 5:22-23
- Philippians 4:6-8

*Why is it important to pray for your parents?*

*How does it influence you when you pray for them?*

MARCH 26                    FROM ANGER TO LOVE
                        (Written by Ariana Matty, age 17)

*"Honor your father and mother"—which is the first command-*
*ment with a promise—"that it may go well with you and that*
*you may enjoy long life on the earth." (Ephesians 6:2-3)*

As you read today's verse, you may have rolled your eyes or let it pass through your head without a second thought. Just a few years ago, I would have done both. Growing up in a Christian home, hearing the same things from the Bible almost every day, I thought it seemed like one big cliché.

On top of that, I hated my parents. I didn't have a good reason, if I'm being honest. They spent time with me, loved me, and tried to listen to me. But their authority made my skin crawl and anger grow. One day I exploded—all over Jesus, that is. I poured myself into him, and for the first time, I wanted to love—and honor—my parents. I asked God to take the anger away, and I felt my heart hollow out.

Over time, God has filled me with more love for my family than for anyone else in my life. If you will reread today's verse, you'll see it isn't just another quotation, but rather a promise. And God never breaks his promises.

*For what are you most angry with your parents?*

*Are you willing to let God replace your anger with love—and*
*forgiveness, if necessary—so that you may honor your parents?*

# MARCH 27  THE HARD RIDE OF PARENTAL CRITICISM

*You can trust a friend who corrects you. (Proverbs 27:6a CEV)*

In this final lecture before dying of cancer, college professor Randy Pausch* talked about a childhood coach who rode him especially hard during one practice. Later, an assistant coach told Randy, "That's a good thing. When you're screwing up and nobody's saying anything to you anymore, that means they gave up."

That lesson stuck with Randy. "When you see yourself doing something badly and nobody's bothering to tell you anymore," he said, "that's a very bad place to be. Your critics are the ones telling you they still love you and care."

Harsh criticism can wound. But not hearing it can cripple. One of the hardest things for parents is to correct their children while also validating them—to challenge questionable behavior and attitudes while showing unconditional love.

When your parents ride you, remember three things:

1. It's a hard ride for them, too.

2. They care more about you than those who will dole out your grades or your paychecks.

3. Along with Jesus, your parents won't give up on you.

*What was the last thing your parents rode you about?*

*How did you respond?*

*Ask God to help you know what to do about it.*

*Professor Randy Pausch gave his last lecture, "Really Achieving Your Childhood Dreams," on September 18, 2007, at Carnegie Mellon University. The lecture inspired the bestselling book *The Last Lecture,* published in thirty-five languages. He died of pancreatic cancer in July 2008 at the age of forty-seven.

# MARCH 28                    I BELONG TO _____

*And you also are among those who are called to belong to Jesus Christ. (Romans 1:6)*

*But you are a chosen people . . . belonging to God. (1 Peter 2:9)*

Do you know the origin of your family name? Is there anyone well-known in your genealogy?

One side of my family's ancestry includes a multiple-great-grandma who, as a five-year-old slave girl, was freed when President Lincoln signed the Emancipation Proclamation on January 1, 1863. On the other side, we have a governor accused of being dictatorial and doing bad things with his state's money. Guess which pedigree I'd rather claim.

Whether noble or notorious, your family heritage isn't what counts in God's eyes. Jesus died so that everyone could belong to him. And while you may enjoy your status in certain clubs, groups, or social networks, the ultimate honor you have in life is to say, "I belong to God."

*In the margin, list every real-life and online group to which you belong.*

*Ask yourself: how would it affect me if I no longer belonged to each of these groups?*

*In what ways does belonging to God affect your life?*

MARCH 29                    UNCONDITIONAL LOVE (PART 1)

*I'm absolutely convinced that nothing—nothing living or dead, angelic or demonic, today or tomorrow, high or low, thinkable or unthinkable—absolutely nothing can get between us and God's love because of the way that Jesus our Master has embraced us. (Romans 8:39 THE MESSAGE)*

You could label today's verse using two words: unconditional love. Though God has holy standards we are to keep, God loves us whether we live up to those standards or we don't.

My friend Mike, parent of three, sums up unconditional love this way:

> My love for [my children] is not based on performance
> in school, athletics, or anything. When I'm at work, I

think of them. It's never bothered me to work fifty-plus hours and hand over a paycheck without even looking at it [in order] to give them a warm home.

Like your parents, Mike is not perfect. He learned some things the hard way in a previous marriage that produced his oldest child. Despite regrets, he appreciates his role as a father.

*Think of a time when your parents showed you unconditional love. What happened?*

*How will you show your own children unconditional love?*

MARCH 30                      UNCONDITIONAL LOVE (PART 2)

*Let love be genuine. (Romans 12:9a ESV)*

*Very rarely will anyone die for a righteous man, though for a good man someone might possibly dare to die. But God demonstrates his own love for us in this: While we were still sinners, Christ died for us. (Romans 5:7-8)*

You'll find nearly seven hundred references to love in the Bible. Although gaining eternal life depends on our surrender to Jesus Christ in response to his sacrifice, God loves us whether we surrender or we don't, as Romans 5:7-8 states.

Like Mike in yesterday's devotion, most parents feel the same way. Privileges may be based on doing chores, respecting boundaries, and so forth, but most parents love their children regardless of their obedience or performance. Don't confuse disappointment or anger with the absence of love.

Unconditional love should go both ways. When my son Denver was about seven years old, he wrote this note:

You're the best mom in the world.
P.S. Even when you're grouchy.

Of course, it made me laugh. What a statement of honesty and unconditional love all in one.

You don't have to agree with everything your parents do or decree, but be the kind of son or daughter who loves them unconditionally, even when—especially when—you don't get your way.

*Are you nice toward your parents only when you're getting your way?*

*How can you show your parents unconditional love?*

## MARCH 31          LAME JOKES AND BIG-FISH STORIES

*I have no greater joy than to hear that my children are walking in the truth. (3 John 1:4)*

I asked my friend Nick, father of five, what he wishes his children knew about him. Thinking I'd get an insightful, heartfelt answer, I shook my head and smiled at Nick's goofy response:

> I wish my kids knew that I really am Santa Claus and that it is hard work getting down my chimney. But those cookies are the greatest!

It makes me think of what my son, Denver, wrote in last year's Christmas letter about his dad: "He enjoys making his trademark 'dad' jokes, and then laughing at them (even if no one else is)."

My husband occasionally claims he's a superhero, ninja, or secret agent. He knows the children don't believe him, but he enjoys provoking some snappy comebacks that get us all laughing.

Parents quote odd sayings, sing silly songs, and tell eye-rolling jokes as only parents can. But do you know what means more to them than your laughing at their lame jokes or believing their big-fish stories? That you understand what God and life are really about, and that you walk in truth.

*What's something ridiculous one of your parents has said (or sung)?*

*How often do you and your parents talk about spiritual things?*

*Write in the margin one example of how you're walking in truth.*

# APRIL

# The Habit of Prayer

## LEANNE CIAMPA HADLEY

APRIL 1                                                    STAY AWAKE

*"Watch and pray.... The spirit is willing but the body is weak."*
*(Matthew 26:41)*

Jesus spoke these words the night of his last supper with his disciples. Following dinner, Jesus invited those he loved to pray with him. He knew that his arrest would happen soon. They wanted to pray. They had good intentions, but they were tired and fell asleep.

Jesus still invites us to spend time in prayer with him. Like the disciples, we are willing and have good intentions but we often end up "falling asleep." We might find ourselves too tired to pray. Or we might find ourselves too busy to pray. With the demands of everyday life—including homework, friendships, and family responsibilities—often we "fall asleep" and forget to make prayer part of our daily life.

April often contains much of Lent (the forty days before Easter) and Easter, and it is designated as a time of prayer and reflection. I invite you to spend time this month trying to "stay awake" and pray. Being intentional about prayer for one month can help you establish the habit of prayer, and the habit of prayer will change your life!

*What keeps you from praying regularly?*

*What changes can you make so that prayer can be a regular part of your life each day?*

APRIL 2                                    ASLEEP AGAIN?

*When he came back, he again found them sleeping, because their eyes were heavy. (Matthew 26:43)*

Three times Jesus asked his disciples to stay awake and pray with him. Three times they fell asleep. It has always amazed me that he did not get angry with them. Instead, he understood how difficult a task he had asked them to do.

When I was in high school, my mother had a serious surgery. I volunteered to stay all night with her. At first I was alert; but as the night went on, I grew tired. The next thing I knew, she was waking me up and asking if I wanted breakfast. I felt so ashamed that I had fallen asleep and that she had to wake me up. But she was grateful to me for trying to stake away and wanted to make sure I had breakfast.

Sometimes we are afraid to commit to increasing our prayer time because we are afraid we will fail. This story reminds us that Jesus invites us to spend time with him, nudges us when we fall asleep, understands when we fail, and always loves us.

*What is your prayer schedule? Do you pray at certain times each day or week?*

*Are you willing to commit to praying more than usual during this month?*

APRIL 3            FINDING A TIME AND PLACE TO PRAY

*After he had dismissed them, he went up on a mountainside by himself to pray. When evening came, he was there alone.*
*(Matthew 14:23)*

Jesus was in demand. Everywhere he went, people lined up—all needing and wanting something from him. He could not pray while all those people were pushing their way toward him, so he would leave the crowds and spend time in quiet.

We face the same challenge today with our technology! When I was a teen, my only messaging service was whoever answered the phone at my home. But you and your friends check messages on Facebook, MySpace, e-mail, voice mail, your cell phone, your home phone, and your computer. If people want to find you, they can! It is difficult for you to find uninterrupted time. You face the same challenges Jesus did as you try to find a quiet time and place to pray.

This story tells us that, for a brief period of time, Jesus would leave the people behind. Perhaps you need to do the same in order to find the quiet time and place you need to pray.

*How and where can you find uninterrupted prayer time each day?*

*Would it be difficult for you to turn off everything and simply be still? Why or why not?*

APRIL 4                                        PRAYER REMINDERS

*Hear, O Israel: The LORD our God, the LORD is one. Love the LORD your God with all your heart and with all your soul and with all your strength. (Deuteronomy 6:4-5)*

This scripture is called the Shema. It is a part of Scripture that Jewish people consider to be extremely holy. In fact, it is so holy that they place it on the doors of their homes, and some Jewish people wear it daily. Each time they look at it, it reminds them to give thanks to God and to live as God invited them to live.

Jesus was Jewish and would have had this scripture posted on the door of his house. As a teen, he would have worn it bound to his wrist and forehead each day. It would have reminded him of God's presence each time he put it on.

What reminds you to think of God and pray? You might wear jewelry or clothing with religious symbols on them. Or you might have religious symbols attached to your skateboard, your car, or your personal items. Each time you look at one of these symbols, you might want to pause and pray for a moment.

*What religious symbols or items do you have that can serve as reminders to pray each day?*

APRIL 5                    TRUSTING GOD WITH YOUR PRAYERS

*"But when you pray, go into your room and shut the door and pray to your Father who is in secret; and your Father who sees in secret will reward you." (Matthew 6:6 RSV)*

One of the most hurtful things about high school for me was that I would share private things with a trusted friend, believing we would be friends forever and this was truly the most trustworthy person I had ever met, and then, for some reason, that person would decide she or he didn't like me, find a new best friend, and tell that person my most private things. I am not saying it happened all the time, but it happened a lot!

This scripture reminds us that God hears our prayers in secret. We can tell God all our private thoughts and know that God will forever hold our prayers in God's heart.

I *hope* your friends never betray your trust. I know God will never betray it!

*Have you ever confided in a friend and later had that person break your confidence?*

*What might be preventing you from telling God all the things you might tell a friend?*

*Is it easier to talk to God or a friend? Why?*

APRIL 6                                        AUTHENTIC PRAYERS

*"And in praying, do not heap up empty phrases as the Gentiles do; for they think that they will be heard for their many words."*
*(Matthew 6:7 RSV)*

It is amazing to me that I write books today, because in high school my writing always seemed simple and bland compared to the writing of so many others! I felt the same way when I was asked to pray in my youth group. I prayed at home, but when it came time to stand and pray out loud, I thought my prayers were too simple. I didn't know enough fancy theological words to make my prayers sound as holy as other people's prayers.

This scripture reminds us that our prayers should not be spoken to impress anyone. In fact, it tells us that God isn't impressed with our fancy words. God wants to hear our authentic needs; when we share that, God is pleased.

Sometimes we hesitate to pray because we feel like our prayers sound simplistic—even when we are alone. I am glad Jesus reminded us to pray from our hearts and forget about the words! Whether we are praying alone or in front of a hundred people, God appreciates when we pray from the heart.

**What makes you self-conscious or uncomfortable when it comes to prayer?**

**What might help you feel more comfortable?**

## APRIL 7                                    WORDLESS PRAYERS

**"Do not be like them, for your Father knows what you need before you ask him." (Matthew 6:8 RSV)**

In Matthew 6:7, Jesus' words remind us that the words of our prayers do not impress God. In this verse, Jesus explains that we don't even need words to pray, because God knows what we need before we ask.

I remember my teen years as some of the most confusing of my life. I was trying to please everyone—my parents, teachers, and friends—and trying to keep up with a schedule that was much too full. There were relationship ups and downs that confused me terribly. I was stressed out over classes and grades. I often found myself beginning to pray and not even knowing what I needed. I was tired, overwhelmed, and unsure. Sometimes I would just sit and cry.

How freeing it is to know that God knows what we need. So, during the times when you are too overwhelmed and not sure of what you need, remember God already knows! Prayer is sometimes simply sitting with God and saying nothing. Even then, our prayers will be answered.

*When have you felt that life was overwhelming and found it difficult to pray?*

*Have you ever prayed without using words?*

*How can sitting still in God's presence be a kind of prayer?*

APRIL 8                                                    WHY PRAY?

*"As the Father has loved me, so have I loved you; abide in my love." (John 15:9 RSV)*

Remember when it would snow when you were little and your mom or dad or whoever cared for you would make you wear layers outside to play? You would have to put on your coat, scarf, mittens, and hat. I always complained because I felt too stiff and couldn't move well or bend my arms and legs. But it kept me warm! I would be outside for a long time because nothing—not wind, cold, or snow—could penetrate those layers!

Prayer is like putting on a lot of layers. Each time you pray, you are adding a layer of God's love to protect you from the things that threaten to harm you—things such as divorce, relationship problems, stress, worry about world issues, finances, the death of loved ones, and on and on. People will tell you that this should be the happiest time of your life, but you know the truth. Teen years are hard years! Prayer will surround you with the presence, love, and care of God. Even when life gets hard, you are protected and shielded by love!

*What stresses do you face?*

*Do you find that regular prayer helps?*

*How and when do you pray?*

APRIL 9                    PRAYING ON THOSE BAD DAYS

*I call upon God. . . . Evening and morning and at noon I utter*
*my complaint and moan, and [God] will hear my voice.*
                              *(Psalm 55:16a, 17 RSV)*

Some days nothing seems to go right. You wake up and get
dressed and nothing fits correctly. You look in the mirror and you
have developed a blemish in a very apparent spot! You get to
school only to find out that you forgot lunch money and your
homework, and that your best friend is angry with you. You look
at your watch and it is only 8:30. You wonder how much worse the
rest of the day is going to get! I have days like that as well. We all
do.

The writer of this psalm was not only having one of those bad
days, he had endured a series of them. Nothing was right, and so
this person called out in complaint to God three times a day for
several days.

Sometimes we feel like we can't complain to God. We think only
prayers of thanksgiving are acceptable; but God wants to hear all
our prayers. So even on those bad days, pray. It is OK to complain!

*Have you ever had one of those bad days? What happened?*

*Did you feel comfortable sharing it with God? Why or why not?*


APRIL 10                    PRAYERS OF THANKSGIVING

*O give thanks to the Lord, for [God] is good; [God's] steadfast*
*love endures for ever! (Psalm 118:1 RSV)*

Have you ever noticed that when things go wrong or you are worried, it is easier to pray than when things are going well? I remember being a teen and meeting my first love. At first I prayed every
night that he would call me. I prayed that I would say the right
things when I saw him in the hall and that I would not get hurt.
But once we started dating and I felt secure, I didn't feel the need
to pray as much about him.

My brother played basketball, and when tryouts were approaching he would pray hard to stay focused and make the shots. But once he made the team, he didn't pray as much.

I guess it is human nature to pray when we are worried, but praying a prayer of thanks each day is just as important. It takes more discipline and planning, though, because for some reason it's harder to remember to give thanks. Try to pray a prayer of thanksgiving each day.

*Do you find it easier to remember to pray when you are worried or upset than when things are going well?*

*How can you remind yourself to pray a prayer of thanksgiving each day?*

APRIL 11                              PRAYERS FOR FORGIVENESS

*Scrub away my guilt, soak out my sins in your laundry.*
                                    *(Psalm 51:2 THE MESSAGE)*

When I was in high school, I went to a football game my parents had forbidden me to attend. At the game, someone spilled a red-colored soda on me! Later, I discovered I had locked my keys in my car and had to call my dad to come and unlock it. I had lied, and now I had gotten busted!

My dad didn't say a word. I cried the whole way home—partly because I was sorry and partly because I was afraid of punishment. When we got home, Dad told me to change my clothes and bring him the shirt with the stain on it. When I gave it to him, he took it to the kitchen sink and scrubbed it until the stain was gone. There were no words spoken, but I knew he had forgiven me. I cried again—but this time because I was really sorry.

We all have done things we are afraid to tell God about—even though God already knows. This scripture reminds us that in God's great love, our sins are washed away and we are forgiven!

*When have you been forgiven by someone for something you knew was wrong? What did that feel like?*

**Do you trust that God loves you enough to forgive you of all your sins?**

APRIL 12                                       EATING AS PRAYER

*O taste and see that the LORD is good! (Psalm 34:8 RSV)*

The movie *Fast Times at Ridgemont High,* filmed in the 1980s, is about a group of teenagers and all the crazy and wild things they did. Back then everyone thought teens had "fast" lives! But that was before the Internet, text messages, and year-round sports. We live in "fast times" now! Fast food is the staple of our diet. If someone calls and we ignore the call, we might have a text message, an e-mail, and a Facebook message waiting within seconds!

This scripture tells us to "taste and see that the LORD is good." To taste and see, though, we will need to slow down! We eat so quickly and on the run that we don't even taste our food. We move so quickly, getting from activity to activity, we don't notice anything! If we slowed down a little, tasted our food, and walked a bit slower, we would notice the beauty of the world and become more aware of God's goodness.

**How difficult would it be for you to slow down when you eat and travel? What other ways might you slow down?**

**How might slowing down help you "taste and see that the LORD is good"?**

APRIL 13                                    PRAYERS FOR THE WORLD

*If my people who are called by my name humble themselves, and pray and seek my face ... then I will hear from heaven, and will forgive their sin and heal their land.*
*(2 Chronicles 7:14 RSV)*

I was listening to a group of older adults talking about the world: war, global warming, and the economy. Suddenly one of them said, "I feel sorry for teens today! We have made a mess, and they will have to clean it up!"

He was telling the truth. Many of the problems you will face as adults are not problems you have caused. You will inherit a world where choices that were made long before you were born have caused problems you will have to solve. Some of you will become politicians or economists or geologists and will try to fix our world. Some of you will be called to other fields and will work on solutions indirectly.

In the meantime, don't forget that God says if we pray, God will heal our land! You certainly don't have to be an adult to work on ways to solve our world problems. So speak out, take these words seriously, and pray hard!

*What problems in the world most concern you?*

*What can you do now to help solve these problems?*

APRIL 14                                        PRAYING FOR OTHERS

*Is any one among you suffering? Let him pray. Is any cheerful? Let [her] sing praise. Is any among you sick? Let him call for the elders of the church, and let them pray over him.*
*(James 5:13-14 RSV)*

In this verse, James reminds us to pray at all times. However, he acknowledges that there are times when people are sick and cannot pray for themselves. People of God are then called to step in and pray for them.

I met with a teen a few months ago whose mother had been killed in a tragic car accident. This teen loved God but was so angry with God that she could not pray. Was she sick? No, not physically. She was filled with grief, and it was getting in the way of her prayer life. I offered to pray for her until she could pray for herself again. I did, and one day recently she came into my office and told me she had prayed the night before.

Praying for the sick means being willing to step in and pray for those who are unable to pray for themselves.

*Have you ever experienced a time when you could not pray?*

*How did the prayers of others help you during this time?*

*Who needs you to pray for them right now?*

## APRIL 15                    PRAYING WITH OTHERS

*Therefore confess your sins to one another, and pray for one another. (James 5:16a RSV)*

When I was a teen, a close friend of mine had an abortion. I was heartbroken. I was not sure I would have made the same choice, I wondered how it would affect our friendship, and I worried about her emotional and physical health. One night in youth group we were in a prayer circle sharing our concerns. I shared about my friend, and we prayed for her.

Later, as I was leaving, I overheard two of the people from the prayer circle talking about my friend. They called her names, made fun of her, and were feeling quite superior to her.

Years later, I found a true prayer circle of trusted friends with whom I can share everything. It has been the greatest gift of my life.

In this scripture, James calls us to pray together. This can happen only when people understand confidentiality and, rather than gossip, pray from a place of caring.

I pray that you have a trusted circle of friends you can share your concerns and prayers with. If you don't, I pray that God will send you one!

*With whom can you share concerns and pray?*

*Are you a trustworthy prayer friend?*

## APRIL 16              PRAY WHEN NO ONE WILL LISTEN

*Even youths shall faint and be weary, and young men shall fall exhausted; but they who wait for the LORD shall renew their strength. (Isaiah 40:30-31a RSV)*

A teen I am very close to came to see me at my office. She was upset, and we talked about many things. Finally, she showed me a series of cuts she had made on her arm. I asked her what had hurt her so badly that she felt she had to begin cutting herself. She said that when her troubles first began, she felt she had many friends to talk to; but as time went on and nothing got better, her friends stopped asking her about her situation and stopped being sympathetic. She decided to try to hide her pain. It didn't work. Eventually she started to cut herself and let the pain out.

Holding pain inside intensifies it. The longer you hold it inside, the stronger it grows. Prayer is a way to express your pain. Everyone grows tired. Sometimes even your closest friends get tired of hearing you talk, but God never wearies of listening. So pray all of your feelings to God and know that God never tires of hearing you.

*Have you ever masked your feelings? Why?*

*Does prayer help? Is it enough?*

APRIL 17                             PRAYING IN THE DRAMA

*The LORD is my light and salvation; whom shall I fear? The LORD is the stronghold of my life; of whom shall I be afraid?*
*(Psalm 27:1 RSV)*

I have so many happy memories of my teen years: shopping at the mall with friends, attending the prom, being in plays, and going to ball games. But I also remember how cruel friends could be and how afraid I was much of the time. I was fearful of wearing the wrong outfit and being made fun of, or talking to the wrong boy and having his girlfriend tell everyone to stop talking to me. Sadly, I hear from the teens in my life that the teen years are still that way.

I remember thinking that when I got older I wouldn't have all this drama. Unfortunately, the drama goes on and on! I still struggle with it. One thing that helps, though, is to focus more and more on God's opinion of me and on what God calls me to do. As I do, God's opinion becomes more important and other people's opinions become less important. Prayer is the time when I am reminded of who it is I need to please.

**What are you fearful of when it comes to other people's opinions?**

**How does prayer help strengthen you against the drama?**

## APRIL 18                    PRAYING WHEN GOD IS SILENT

*To thee, O LORD, I call; my rock, be not deaf to me.*
*(Psalm 28:1a RSV)*

I am not proud of this, but I had a crush on the same person from fourth grade until college. I was sure that he was the one for me and that I was the one for him. Every night I prayed to God to help me either get over this guy or make him fall madly in love with me, but for years nothing changed. I wondered if God was angry with me, or if I was doing something wrong.

You will be happy to know that I am no longer in love with that same guy! I still wonder why God never stepped in and helped me. I have many theories. Maybe it taught me to pray regularly. Maybe it made me appreciate other people who have returned my love.

Sometimes when we pray, God is silent. We wonder why. The writer of this psalm felt the same way and called God "deaf." I don't know why God is sometimes silent, but I know God loves and hears our prayers. So I keep praying, and I hope you will, too!

**What have you been praying about that God has not given an answer?**

**Why do you think God is sometimes silent?**

APRIL 19                                    PRAYING LIKE A CHILD

*"Truly, I say to you, unless you turn and become like children,*
*you will never enter the kingdom of heaven."*
*(Matthew 18:3b RSV)*

Each Palm Sunday at my church we do a little dance with palm branches. The children make the Alpha and Omega signs using large motions to remember how Jesus called himself the Alpha and Omega, the beginning and the end. Our teens help teach Sunday school and do a great job. However, they don't really like doing the yearly dance. They are self-conscious and feel childish making huge letters in the air.

A few weeks ago, we were all doing the dance when I noticed that none of the teens were doing it. They were gathered and pointing at one child, a four-year-old. I looked, ready to tell them to get back to work, but I was frozen as well. This little girl had her eyes closed and was doing the most beautiful dance I have ever seen. She moved and swayed as her whole body prayed. And she had no idea anyone but God was in the room. After that, even the teens did the dance! We were all reminded of Jesus' words that we must become like children!

*What does it mean to pray like a child?*

*What can you do to become more childlike when you pray?*

APRIL 20        TRUSTING WHEN YOU HEAR GOD SPEAK

*And Samuel grew, and the LORD was with him and let none of*
*his words fall to the ground. (1 Samuel 3:19 RSV)*

Usually when we think of prayer, we think of being still and reaching out to God. However, in this story Samuel, a teen, is sleeping, and God speaks to him. Samuel is so used to being called by Eli that he does not recognize God's voice. Eventually he does. God calls him to be a great leader, and he becomes one.

I wonder how many times God calls us each day. A beautiful

bird sits singing on a branch, and we walk by and don't notice. God gently nudges us to make a good choice, but we are so set on doing it our way that we don't feel the nudge. God calls us to ministry, but we are so busy trying to impress our friends that we don't hear the call. God sends a friend to listen to us at the very moment we need it, and we think it is a weird coincidence.

God speaks to you each day. God calls you. Are you missing it?

**What are some ways God communicates with us?**

**When and how have you heard God "speak" to you? What did God say?**


APRIL 21                    PRAYING AS JESUS TAUGHT US

*"In this manner, therefore, pray: Our Father in heaven, Hallowed be Your name. Your kingdom come. Your will be done on earth as it is in heaven. Give us this day our daily bread. And forgive us our debts, as we forgive our debtors. And do not lead us into temptation, But deliver us from the evil one. For Yours is the kingdom and the power and the glory forever. Amen."*
*(Matthew 6:9-13 NKJV)*

I remember memorizing the Lord's Prayer in third-grade Sunday school. It took me weeks! On the Sunday we were to say it in front of the class, I did it perfectly. I said every word, and I won a bracelet with a little cross on it that I had worked so hard to get. The only problem was that I did not understand a word of what I had just said so proudly.

Many of us have said the Lord's Prayer for years, and many of us have memorized it. But for some of us it has become so common that we have forgotten its power and beauty. This is the prayer Jesus taught us to pray. In the next few days let's explore it and rediscover its meaning.

**Focus on the Lord's Prayer. Read it several times out loud.**

**Do you understand it? What parts do you find confusing?**

APRIL 22                                    OUR FATHER

*"Our Father in heaven, Hallowed be Your name."*
*(Matthew 6:9b NKJV)*

Political elections tend to be emotional. It is always interesting to me to hear the responses of people when their candidate's name is spoken. For some a name inspires hope and security, while for others it inspires fear, doubt, and even anger.

Names do that. They can evoke positive feelings or negative feelings when we hear them. They are powerful!

In the Lord's Prayer, Jesus begins with a name for God: Father. For Jesus it meant a loving, caring One who wants the best for us.

If you have or had a good relationship with your father, you probably associate joy, security, and delight with this description of God. If you have or had an absent or abusive father, you may not be able to understand this name. The point is not the name Jesus chose, but the feeling that comes from the name. By using the name *Father*, Jesus was telling us that we have a loving God.

*How would you describe someone who really loves you? Make a list of characteristics.*

*Now, begin the Lord's Prayer, and after you say "Father," add those words. Is that how you usually describe God?*

APRIL 23                              DOING THE WILL OF GOD

*"Your kingdom come. Your will be done On earth as it is in heaven." (Matthew 6:10 NKJV)*

Many times heaven is described as being far away, but the kingdom Jesus describes is coming to us. It will not be a place we go to when we die but something we experience on earth.

Mother Theresa spent her life caring for the dying people of Calcutta, and she used to say that when she looked into their eyes she saw God. In those eyes she found the kingdom of God on earth. When she was asked how others should change the world, she simply told them to take care of their corner of the world by doing simple things such as loving others and being kind.

I think doing the will of God is in loving others. We don't live in a very loving time. We live in an angry time, so the task is even more challenging. But when we love others, we experience the kingdom of God on earth. By doing the will of God, loving one person at a time, the kingdom comes closer.

*What are the obstacles that keep you from loving others?*

*Do you experience God's kingdom in loving relationships?*

*How would you describe the kingdom of God?*

APRIL 24                                    GOD WILL PROVIDE

*"Give us this day our daily bread." (Matthew 6:11 NKJV)*

I was listening to a story on National Public Radio about a group that was taking children to farms to teach them how bread is made. This group had conducted a survey and discovered that more than half of the children surveyed had no idea that bread is made from wheat. It made me think about what Jesus is saying in this prayer when he asks God to give us our daily bread.

Long before bread is made, the soil is tended and wheat seeds are planted. The wheat is watered and cared for, harvested, ground, mixed with water and yeast, given time to rise, and then, after all that, baked into bread. Likewise, long before we receive the bread God gives us, God has been hard at work making it for the moment we need it.

It is comforting to know that we have a God who is always working for our good and that God plans ahead to make sure we have what we need, when we need it.

*What is bread a symbol for in your life?*

*What do you need from God? Do you believe God is already working to provide what you need?*

APRIL 25                                        FORGIVENESS

*"And forgive us our debts, As we forgive our debtors."*
*(Matthew 6:12 NKJV)*

The word *debts* means "sins" or "things that we have done wrong." Admitting our sins to God can be very difficult, but I wonder which is more difficult: admitting our sins to God, or forgiving those who sin against us?

I have noticed that when I sin, I usually can have mercy toward myself, vow not to do it again, and let it go. But when someone does something to me, I have a hard time letting it go. Forgiveness is especially hard for teens these days because arguments are so public. Comments on both sides are posted for everyone to see on Facebook and MySpace, and text messages about the conflict are sent to multiple people. Not only are you trying to forgive the person who has wronged you, but you also are managing rumors and defending yourself to others who have nothing to do with it.

Jesus was always accused of wrongdoing. He knew what it was to be publically embarrassed and misrepresented. Yet still he forgave those who hurt him. Even on the cross, his last words were ones of forgiveness. Christ calls us to forgive, no matter how hard it might be.

*What sins do you need to be forgiven for?*

*Who has wronged you? How can prayer help you forgive this person?*

APRIL 26                                        TEMPTATION

*"And do not lead us into temptation." (Matthew 6:13a NKJV)*

If there is a word that describes the teen years, it is temptation—not because teens are more susceptible to temptation than everyone else, but because it's a time of transition, from being dependent on your parents and other adults to making your own choices.

No longer do teachers explain each assignment and read aloud to you. You are expected to follow the class syllabus, read on your own, and get everything done on time. Once you're sixteen, no longer do your parents drive you everywhere. You drive yourself or ride with friends, and you have many choices about where to go and what to do when you arrive. No longer do you go along with everything your parents believe about politics, God, and what is right or wrong. You are deciding for yourself what you believe and value.

It is an exciting and necessary time, but it's also a time of being tempted like never before. So pray these words boldly! God will help you make life-giving choices for yourself!

***What new freedoms have you experienced since becoming a teen?***

***When do you find temptation is strong? What do you do in those times?***

APRIL 27                                                                          EVIL

***"But deliver us from the evil one." (Matthew 6:13b NKJV)***

Evil is a tricky thing! None of us sets out to get ourselves into an evil situation. It is sort of like swimming. You decide to go swimming and at first everything is fine. Then someone invites you to swim out farther. You start to get out there, but they are farther than you thought. You get tired, and once you get there, the water is deeper than you thought it would be. Suddenly, you are in danger. You are drowning!

Finding yourself surrounded by evil happens before you know it! You go to a party and someone offers you a drink with alcohol in it. You know you shouldn't drink it, so you decide to just take one sip. Before long, the glass is empty and you have had too much!

None of us is immune to evil. By asking God to deliver us from evil, we are reminded that we need to be mindful of placing ourselves in situations where evil might sneak up on us. God, who hears our prayers, is with us to help us get out of situations where evil is present.

*When have you found yourself in need of God's help?*

*What steps can you take to protect yourself from evil situations?*

APRIL 28                                                      FOREVER

*"For Yours is the kingdom and the power and the glory forever. Amen." (Matthew 6:13b NKJV)*

When I was in junior high school, my teacher drew a line on the chalkboard with arrows at both ends and explained that lines go on in each direction for infinity. That is how God is. God has always been and will always be. It is the same with people.

The times you live in are unique. The Internet, iPods, CDs, and cell phones had not been invented a generation ago. You face troubles, challenges, and opportunities that people born even twenty years before you could not have imagined. However, many struggles you face—finding time to pray; not understanding why God is sometimes silent; struggling to become independent; knowing that we need forgiveness; having a hard time forgiving those who have hurt you—are things teens have struggled with forever.

The Lord's Prayer is old, but it is not outdated. It addresses the needs of ancient people while articulating the needs of teens today. Keep praying this prayer, for like those who prayed it long ago, God will hear you and answer you!

*How do you think the prayers of teens have remained the same throughout all time?*

*How do you think the prayers of teens today are different?*

APRIL 29                    PRAYING WHEN WE ARE ANXIOUS

*"Therefore I tell you, do not be anxious about your life. . . . Look at the birds of the air. . . . Are you not of more value than they? And which of you by being anxious can add one cubit to his [or her] span of life?" (Matthew 6:25, 26-27 RSV)*

If you asked most adults, they would tell you that teenagers are too carefree, party too much, and refuse to grow up. That is not my experience of teens today. As you understand all too well, the world today is a difficult one. Far from the carefree experience adults seem to think teens are having, anxiety is a huge part of your everyday life. It is tempting to begin using negative behaviors as a way to cope. Drinking too much, driving too fast, experimenting with drugs, developing eating disorders, and cutting yourself are all ways of coping. The problem is that they don't work. In fact, they lead to more stress because you have to hide what you have been doing.

Prayer is a positive way of coping. You take all your anxiety, stress, and worries to God, place them in God's loving hands, and find assurance that God will provide for you. God is watching over you, caring for you, and protecting you.

*What are the stressful situations in your life? How can praying help?*

APRIL 30          EXPECTING GOOD THINGS FROM GOD

*"Or what man of you, if his son asks him for bread, will give him a stone? . . . How much more will our Father who is in heaven give good things to those who ask him!"*
*(Matthew 7:9, 11 RSV)*

We recently had an Easter egg hunt at our church. The children were so excited to find the eggs! When we gathered back together, most of the children sat on the ground opening their eggs, anticipating a different treat inside each one. They knew that each egg contained something sweet just for them. It never occurred to them that there might be something bad in one of the eggs.

When we approach God in prayer, I wish we would always pray like a child opening an Easter egg—expecting something good. But somewhere along the way we began to believe that we don't deserve good from God, or that God might be angry if we ask for too much or for the wrong thing. Jesus reminds us that God will only give us good things. So when you pray, pray expecting the goodness that God promises!

**Do you think God ever gets angry because of our prayers? Why or why not?**

**Do you think there are prayers we should not pray?**

**Why and how do you think we learn to fear God?**

# MAY

# Who Are You and Why Are You Here?

## MARY LYNN JOHNSON

MAY 1                                        UNCOVERING THE MYSTERY

*Beloved, we are God's children now, and what we will be has not yet appeared; but we know that when he appears we shall be like him, because we shall see him as he is.*
*(1 John 3:2 ESV)*

As teenagers, our lives can be pretty complicated. With our hectic schedules, we barely have time to ask the questions *Who are we?* and *What is our purpose?* much less to seek the answers.

We long to know and understand our purpose and to believe we can make a difference. We also want people to know and understand us, but sometimes we don't really know and understand ourselves.

Come along with me this month as we journey together to uncover the mystery of our identity and our purpose. We'll take a closer look at our map for life and turn to our own personal tour guide. We'll also meet some people along the way, and we'll dig deeper into their identity and the mastermind behind it all. Our time together will be filled with thought-provoking facts and comforting answers. All the while we will get to know a little better the artist who intricately concocted this masterpiece known as you.

*What are some things in our lives that define who we are?*

*How does knowing God help us know ourselves?*

MAY 2                                    A BEAUTIFUL REFLECTION

*Be imitators of God, therefore, as dearly loved children.*
*(Ephesians 5:1)*

When we think about our identity, our instinct is to question who
we are. People may say you're the one who knows yourself best,
but I know someone who knows you *completely*.

If we want to better understand a specific painting, we research
the artist. Likewise, to better understand a competitive team, we
turn to the coach. When examining a book, we learn about the
author. So when trying to understand our own identity, why not
turn to our Creator?

When we turn to the One who created us, he tells us everything
we need to know. After all, no one knows us better than the One
who created our hearts and minds! God created us in his image
(Genesis 1:27) so that we can reflect who he is in our lives. The
more we know God, the more we know and understand who he
created us to be.

*What are some ways we can help ourselves understand God's
character?*

*What are some characteristics of God you already understand?*


MAY 3                                    CREATOR OF THE WORLD

*The Lord God took the man and put him in the garden of Eden*
*to work it and keep it. (Genesis 2:15 ESV)*

In the beginning, when God created human beings and everything
in this world, God gave Adam and Eve a very important job: to
take care of the Garden of Eden. In the same way, God has given
us the responsibility of taking care of where we live. This means
it's our purpose to nurture our family, friends, home, church,
school, and workplace, so that where we live pleases God.

One way we help nurture and take care of our family is by helping around the house with chores and responsibilities. Similarly,
we can care for our community by volunteering our time and tal-

ents to help our church, school, or friends. When we look after these things, we have the power to do good or to cause chaos.

God wants us to love and take care of one another and the world around us. We shouldn't take this responsibility lightly.

*How are we creating chaos where we live?*

*How can we make our lives and actions pleasing to God?*

*How can we be leaders in every aspect of God's creation (e.g., church, school, home, family, government, and education)?*

## MAY 4                        A WONDERFUL MASTERPIECE

*I praise you because I am fearfully and wonderfully made; your works are wonderful, I know that full well. (Psalm 139:14)*

In Jeremiah 1:5, God tells Jeremiah, "I knew you before you were formed within your mother's womb; before you were born I sanctified you and appointed you as my spokesman to the world" (TLB). As with Jeremiah, the Great Artist painted a beautiful and wonderful person in you. God created you and planned for your life purpose, including your gifts, talents, and physical and emotional qualities. God laughed and smiled when shaping your laugh and your smile. God wanted to put your personality on display for the entire world to see. God is proud of you for who you are, because you are completely his fearfully and wonderfully made creation. There is no one else like you.

No creation of God is an accident, including you! Because God authored your life, there is a reason you were born, a reason you live where you do, and a reason you are who you are. Though sometimes these things are hard to understand, God can use you in amazing ways. God will accomplish great things for you and through you.

Read Psalm 139:1-18.

*What are some talents and gifts God has given you?*

*What are some ways you can thank God by using your talents and gifts to serve him?*

MAY 5                                  NEVER-ENDING LOVE

*With a mighty hand and outstretched arm; His love endures forever. (Psalm 136:12)*

God created us to love and to be loved. God wants us to see and feel his great love for us, and to show that love to others. The good things we do may or may not be motivated by love. In order to show Christlike love, we need to learn about God's love. When we understand how God loves us, we are more capable of showing other people Christlike love.

Sometimes it's hard to see and feel God's love. This is why God left some clear, physical reminders of his caring and faithful love. God gave us his word and blessings all around us that describe and proclaim this love. No matter what we do, we cannot lose God's love or make God love us any less.

In Psalm 136, the words "His love endures forever" appear in every verse—a total of twenty-six times! The psalm impresses upon us how God's love is great and powerful. The Lord's love withstands all of our flaws and mistakes. God's love endures forever.

*When love is not our motivation, what are some other reasons we do good things?*

*What blessings in your life show God's love?*

*Read Psalm 136. If you like, write a poem or prayer about God's blessings.*

MAY 6            NO RETURNS OR EXCHANGES ACCEPTED

*God decided in advance to adopt us into his own family by bringing us to himself through Jesus Christ. This is what he wanted to do, and it gave him great pleasure.*
                                                   *(Ephesians 1:5 NLT)*

All around us, things change. The weather changes from calm to stormy and warm to cold. Music, movies, and styles are constantly being modernized. We grow and progress through grades in school while our interests and personalities are refined. Friends move away or grow apart, and other relationships change. The loss of a pet or family member, or a serious illness, can be a difficult change.

Some changes are natural and provide new opportunities. Maybe you played a sport in middle school but in high school you didn't make the team. Now you have time to join a club, volunteer, or work an after-school job. Sometimes change is exciting and good, but many times it hurts and makes our life feel unstable. When we go through a lot of changes at once, our emotions are in for a pretty tough ride.

There is one thing you can be sure will never change: God's incredible love and care for you. God will never give up on you or walk away, no matter the changes you experience throughout life. You are a member of God's family, and that is unchanging.

***How does God's unchanging love provide security for your life?***

MAY 7                                    YOU'RE NEVER INVISIBLE

*O LORD, you have examined my heart and know everything about me. You know when I sit down or stand up. You know my thoughts even when I'm far away. (Psalm 139:1-2 NLT)*

God knows your heart, inside and out. He knows everything about you, and nothing is ever hidden from him.

When we do something kind for someone else and are recognized and thanked, we feel appreciated. There's nothing wrong with that! (See 1 Corinthians 16:17-18.) But sometimes we try so hard to receive praise for the good things we do that we put our good works on display. Colossians 3:23 says we should work for the Lord, not for other people. Even though sometimes our good deeds go unseen by the people around us, they can still make a big impact on the people we help, and they are never hidden from the Lord because he knows our hearts.

God will be pleased with the good things we do, for God sees it all. God also sees the things that we shouldn't be doing—the things we want no one else to see. We cannot escape the consequences of our actions, but we can always ask for God's forgiveness.

*How do the things you do when no one is watching influence who you are?*

*Do you think God is pleased with what you do?*

MAY 8                                    A POWERFUL PROTECTOR

*"O Sovereign LORD! You made the heavens and earth by your strong hand and powerful arm. Nothing is too hard for you!"*
*(Jeremiah 32:17 NLT)*

What do you think of when you hear the word *powerful*? Throughout history, people have risen and fallen from power. Politicians have power, although it is limited and temporary. Dictators are powerful because they impose nearly complete control over people's lives.

God is not a politician or dictator, but God is all-powerful. God has the power to do anything. God spoke and our world came into existence. God's word, the Bible, is also powerful.

It's comforting to know that the all-powerful God cares about our lives. There is no problem or trial too difficult for God! God is bigger and more powerful than anything and anyone. No matter what's going on in our lives, God is always in control. So we never have to worry. "The LORD is my light and my salvation—whom shall I fear? The LORD is the stronghold of my life—of whom shall I be afraid?" (Psalm 27:1).

God is our protector. A God who is that powerful is the absolute best comfort.

*How does knowing that God is all-powerful comfort you or give you a sense of awe?*

*What situation or circumstance in your life or the life of someone else shows the power of God?*

MAY 9                                    HE REIGNS…FOREVER

*"During the reigns of those kings, the God of heaven will set up a kingdom that will never be destroyed or conquered. It will crush all these kingdoms into nothingness, and it will stand forever." (Daniel 2:44 NLT)*

When I think about how great our God is, my mind is completely blown away. We serve a God who always was and always will be.

Our bodies and lives have limits of time and space, beginnings and endings. Every person has a day of birth and a day our earthly journey ends; our days are numbered. Since everything around us is mortal, it's all we've ever known. Our minds are limited, so the fact that God never had a beginning and will never end seems incomprehensible, but it's true.

Because our life on earth is temporary and seems so short, every day counts. Having a close relationship with God matters in our lives right now. When we've accepted Christ as our Savior, we receive the gift of eternal life. Although our earthly bodies and lives here are limited, we will live forever in heaven with God.

*How do you think we would view things that happen in the world and our lives if we embraced the truth that God reigns forever?*

*How should we live each day and prioritize our time knowing that our time on earth is limited?*

MAY 10                                      IN HIS FOOTSTEPS

*Live a life filled with love, following the example of Christ. He loved us and offered himself as a sacrifice for us; a pleasing aroma to God. (Ephesians 5:2 NLT)*

So far in our journey to discover our identity, we've looked at our Creator and who he is. Now we're going to take a closer look at Christ and trace his footsteps. God sent his Son not only as a sacrifice, but also as an example. Jesus was the only perfect human, without sin, ever to walk this earth. Christ was God, yet he also was a man. He had earthly parents he had to obey; he was a boy and a teenager before he was a man; he had emotions; he had friends; and he felt pain. He was tempted, misunderstood, and questioned; and he suffered. "No one needed to tell him what mankind is really like" (John 2:25 NLT).

During his lifetime, Jesus displayed every characteristic we need as Christians—as Christ's followers. When we display the same characteristics that Christ displayed, by following in his footsteps and allowing the Holy Spirit to live in and through us, we are fulfilling aspects of our identity. We are being who we were created to be.

**What are some characteristics Jesus displayed while he was on earth?**

**How can we be more Christlike?**

MAY 11                                    YOUR NUMBER-ONE FAN

*"If the world hates you, know that it has hated me before it hated you." (John 15:18 ESV)*

The Bible talks about things Jesus did, and he wasn't always doing glamorous jobs or walking around with adoring fans. He went to places no one else wanted to go and hung out with people no one else wanted to be with. Needless to say, that didn't exactly make Jesus popular with everyone. As he said himself in the book of John, he was hated. Jesus wasn't distracted by what the world thought. It was hard, though. Some people laughed at him, some rejected him, and even his followers denied him! He didn't do things to call attention to himself or to put his works on display. He sincerely went around helping and loving anyone who needed him.

Any popularity here on earth will not last very long and does not even matter. Proverbs 27:20 says that humans are never satisfied. We have a heavenly Father who already adores us and is proud of us.

*Why did Jesus hang out with the unpopular people? (Read Matthew 9:10-13.)*

*What are things you do in your daily life that show that popularity isn't important?*

*How is having a good reputation (for example, character, morality, integrity) important? (Read Proverbs 22.)*

MAY 12                         CARING AND COMPASSIONATE

*When he saw the crowds, he had compassion for them, because they were harassed and helpless, like sheep without a shepherd.*
*(Matthew 9:36 ESV)*

Jesus truly cared for people and met their needs. He fed the five thousand (John 6:1-14); healed a paralyzed man and forgave his sins (Matthew 9:1-8); and wept when Lazarus died, before raising him from the dead (John 11:33-36, 43-45). Jesus showed compassion.

Inviting someone who normally sits alone to sit with you, or greeting someone who is new or shy, are ways to show compassion. Just letting someone know you thought about him or her is also compassionate. When we see someone who's hurting, we can offer comfort. When we know someone who may not be able to perform a task alone, such as someone who is moving, we can choose to have compassion and offer help. There are many ways we can show compassion. When we serve people, we encourage them.

If we will keep watch for those who need care and compassion, then we can put into practice in our daily lives what Jesus did while on earth. We can be the hands and feet of Jesus Christ.

*What are some other instances in the Bible illustrating that Jesus is compassionate?*

*Think of someone who needs your compassion now. What can you do to care for that person?*

MAY 13                                          SLOW TO ANGER

*"But to you who are willing to listen, I say, love your enemies!
Do good to those who hate you. Bless those who curse you. Pray
for those who hurt you." (Luke 6:27-28 NLT)*

When someone hurts us, it's easy to get very upset and angry.
Sometimes we display that anger or take it out on someone else.
We may have different ways of showing anger, but we all have
something in common: we tend to let our frustration dictate our
actions.

As sinners, we persistently do things that hurt Christ. Every
time, he is never quick to anger. Psalm 86:15 says, "But you, O
LORD, are a compassionate and gracious God, slow to anger,
abounding in love and faithfulness." During his years of ministry,
Jesus told people to repent of their sins. Jesus will forgive us and,
likewise, we are to forgive others.

In John 2:13-16, Jesus was angry and stopped the money chang-
ers from dishonoring the temple. Getting mad isn't wrong as long
as we don't sin (Ephesians 4:26). We can turn that anger into motivation to do something good, such as showing patience and forgiveness (Matthew 18:18-35). How we handle anger can define
whether we have a Christlike character.

*What are ways you can manage anger without sinning?*

*How can you show patience and forgiveness to others when
they frustrate you?*

MAY 14                                          CIRCLE OF FRIENDS

*And when day came, he called his disciples and chose from
them twelve, whom he named apostles. (Luke 6:13 ESV)*

Jesus values friendship and close relationships with people. He
loved everyone. However, he chose twelve disciples to spend the
most time with while on earth. In Luke 6:12, Jesus prayed and
then selected twelve disciples. They came from different back-

grounds, but what they had in common was being followers of Christ.

It's really important that we choose our friends carefully. Eventually, we talk and act like the people we hang out with. When we spend an excessive amount of time with people who don't believe in Christian values, eventually they can take us away from following Christ.

Your Christian friends are essential to your faith; they can comfort and encourage you when times get hard, and they can rejoice with you in the good times. My close Christian friends have always been my source of encouragement and support when something is bothering me or when I'm trying to figure out how to help another friend who is struggling in her or his faith. They are always there with a hug, a prayer, and a passage from the Bible.

*What qualities should you consider when looking for a good friend?*

*How do you and your close Christian friends encourage one another in your spiritual growth?*

MAY 15                                    THE GREAT TEACHER

*Jesus answered him, "I have spoken openly to the world. I have always taught in synagogues and in the temple, where all Jews come together. I have said nothing in secret." (John 18:20 ESV)*

Wherever Jesus went, he was teaching. He was constantly showing his followers God's love and telling us how to live as God intended. Jesus told parables to illustrate concepts to people so he could communicate in a way that everyone could understand.

Paul writes, "I pray that the sharing of your faith may promote the knowledge of all the good that is ours in Christ" (Philemon 1:6 RSV). Christians are called to teach wherever we go. In order to do so, first study God's word carefully to know it well and to increase your own understanding. Simply communicating your faith to a friend and reading Bible stories to younger children (even your siblings) can be opportunities to teach. But, ultimately, we teach by living out our faith rather than hiding it. Our lives and actions are testaments to what we know and believe about our Lord. When we reflect Christ, we are teaching and, we hope, leading and pointing people to Christ.

*Using words, how can we teach others about Christ?*

*With our actions, how can we teach others about Christ?*

MAY 16                                              GOD'S WILL BE DONE

*He went on a little farther and bowed with his face to the ground, praying, "My Father! If it is possible, let this cup of suffering be taken away from me. Yet I want your will to be done, not mine." (Matthew 26:39 NLT)*

Before Jesus was arrested and brought to trial, he took his disciples and went to pray (Matthew 26:36-45). Jesus didn't just say a quick prayer; he went to be alone, praying three times.

Often we find ourselves doing what we want and hoping that it is God's will—or hoping that God will bring good out of it anyway. To understand God's will, we have to seek it and, like Jesus, pray and obey. "Watch and pray that you may not enter into temptation. The spirit indeed is willing, but the flesh is weak" (Matthew 26:41 ESV).

Sometimes we have to do things that we really don't want to do, whether it's something our parents or teacher tells us to do, or something God has called us to do. Like Jesus, we need to earnestly pray and then obey.

*Have you ever had to do something that you really didn't want to do?*

*Did you follow Jesus' example in the situation?*

*How did it turn out?*

MAY 17                                    A LIVING SACRIFICE

*And so, dear brothers and sisters, I plead with you to give your bodies to God because of all he has done for you. Let them be a living and holy sacrifice—the kind he will find acceptable. This is truly the way to worship him. (Romans 12:1 NLT)*

Jesus gave himself as a sacrifice. He left his Father, lived on earth, and put the needs of people before himself. He was wrongly accused; he suffered physical, spiritual, and emotional pain; and he was humiliated. Ultimately, Christ died so we could be forgiven and live forever.

Following in Christ's footsteps, we may not be called upon to give our lives, but we can give ourselves as a living and holy sacrifice, "just as the Son of Man did not come to be served, but to serve, and to give his life as a ransom for many" (Matthew 20:28).

Making a sacrifice means putting others before ourselves. Volunteering to rake leaves or babysitting for a family in a difficult or emergency situation could be a sacrifice. Being willing to compromise puts aside what we want. Helping our family by taking on extra responsibilities we are not expected to do; tutoring a student; or giving our money beyond our normal tithe, perhaps to a Christian ministry, can also be ways to sacrifice for others.

*How can you sacrifice for someone else?*

MAY 18                                    GOD'S SPIRIT IN US

*"But the Helper, the Holy Spirit, whom the Father will send in my name, he will teach you all things and bring to your remembrance all that I have said to you." (John 14:26 ESV)*

We've talked about God the Father and God the Son, but we have not fully explored the third person of the Trinity: the Holy Spirit. Jesus promised us a helper—also known as our advocate to the Father—to be with us on earth. The Holy Spirit completes the Trinity, which is God in three persons. One person of the Trinity is not more important than another; they work together. Some might think that the Holy Spirit is a myth, a ghost, or a theoretical idea, but the Holy Spirit is alive.

The Spirit lives in us when we accept Christ. "Don't you know that you yourselves are God's temple and that God's Spirit lives in you?" (1 Corinthians 3:16). Jesus said the Spirit would be with us always, to encourage and counsel us, to guide, comfort, and empower us. The Spirit is always congruent with Scripture, God's word, so that a false spirit will not mislead us. The Spirit of God is greater than any in the world (1 John 4:1 ESV).

For more about the Holy Spirit, read John 14:15-21 and 16:5-15.

**How does the Holy Spirit affect our daily lives?**

MAY 19                                                    OUR GUIDE

*"When the Spirit of truth comes, he will guide you into all truth. He will not speak on his own but will tell you what he has heard. He will tell you about the future." (John 16:13 NLT)*

Life can give us some pretty big and challenging decisions to make. Sometimes it's really hard to know which is the right or best choice. We go over the situation countless times and analyze every possible scenario. How will the choice affect us? What will happen if we make a particular choice?

Fortunately, the Holy Spirit is our guide and always is consistent with God's word and character (John 14:26). We may be facing a decision that involves right and wrong, or we simply may be trying to decide which choice is best for us. Either way, the Holy Spirit will guide us in the right direction.

We can receive guidance by reading God's word, praying, listening to a pastor or Bible study teacher, and discussing choices with our parents and mature Christians in our lives. God knows what is ahead for us and promises to guide us. We never have to make decisions on our own and, in fact, we shouldn't without seeking the Spirit of Truth.

**What big decision is on your mind now?**

**How can you seek the guidance of the Holy Spirit?**

MAY 20                                    SPIRITUAL GIFTS

*Now there are varieties of gifts, but the same Spirit; and there are varieties of service, but the same Lord; and there are varieties of activities, but it is the same God who empowers them all in everyone. (1 Corinthians 12:4-6 ESV)*

When we accept Christ's gift of eternal life and the Holy Spirit lives in us, we are given at least one spiritual gift. Each gift has a unique role of service in the body of Christ. We have spiritual gifts so that we can be who we were created to be.

In the Old Testament, Bezalel was filled with the Spirit of God and was able to do artistic craftsmanship (Exodus 35:30-34). God called Bezalel to use the skills he had been given to assist in the construction of the temple (Exodus 36:1). Likewise, God calls each of us to use our gifts in specific ways.

Different people are given different gifts. Some may be geared for up-front serving, and others may prefer behind-the-scenes work. Your gift is part of God's plan for your life, and you can use it throughout your lifetime.

No matter what our gifts are, we are called to use them to make a difference. Our gifts are blessings sent directly from God.

*What do you think your spiritual gift is and why?*

*How can you use it for God's glory?*

MAY 21                                           INTERCESSOR

*And the Holy Spirit helps us in our weakness. For example, we don't know what God wants us to pray for. But the Holy Spirit prays for us with groanings that cannot be expressed in words. And the Father who knows all hearts knows what the Spirit is saying, for the Spirit pleads for us believers in harmony with God's own will. (Romans 8:26-27 NLT)*

The Holy Spirit not only guides us but also intercedes for us. The Spirit steps in for us when we are at a loss for words and don't know what to pray. The Spirit speaks for us according to God's will.

Whenever you don't know what or how to pray—perhaps because you are sad, hurting, confused, uncertain, or numb—you can still call out to God and ask the Holy Spirit to help you, to intercede for you. Knowing that the Spirit is praying for you can be very comforting. It helps keep the communication going between you and God.

*Has there ever been a time when you were aware that the Holy Spirit was interceding for you or someone else?*

*What happened?*

MAY 22                                          A MASQUERADE PARTY

*What you learn from them will crown you with grace and be a chain of honor around your neck. (Proverbs 1:9 NLT)*

God is the most reliable source for discovering our identity. Yet because God is sinless, it can be hard for us to relate. Fortunately, people have been following God's laws and commandments for thousands of years, striving to know him more. Although there may be people around you who are great examples of God's followers, we're going to take a look at some of the early followers. Their history shows their love and devotion to God, and they are great examples of who we are in Christ.

You may have some preconceived ideas about characters in the Bible, but those are only masks that we put on them. In order to really study them, we have to get straight to the heart of the matter and read their life stories firsthand in the Bible. They weren't perfect, but they sought after God nevertheless. It's a privilege to be able to study their courage, strength, loyalty, and even sinfulness. Over the next several days we will take off their masks and start looking at who God made them to be and how they lived, which will help us understand our own identities.

*Think of a specific person in the Bible. What can you learn from this person?*

## MAY 23          CONSEQUENCES

*But God did say, "You must not eat fruit from the tree that is in the middle of the garden, and you must not touch it, or you will die." (Genesis 3:3)*

Adam and Eve were the first people to walk the earth. They were perfect, without sin, and able to make choices. God had given them everything they needed. God gave them the responsibility to take care of the garden, and they were free to eat from any tree except one. They were not to eat from the tree of the knowledge of good and evil (Genesis 2:15-17).

Unfortunately, evil was lurking. The serpent tempted them to do what they shouldn't, and they chose to disobey God. The serpent told Eve she would be like God, knowing good and evil (Genesis 3:4-5). Eve ate and gave some to Adam, making them the first sinners. They chose to disobey God, giving in to the temptation and the lies of the serpent. There were consequences for their choice.

Like Adam and Eve, we are tempted to sin, and if we do, we fall into the consequences of those sins. When Adam and Eve sinned, they were separated from God, which is the ultimate and inevitable consequence.

*Read Genesis 2 and 3. What can you learn from Adam and Eve?*

*What kinds of consequences have resulted from your sins?*

## MAY 24          EXACTLY THE WAY I'M CREATED TO BE

*"Now therefore go, and I will be with your mouth and teach you what you shall speak." (Exodus 4:12 ESV)*

Moses approached the burning bush that was on fire but didn't burn up, and God spoke to him. Moses was called to approach Pharaoh and demand God's people be released from captivity. Maybe we imagine Moses settled on his donkey with his game face on—staff in one hand and bullhorn in the other—ready to give

Pharaoh a piece of his mind; but that is far from what happened. Moses tried to convince God that he wasn't the right person because he couldn't speak eloquently. God said he would be with Moses and tell him what to say. Moses still asked God to send someone else! But God wanted Moses.

No flaw is too big an obstacle for God, even if it seems that it will make the task at hand impossible. Moses thought he wasn't the right person for the job God had called him to do; but God was with Moses, and Moses succeeded in bringing the people out of captivity.

**What might be holding you back from fulfilling God's call?**

**Do you believe that nothing is too big for God, and that God will supply your need?**

MAY 25             EXACTLY WHERE I'M SUPPOSED TO BE

*"If you keep quiet at a time like this, deliverance and relief for the Jews will arise from some other place, but you and your relatives will die. Who knows if perhaps you were made queen for just such a time as this?" (Esther 4:14 NLT)*

Hadassah, more commonly known as Esther, was an orphan being raised by her uncle, Mordecai. The Jews had been taken captive and were away from their homeland. The king wanted a queen, and Esther, along with many other girls, was taken so that he might choose a bride. Esther won the heart of the king and was chosen queen. But no one knew her Jewish identity, for Mordecai had advised her to keep it secret.

Meanwhile, Haman, an official of the king, was plotting to kill all the Jews—Esther's people. She needed to ask the king to spare the lives of her people. But if Esther approached the king without being summoned, even though she was the queen, she could be killed.

Esther struggled, but God gave her courage. She determined that God had put her in this foreign land as queen to save her people. Although Esther was in captivity, she was in the right place, family, and time for God to fulfill his plan. God has put you where you are for his purpose, as well.

*Why do you think God has put you where you are—in this time and place?*

MAY 26          FOREVER CHANGED AND NEVER THE SAME

*All those who heard him were astonished and asked, "Isn't he the man who raised havoc in Jerusalem among those who call on this name? And hasn't he come here to take them as prisoners to the chief priests?" (Acts 9:21)*

Paul, formerly known as Saul, has a pretty cool testimony. When Saul is first mentioned in the Bible, he isn't a follower of Jesus. In fact, he was plotting to murder some of Christ's disciples, which he thought was his duty as a Pharisee. As he was traveling to Damascus, a light from heaven flashed around him and he heard a voice: "I am Jesus, whom you are persecuting" (Acts 9:5b).

God took away his sight for three days, and when he could see again, he began preaching that Jesus was the Son of God. Naturally, people questioned him when they heard him, and they even conspired to kill him. He escaped over the city wall in a basket. Paul, sent by God, became the first missionary, teaching and preaching wherever he went.

Paul is an example for us of being made new in Christ. His past didn't matter; he gave his life to the Lord and was ready to fearlessly make known the gospel all over the world.

*Is something from your past holding you back from embracing a new life in Christ?*

MAY 27          A HOSPITABLE HEART

*When God's people are in need, be ready to help them. Always be eager to practice hospitality. (Romans 12:13 NLT)*

While Paul was traveling, he encountered a woman named Lydia. She was a respected businesswoman and a worshiper of God.

When she heard Paul, she believed in the Lord and was baptized. She went and told others what had happened to her, and they believed. She also offered her house as a place for Paul to stay. After Paul and Silas were miraculously released from jail, the jailer and his family believed in God. Paul and Silas returned to Lydia's house to offer encouragement (Acts 16:11-15).

Lydia not only shared the news of the gift of life in Christ, but she also was able to support Paul and Silas. Everyone needs support and encouragement. Lydia was able to offer a place where they could rest. It may not seem like much, but it was vital. God took something as simple as a place to sleep and used it to bring great benefit.

*What are some ways that you can serve and encourage fellow Christians?*

*What gift, whether small or large, do you have that God can use?*

MAY 28                                    UNWAVERING DEVOTION

*"If this be so, our God whom we serve is able to deliver us from the burning fiery furnace, and he will deliver us out of your hand, O king." (Daniel 3:17 ESV)*

King Nebuchadnezzar passed a decree that everyone had to bow down to a golden idol. When he heard that Shadrach, Meshach, and Abednego would not comply, he threatened to throw them into a fiery furnace. They said God could save them, and even if God did not, they still would not bow down. When the soldiers threw them into the furnace, the soldiers were killed because it had been heated to seven times its normal temperature. The king saw four men, not three, walking around in the furnace and called them to come out. The three men were completely unharmed. King Nebuchadnezzar believed that their God was the only One who could save, and he even promoted them.

Shadrach, Meshach, and Abednego would have lost their lives rather than break God's commandments. And because of their faithfulness, God changed the heart of the king, who passed a decree to all nations and no one was to speak against God (Daniel 3).

*What is something you have given in to that goes against God's commandments?*

*What would it take for you to have the courage to stand against our culture and stand up for God like Shadrach, Meshach, and Abednego did?*

MAY 29                ONLY ONE THING IS NECESSARY

*But the Lord answered her, "Martha, Martha, you are anxious and troubled about many things, but only one thing is necessary. Mary has chosen the good portion, which will not be taken away from her." (Luke 10:41-42 ESV)*

While Jesus and his disciples were traveling, they came to a village where two sisters, Mary and Martha, lived. Martha invited Jesus to their home. While there, Martha scurried around, preparing and serving food for Jesus and his disciples. She wanted everything to be perfect. Mary, however, sat at Jesus' feet to listen, and she hung onto every word he said (Luke 10:38-42).

You may think that Martha was the smart one. After all, you'd probably want everything perfect if the Son of God was spending the afternoon at your house! Yet Jesus himself said that only one thing is important: spending time with him. Mary chose not to worry about the details and thrived on learning from the Lord. She understood what was important and focused on spending time with Jesus.

*Are you sometimes too busy to listen to Jesus? Do you worry about the details and miss what God is teaching you?*

*What in your life keeps you too busy or too anxious to spend time with God?*

MAY 30                                    CALMING THE DOUBT

*Jesus immediately reached out his hand and took hold of him,*
*saying to him, "O you of little faith, why did you doubt?"*
*(Matthew 14:31 ESV)*

Follow me" is what Jesus, the Son of God, told his disciples. And
that's exactly what Peter did. After Jesus fed the five thousand, he
sent the disciples ahead in a boat. Jesus was alone to pray, and
evening came. Then Jesus walked on the water to them, and they
were terrified. Jesus told them not to be afraid and called for Peter
to come to him. Peter stepped out of the boat and walked on the
water, but he began to sink because he was afraid. He called to
Jesus and reached out for him. When they saw that Jesus had
saved Peter, everyone in the boat believed that Jesus truly was the
Son of God. Though Peter was scared, he had faith in the Lord and
believed Jesus would save him. Jesus showed Peter that there was
no need to doubt him (Matthew 14:22-33).

Peter became afraid when the winds from the storm around
him grew stronger. But when Jesus entered the boat, the storm
calmed. When we have faith in Jesus, he can calm the storms in
our lives.

*When have you doubted Jesus or his power? What happened?*

MAY 31                                      MORE THAN A MASK

*For the word of God is alive and powerful. It is sharper than*
*the sharpest two-edged sword, cutting between soul and spirit,*
*between joint and marrow. It exposes our innermost thoughts*
*and desires. (Hebrews 4:12 NLT)*

This month we've seen that the key to our identity is found in
God's word. We know ourselves when we know our Creator. God
created each one of us with a plan and for a purpose, and God
loves us more than we can imagine.

We've considered that Jesus is the Son of God. He is patient and
he loves the unlovable. Christ sacrificed his life so that we might

live. He taught and served, just as we should. His identity is the outline of our own.

We've learned that the Holy Spirit is with us to guide, comfort, and intercede on our behalf. The Holy Spirit guides us into all truth (John 16:13).

And we've looked at people in the Bible who can encourage us. Like them, we all are sinners, but we can be forgiven. God has called us to leave our past behind and embrace new life. We do not have to give in to evil, and there is no reason to doubt. No flaw we might have is too big for the Lord. We are exactly who God created us to be!

***How can you continue to grow in your faith?***

# JUNE

# Thirty Days with Jesus

## BRENT PARKER

JUNE 1                                    IN THE BEGINNING

*In the beginning was the Word, and the Word was with God, and the Word was God. He was in the beginning with God. All things came into being through him, and without him not one thing came into being. (John 1:1-3a NRSV)*

When we hear the story of creation in Genesis, we think about God creating stars and skies, water and land, animals and plants, and so forth. We think about God creating Adam and Eve and the Garden of Eden. This story of creation is very familiar to us.

In John 1, though, we are reminded that Jesus was there at creation too! In fact, Jesus was God's partner in creation. Can you imagine God and Jesus deciding together what animals they would make first? Jesus' favorite creation was us!

This month we will experience thirty encounters that Jesus had with people in the Bible, including Jesus with his family, his disciples, his friends, and with strangers who needed a miracle. As you witness these encounters, I hope you will be reminded of the many ways in which Jesus is reaching out to you.

*When was the last time you experienced Jesus?*

*What was it like to be with him?*

JUNE 2                                           MOMMY'S BOY

*And Mary said, "My soul magnifies the Lord, and my spirit rejoices in God my Savior, for he has looked with favor on the lowliness of his servant. Surely, from now on all generations will call me blessed; for the Mighty One has done great things for me, and holy is his name." (Luke 1:46-49 NRSV)*

The first person to ever see Jesus was his mother, Mary. Today's verses are a part of Scripture called the Magnificat, and they are the words to a song that Mary sang when she found out she was going to be Jesus' mom. She was excited to meet her first child.

When Jesus was born, Mary was so proud and happy. She looked down into her arms and saw the Savior of the world looking back up into her eyes. Can you imagine what it would be like to look the baby Jesus in the eyes?

Mary's life was changed forever by her experience of having her new son Jesus. She received a miracle from God and loved Jesus with everything she had.

*When you picture Jesus and Mary seeing each other for the first time, how would you describe it?*

*How have you been forever changed by your experience with Jesus?*

JUNE 3                                           A TIME TO LEARN

*After three days they found him in the temple, sitting among the teachers, listening to them and asking them questions. And all who heard him were amazed at his understanding and his answers. (Luke 2:46-47 NRSV)*

Sometimes we forget that Jesus went to church and Sunday school just like we do. Maybe he didn't like to wake up early, either. We picture Jesus as a grown-up who had all the right answers and who never made mistakes. Jesus was perfect.

In this story, we find Jesus spending time with those who were the Bible teachers for his worshiping community. Jesus was not teaching; he was listening and learning. Even Jesus knew how important it was to ask questions of those who had knowledge and experiences different from his own.

Is there someone in your life who has something to teach you today? Choose to be a good listener today and be amazed by what you might learn about our God, who has so much to teach us each day.

*What was the last thing you learned about Jesus?*

*How did the new information change what you believed about him?*

## JUNE 4                    JESUS WITH THE PREACHER

*Then Jesus came from Galilee to John at the Jordan, to be baptized by him. John would have prevented him, saying, "I need to be baptized by you, and do you come to me?" But Jesus answered him, "Let it be so now; for it is proper for us in this way to fulfill all righteousness." (Matthew 3:13-15 NRSV)*

Just as we saw in yesterday's devotion, today we see Jesus once again joining other believers in the religious practices of his community. His cousin, John the Baptist, is out by the river baptizing believers and preaching to them about purifying themselves before God. Jesus wants to share in this important act of faith.

Even though Jesus was God's perfect Son, he knew how important it was to follow God's commands. Jesus wanted to live in a way that would please God and would serve as an example to other believers.

We all have the chance to lead the way in living righteous lives of faith. God invites us to be faithful in our journey and desires for us to be good role models for those who walk with us.

*How is Jesus asking you to be faithful to him today?*

*What is keeping you from following what he asks of you?*

JUNE 5                              AWAY FROM ME, SATAN!

*Jesus, full of the Holy Spirit, returned from the Jordan and was led by the Spirit in the wilderness, where for forty days he was tempted by the devil. (Luke 4:1-2a NRSV)*

After Jesus' cousin John baptized him, the Bible says that Jesus was taken out into the wilderness and tempted. When we read Luke 4, we find out that Jesus was tempted in three ways: to prove himself by doing something special; to prove himself by being who others said he was; and to prove himself by gaining a lot of possessions.

Jesus knew that he was the Beloved of God, and he did not accept any of the temptations. He didn't have to do something. He didn't have to live up to someone else's expectations. And he didn't need any more stuff! He had God's favor, and that was enough.

Did you know that you are God's beloved, too? You do not have to prove yourself to anyone. The evil one lies to you just as he lied to Jesus. You are enough just as you are!

*When you think about yourself, do you think you are enough?*

*How would you live life if you believed you were enough?*


JUNE 6                              BACK IN HIS HOMETOWN

*He unrolled the scroll and found the place where it was written: "The Spirit of the Lord is upon me, because he has anointed me to bring good news to the poor. He has sent me to proclaim release to the captives and recovery of sight to the blind, to let the oppressed go free, to proclaim the year of the Lord's favor." (Luke 4:17b-19 NRSV)*

Jesus returned to his hometown for worship. He read the Scriptures and then announced that he had been sent to fulfill the words he had just read. This made the people around him very upset.

We all have been created to fulfill God's kingdom purposes that we find in the Bible. God has commanded that we continue to live as Jesus lived so that the world can be a better place and others can come to know Jesus. Jesus was chased out of town for proclaiming that he was going to take God's words seriously.

Every day we have the chance to boldly live as committed children, created in God's image. Are we willing to really be like Jesus?

*How have you lived out your Christianity in unpopular ways?*

*What would your friends say or do if you followed God's commands to be like Jesus?*

## JUNE 7                    THE FIRST TO FOLLOW JESUS

*Then Jesus said to Simon, "Do not be afraid; from now on you will be catching people." When they had brought their boats to shore, they left everything and followed him.*
*(Luke 5:10b-11 NRSV)*

These guys were out in their boats fishing, just as they were every day, when Jesus came along. This rabbi, Jesus, walked onto their turf and started telling them what to do, suggesting that he knew their trade better than they did. Since he wouldn't let up, they went ahead and tried his way of doing things. And they caught more fish than they could pull into the boat.

After an experience like that, wouldn't you leave it all behind, too? Jesus told them that they should not be afraid of him and should leave their old lives to join him in a new way of life.

Are you ready to drop everything to follow Jesus? What are you afraid of? What does Jesus need to do in your life that would give you the confidence to follow right now? Ask him to do it, and get ready to follow!

*What have you given up to follow Jesus—or what are you willing to give up?*

*What does Jesus need to do in your life to give you the confidence to follow him?*

JUNE 8                                              HE TOUCHED ME

*Once, when he was in one of the cities, there was a man covered with leprosy. When he saw Jesus, he bowed with his face to the ground and begged him, "Lord, if you choose, you can make me clean." Then Jesus stretched out his hand, touched him, and said, "I do choose. Be made clean." Immediately the leprosy left him. (Luke 5:12-13 NRSV)*

Leprosy was one of the most dreaded diseases in Jesus' day. People with this disease lost feeling in the skin on most parts of their bodies. When they scratched themselves or twisted an ankle, they would not feel the pain. This left their bodies injured and rough looking. They became the "untouchables" of their communities.

When Jesus encountered people, he liked to touch them. No matter the ailment or disease, Jesus would not let the problems of another person keep him away. He knew that people could be healed of physical, emotional, and spiritual sicknesses simply as the result of being offered a loving touch.

Each day we encounter people who are waiting to be touched by the love of Jesus. We may be the right person at the right time to share the love of God with a stranger in need.

*Who are the untouchables in your school, church, or community?*

*How might you offer them your healing presence?*

JUNE 9                                              ON BENDED KNEE

*She stood behind him at his feet, weeping, and began to bathe his feet with her tears and to dry them with her hair. Then she continued kissing his feet and anointing them with the ointment. (Luke 7:38 NRSV)*

A woman found out that Jesus was near and found her way into his presence. She was a sinner but knew that Jesus was capable of forgiving her in ways that no one else would even consider. She entered his presence and fell on her knees.

Being at the feet of Love, she found the only way she knew to express her need for forgiveness; she knelt at Jesus' feet and cleaned them, anointed them, and kissed them.

Jesus calls us to sit at his feet. Sometimes we will be bowed in adoration and other times in confession. Regardless of the reason, once we kneel at his feet, we are then able to stand with him in the fullness of his grace.

*If you were to be at Jesus' feet, what would you say or do?*

*How do you think Jesus would respond to you?*


## JUNE 10                                                    BE STILL!

*They went to him and woke him up, shouting, "Master, Master, we are perishing!" And he woke up and rebuked the wind and the raging waves; they ceased, and there was a calm.*
*(Luke 8:24 NRSV)*

The disciples were in a boat with Jesus when a big storm came up. Though they were very scared and worried, Jesus was asleep. They woke him up and wanted to know why he wasn't trying to help them. And then he calmed the waves—and their fears.

You would think that those guys, who had seen Jesus at work in their lives, would have had more confidence that he would not let them perish. Jesus has been at work in our lives, too! Have we forgotten about the many times Jesus has been there for us?

Jesus sits in life's "boat" with us. He knows when it is calm and when a storm is coming. He reminds us that in all of life's storms, we can trust him to bring us peace.

*What storm are you experiencing right now?*

*How will you ask Jesus to calm that storm today?*

JUNE 11                                    DEALING WITH DEMONS

*Now there on the hillside a large herd of swine was feeding; and the demons begged Jesus to let them enter these. So he gave them permission. Then the demons came out of the man and entered the swine, and the herd rushed down the steep bank into the lake and was drowned. (Luke 8:32-33 NRSV)*

Jesus was getting out of a boat and was approached by a man with demons. The community said that the man went about yelling and thrashing. He clearly was tormented by evil spirits but believed that Jesus could heal him and rid him of the demons.

Jesus had compassion on the man and allowed the evil spirits to go into some nearby pigs. It shouldn't surprise us that Jesus would get rid of evil from anyone at anytime, using any means necessary.

Just as he taught us to pray, "Deliver us from evil," Jesus reminds us that God wants to help us keep away from the things that prevent us from experiencing God's love within us. Jesus desires that we experience peace in this life, and he will do whatever we ask of him if it means we will have a better relationship with him.

*What stands between you and the peace you desire?*

*How will you ask Jesus to bring more peace into your life?*

JUNE 12                                                        WAKE UP!

*But he took her by the hand and called out, "Child, get up!" Her spirit returned, and she got up at once. (Luke 8:54-55a NRSV)*

This story, which begins in verse 40, tells of Jesus meeting a man named Jairus whose daughter was dead. Jairus pleads with Jesus to come to his home to heal her. Jesus arrives and restores the girl to life.

Even though we may not be dead, many of us do sometimes walk through life not fully alive to the presence of God around us. We go through the motions of our daily routine and miss God offering love, forgiveness, hope, and life to us. We get caught up in the anxiety, fear, and chaos of the world, and before we know it we find ourselves completely sidetracked.

God spends all day trying to break into our worrisome lives to remind us of the grace and peace that can revive us and help put the spring back into our step.

*Each day, are you excited to see where God might show up?*

*When was the last time you asked God to reveal the abundant life that is promised to us?*

## JUNE 13                    THE BOY WHO SAVED THE DAY

*One of his disciples, Andrew, Simon Peter's brother, said to him, "There is a boy here who has five barley loaves and two fish. But what are they among so many people?"*
*(John 6:8-9 NRSV)*

You may remember this story about five thousand hungry people who showed up on the hillside to hear Jesus. The disciples came to Jesus and told him that the people who had gathered were all hungry. Jesus instructed the disciples to gather food for the people, but the only one who offered food to share was a little boy.

Jesus performed a miracle in front of the crowds, feeding all of them with what was available. Jesus took what the little boy offered, gave thanks to God for the boy's food, and then shared it with the entire crowd. Have you ever wondered what would have happened if the little boy had not shared his belongings?

Sometimes we forget how important the contributions of teenagers are to a well-functioning society. You have a very important role to play in our world.

*Have you ever thought about how you are needed to help change the world?*

*If you could start changing the world today, how would you do it?*

JUNE 14                    WHO DO YOU SAY THAT I AM?

*Once when Jesus was praying alone, with only the disciples near him, he asked them, "Who do the crowds say that I am?" They answered, "John the Baptist; but others, Elijah; and still others, that one of the ancient prophets has arisen." He said to them, "But who do you say that I am?" (Luke 9:18-20 NRSV)*

Jesus and the disciples were together when he asked them to tell him what others thought of him. After they had given their answers, he turned to Peter and asked him. All of the answers revealed something about how Jesus had affected people. Jesus was a prophet, a preacher, and a healer.

Jesus ended his questioning with these words: "Who do you say that I am?" This is a great question for us to ask ourselves every day. Who is Jesus to us? Who is he to our world? It is important to look back at our experiences with Jesus and to think about the ways that he has influenced our lives. The world needs us to be ready with an answer; it might change the world.

*How would you reply if someone were to ask you the question, "Who is Jesus to you?"*

*Who is Jesus for our world?*

JUNE 15                                          LIKE A CHILD

*An argument arose among them as to which one of them was the greatest. But Jesus, aware of their inner thoughts, took a little child and put it by his side, and said to them, "Whoever welcomes this child in my name welcomes me, and whoever welcomes me welcomes the one who sent me; for the least among all of you is the greatest." (Luke 9:46-48 NRSV)*

Getting to be on the front row for every miracle, in the best seats for his times of teaching, and at the table with him at every meal was surely a blessing to the disciples. Yet it wasn't good enough for the disciples to be one of the twelve; each wanted to be number one.

Jesus reminds them (and us) that Christians are to look out for those who do not get enough attention and to let them be first in line to receive our attention. The Christian life is never about becoming greater than those around us; it is about becoming less, so that others, and ultimately Jesus, can be lifted up.

*How have you offered your life as a gift to those around you?*

*How can you do so from now on?*

JUNE 16                                                    LOOKING FOR US

*He was trying to see who Jesus was, but on account of the crowd he could not, because he was short in stature. So he ran ahead and climbed a sycamore tree to see him, because he was going to pass that way. (Luke 19:3-4 NRSV)*

Of course, this story is about the tax collector Zacchaeus. The large crowd surrounded Jesus, but this short man wanted to see what all of the commotion was about. So he climbed a sycamore tree to see Jesus. The familiar children's song continues the story this way: "And as the Savior walked that way, he looked up in the tree. And he said, 'Zacchaeus, you come down, for I'm going to your house today.'" It should not surprise us that even as we try our best to get to Jesus, he is the one who is looking for us.

Jesus is always on the lookout for those who seek him. In his own words, Jesus tells us, "Search, and you will find" (Matthew 7:7 NRSV). By God's grace, even those who are not seeking may, in fact, be found!

*How would you have felt to be seen by Jesus?*

*When was the last time Jesus "found" you?*

JUNE 17                                                           TOO BUSY?

*But Martha was distracted by her many tasks; so she came to him and asked, "Lord, do you not care that my sister has left*

*me to do all the work by myself? Tell her then to help me." But
the Lord answered her, "Martha, Martha, you are worried and
distracted by many things; there is need of only one thing."*
*(Luke 10:40-42a NRSV)*

You have likely read the story about the time Jesus came to visit
Mary and Martha in their home. Martha was so busy getting
things together that she was unable to spend any time with Jesus.
She looked up from her work and found Mary sitting at Jesus' feet,
listening to him speak. Looking for a little sympathy, she asked
Jesus to send Mary to help her.

Jesus not only didn't ask Mary to go and help, he told Martha
that Mary was doing what he wanted her to do. Jesus said that sitting with him was all Mary needed to be doing at that time. He
seemed to be suggesting that just being in his presence and listening to his words were enough.

*Have you been so busy doing things for God that you have
missed the chance to just sit with Jesus?*

*What does Jesus have to say to you today?*

JUNE 18                                   TRUSTING THE SPIRIT

*"Very truly, I tell you, we speak of what we know and testify to
what we have seen; yet you do not receive our testimony. If I
have told you about earthly things and you do not believe, how
can you believe if I tell you about heavenly things?"*
*(John 3:11-12 NRSV)*

Sometimes it is difficult to believe the stories that people tell us
because the details seem so farfetched or because we could never
imagine having the same experience. Some things just seem
impossible. The multiple experiences that people had with Jesus
during his lifetime seemed to fall into this category.

Jesus was trying to let Nicodemus in on the little secret about
God's love, and Nicodemus could not believe what he was hearing.
God's love sounded too easy. God could not possibly let humans

experience the kingdom of God on earth; that would be scandalous!

God's love is scandalous. And when Nicodemus heard what Jesus said next (verse 16), he just might have begun to realize that the kingdom of God was in his midst—and he finally might have believed.

*How do you respond to testimonies of faith that exceed your understanding?*

*Do you have experiences of God that your friends need to hear so that they might believe?*

## JUNE 19                                    SELL IT ALL

*When Jesus heard this, he said to him, "There is still one thing lacking. Sell all that you own and distribute the money to the poor, and you will have treasure in heaven; then come, follow me." (Luke 18:22 NRSV)*

Doing what we think God wants us to do can sometimes become a very difficult task when we think of all of the ways that we could serve others, love our enemies, read and study the Bible, and pray without ceasing. It would seem that our whole day would be spent thinking about everything but ourselves.

The rich man was confronted by Jesus and was proud to say that he had followed all of the commandments since birth. He was very surprised when Jesus seemed unimpressed and then told him he must sell everything he owned and give to the poor.

Following the commandments of God doesn't appear to be enough. Jesus tells us that we must be willing to leave everything behind—even our possessions—if we want treasure in heaven.

*What possessions do you own that keep your attention away from your relationship with God?*

*Are you ready to give them away if it means knowing God in a deeper way?*

JUNE 20                                                  THIRSTY?

*Jesus said to her, "Everyone who drinks of this water will be thirsty again, but those who drink of the water that I will give them will never be thirsty. The water that I will give will become in them a spring of water gushing up to eternal life."*
                                             *(John 4:13-14 NRSV)*

A thirsty Samaritan woman and a thirsty Jewish man meet at the middle of town to draw water from a well. The woman has a jug for water and the man has the keys to the kingdom of God. He asks her for a drink. She replies with a question as to why he would even talk to her (as she is considered unworthy by most of her townspeople and by presumably all Jews).

Jesus takes an ordinary encounter of two people and turns it into an opportunity for a woman to regain her dignity, to experience the love of another, and to receive more than she came for.

Jesus invites us into daily encounters so that he can give us more than we ever expected to find.

*What "thirst" are you hoping to have quenched for you today?*

*Where might you find Jesus waiting to encounter you today?*

JUNE 21                                          DROP YOUR STONE

*When they kept on questioning him, he straightened up and said to them, "Let anyone among you who is without sin be the first to throw a stone at her." And once again he bent down and wrote on the ground. When they heard it, they went away, one by one, beginning with the elders; and Jesus was left alone with the woman standing before him. (John 8:7-9 NRSV)*

Forgiveness is a treasured gift that we all long to receive. Each day we begin by saying to ourselves that we will be more careful to do only the things that God would like for us to do and to say only the words that God would like for us to say. Then we leave our homes and it all goes downhill.

The woman in today's verses had been caught in adultery, and the religious leaders wanted to discipline her. By asking them to take inventory of their own lives instead of looking at the sins of this woman, Jesus turned the spotlight away from the sin of this woman and onto the sins of those who brought her.

*How would it feel to have Jesus stand with you and offer compassion to you when you made mistakes or sinned?*

*For what will you ask Jesus for compassion today?*

## JUNE 22                                        DIRTY FEET

*And during supper Jesus, knowing that the Father had given all things into his hands, and that he had come from God and was going to God, got up from the table, took off his outer robe, and tied a towel around himself. Then he poured water into a basin and began to wash the disciples' feet and to wipe them with the towel that was tied around him. (John 13:2b-5)*

Oftentimes the dirtiest part of the human body is the feet. Whether the feet have been surrounded by sweaty socks or left free to pick up dirt and mud in sandals, they can be really disgusting. The last thing most of us want to do with anyone else's feet is get down next to them and wash them—especially at the dinner table!

Jesus gathered with his disciples for a final meal before his death. As a way of reminding them what selfless love looks like, he went to each of them and washed their feet. He didn't give a sermon, heal a sick person, or perform a miracle; he washed their feet.

*When was the last time you experienced selfless love from another?*

*How is Jesus calling you to serve the people around you?*

JUNE 23                                              PASS HIM ON

*Jesus said to her, "Do not hold on to me, because I have not yet ascended to the Father. But go to my brothers and say to them, 'I am ascending to my Father and your Father, to my God and your God.'" Mary Magdalene went and announced to the disciples, "I have seen the Lord"; and she told them that he had said these things to her. (John 20:17-18 NRSV)*

Jesus' family and his disciples had just gone through the most difficult three days of their lives and were still deep in grief after the crucifixion of the one they loved. More than anything, each of them would have loved to have just one more opportunity to touch him or see him or hear him.

Mary showed up at the tomb, and there he was! She ran to hold him, and he confused her with the verses we just read. Jesus sent her away to tell the others what she had seen.

Jesus asks us to do the same. We are to hold our experiences of him closely, yet gently, so that we are able to pass along to others what we have seen and heard.

*What experience of Jesus do you need to pass along to others?*

JUNE 24                                                  I DOUBT IT

*A week later his disciples were again in the house, and Thomas was with them. Although the doors were shut, Jesus came and stood among them and said, "Peace be with you." Then he said to Thomas, "Put your finger here and see my hands. Reach out your hand and put it in my side. Do not doubt but believe." Thomas answered him, "My Lord and my God!"*
*(John 20:26-28 NRSV)*

In this text, we are introduced to the one they called "Doubting Thomas." Almost every time you hear the name of the disciple Thomas, you hear about how he doubted Jesus. Consider how you would feel if a person who had died three days earlier walked into the room without using the door. You might either run in fear or ask to touch him to make sure you weren't dreaming.

Instead of pinching himself, Thomas reached out and touched the wounds of Jesus. Immediately, Thomas remembered and exclaimed that Jesus was his Lord.

Every day Jesus shows up in our midst and we miss the chance to touch him. Be on the lookout for Jesus today!

*If Jesus showed up in your room right now, how would he prove to you that he was Jesus?*

*If you could reach out and touch him and speak to him, what would you say?*

## JUNE 25                    SURROUNDED BY FRIENDS

*Then some people came, bringing to him a paralyzed man, carried by four of them. And when they could not bring him to Jesus because of the crowd, they removed the roof above him; and after having dug through it, they let down the mat on which the paralytic lay. When Jesus saw their faith, he said to the paralytic, "Son, your sins are forgiven." (Mark 2:3-5 NRSV)*

The crowd had gathered around Jesus again. So many people had arrived to hear him that the friends of a man who was paralyzed had to go to extreme measures to get the man in front of Jesus. And when Jesus saw how much faith and love the four friends exhibited, he healed the paralytic.

The man was healed because of the faith of his friends. Imagine being lowered down on a mat to the feet of Jesus and looking up into the eyes of the four friends who you know will be there helping you. Jesus invites us to bring one another into his presence so that each of us can be healed.

*Who are the friends you know would take you to Jesus?*

*Is there someone who would name you as the person who brought them to Jesus?*

JUNE 26                                    JUST TO TOUCH HIM

*She had heard about Jesus, and came up behind him in the crowd and touched his cloak, for she said, "If I but touch his clothes, I will be made well." Immediately her hemorrhage stopped; and she felt in her body that she was healed of her disease. (Mark 5:27-29 NRSV)*

Word had spread about Jesus and his abilities to heal. Word was that merely touching the clothes of Jesus healed some people. A woman who had been bleeding for a very long time trusted that she, too, would be healed. She could not get his attention, but she got close enough to touch his garment; and she was healed.

All of us are in need of some sort of healing. The struggles of each day sometimes make it difficult to clear a path to Jesus' presence. This story tells us that if we just try to get within reach of Jesus, we can be healed. The experience of this woman can give us the confidence that our healing may be right at our fingertips!

*How does it feel to know that your ability to have Jesus heal you is always right at your fingertips?*


JUNE 27                            THE BIBLE AND SOME BREAD

*When he was at the table with them, he took bread, blessed and broke it, and gave it to them. Then their eyes were opened, and they recognized him; and he vanished from their sight. They said to each other, "Were not our hearts burning within us while he was talking to us on the road, while he was opening the scriptures to us?" (Luke 24:30-32 NRSV)*

This story is another instance in which Jesus revealed himself to his followers after he had risen from the dead. He walked up alongside two disciples as they journeyed toward their home and began to ask them about what had been going on. They could not believe that anyone was unaware of the horrible crucifixion of Jesus.

All along, the man they talked to was Jesus. He had communion with them and recited Scripture to them, and only then did they realize they were in his presence.

We have the same opportunity to be in the presence of the risen Jesus. Each time we seek communion with him and read the Bible, we find Jesus waiting to be with us.

*How have you experienced Jesus when you read the Bible?*

## JUNE 28                                                    LOOK AROUND

*While he was going and they were gazing up toward heaven, suddenly two men in white robes stood by them. They said, "Men of Galilee, why do you stand looking up toward heaven? This Jesus, who has been taken up from you into heaven, will come in the same way as you saw him go into heaven."*
*(Acts 1:10-11 NRSV)*

At this, the last moment that the disciples would be with Jesus, we find Jesus being taken away into a cloud at what we call the Ascension. As Jesus is going away, the disciples' eyes are fixed upon the sky. It must have been a sight to see the risen Jesus being taken away again, and there surely was some curiosity about whether he would come back soon.

The men told them—and they tell us—not to worry about his departure because he will come back again. Instead, Jesus commands that we look around for ways to see him in other people and to be the type of people who reveal him to others.

*If you were to look around the halls of your school, where might you find Jesus?*

*Where does the kingdom of God show up in your daily routine?*

## JUNE 29                                                  A JOB FOR JESUS?

*When the wine gave out, the mother of Jesus said to him, "They have no wine." And Jesus said to her, "Woman, what concern is that to you and to me? My hour has not yet come." His mother said to the servants, "Do whatever he tells you."*
*(John 2:3-5 NRSV)*

This story is of the first recorded miracle that Jesus performed. Jesus, his mom, and the disciples were at a wedding in Cana when the wine ran out. It would have been very embarrassing to the hosts of the wedding if the guests noticed this, and Mary wanted Jesus to save the day.

We all run into day-to-day struggles that lead us to pray that Jesus will come and save the day for us too. Whether it is prayers for help on a test for which we did not prepare or for the well-being of a sick relative, we often ask Jesus to come into our situation and make it better. Even if we think that our request is not something that is worth Jesus' time, we are encouraged to ask him anyway.

*For what could you use the help of God right now?*


JUNE 30                                   JESUS IS LOOKING FOR YOU

*I pray that, according to the riches of his glory, he may grant that you may be strengthened in your inner being with power through his Spirit, and that Christ may dwell in your hearts through faith, as you are being rooted and grounded in love. I pray that you may have the power to comprehend, with all the saints, what is the breadth and length and height and depth, and to know the love of Christ that surpasses knowledge, so that you may be filled with all the fullness of God.*
*(Ephesians 3:16-19 NRSV)*

Throughout these thirty days of reading about and witnessing how many people in the Bible experienced Jesus, we have seen the power of an encounter with the Son of God. People have been healed physically, spiritually, and emotionally. They have expressed deep faith and have put great trust in him.

All of the encounters with Jesus resulted in the giving and receiving of God's love. Through Jesus, God found the most meaningful ways to let the people of the world know how much they are loved. If you have learned nothing else this month, I pray that you have realized the power of God's love revealed in Jesus.

*When was the last time you experienced the profound love described in today's verses?*

# JULY

# Lessons from the TV and Movie Screen

## DEVIN PENNER

DON'T LET YOUR FAITH BE
                                         SCRUBBED OUT

*Trust in the LORD with all your heart and lean not on your own understanding; in all your ways acknowledge him, and he will make your paths straight. (Proverbs 3:5-6)*

Like most teens, I love watching TV and movies. Although we should try to avoid as much "junk" as possible—and there's plenty of it out there—there are some great lessons to be found in many television shows and movies. This month we'll take a look at some of these lessons and how they can encourage us in our faith.

Let's start with *Scrubs*. In season six, the faith of Nurse Roberts, a very spiritual and God-loving nurse, is put to the test. Throughout one episode she is put through a rigorous faith workout from the cynical and angry Dr. Cox (admittedly my favorite character). Dr. Cox questions Nurse Roberts's faith, and she always proves how strong her faith is.

When an eight-year-old girl is shot, Dr. Cox comments to the nurse, "What was your God's plan when this happened?" She shakes her head and tells Dr. Cox that she doesn't know but that God will show them eventually. After a series of tests, it is discovered that the little girl has a tumor. If she had not been shot,

*151*

they never would have found it and the little girl would have died.

Many times in our lives things happen that make us question our faith. But like Nurse Roberts, we should stay strong in our faith and trust God to show us the plan.

*When have you questioned your faith?*

*What can help you hold on to your faith regardless of what happens?*

JULY 2                                                    A CRICK IN FATE

*God has not given us a spirit of fear, but of power and of love and of a sound mind. (2 Timothy 1:7 NKJV)*

The movie *Stranger than Fiction* places Will Ferrell in the shoes of the main character, Harold Crick, an obsessive-compulsive IRS auditor who hears his life being narrated. Mr. Crick does not notice the voice until he hears about his "imminent death." He begins to panic at this news, as most of us would, and he searches for ways to stop his death. When Mr. Crick realizes that there is no stopping his death, he makes the best of the life he has left, instead of living in fear.

One of the things we can gather from this is that we should not live in fear. When we talk about our faith as Christians, we are referring to our belief that God is good and that God's plan is much bigger and better than our plan. God has given us a spirit of power and love, and a sound mind, so that we can handle whatever our circumstances may bring. So, instead of living in fear about what could happen tomorrow, we should be strong in the Lord and trust that God's plan is always best.

*What are some things you worry about?*

*What can help you put all your faith in God?*

JULY 3                                SOAP OPERAS FOR THE WIN

*"Remain in me, and I will remain in you. No branch can bear fruit by itself; it must remain in the vine. Neither can you bear fruit unless you remain in me." (John 15:4)*

I need to admit something: I'm a fan of teen soap operas like *The O.C.* (now off the air). Despite all the drama that happened within the series, I learned something from Ryan and Marissa's relationship. I learned that it was a very unhealthy relationship in which they only came to each other in times of need and want, such as when one of them needed a hug because something had gone wrong.

I realized that often that's how we perceive our relationship with God. So often we come to God when times are rough, expecting God to help, which he does; but then we abandon God when we feel like everything is better. We use God like the miscellaneous items we use every day to get by. God deserves more than that. God deserves to have our attention all the time. Jesus said we are to remain or abide in him. He wants to be the One we turn to all the time, no matter the circumstance. God wants a healthy relationship with us.

*What are the unhealthy relationships in your life?*

*What are some ways in which you can improve your relationship with God?*

JULY 4                                          "BE PERFECT"

*"Be perfect, therefore, as your heavenly Father is perfect."*
*(Matthew 5:48 NRSV)*

Why does a group of guys or girls get together to hit, kick, shoot, run, fight, or aim better than others? It's because of the gratification they get from giving their all. As an athlete myself, I can vouch for this. So could the 1988 Permian Panthers football team. *Friday Night Lights* is the true story of this high school football team and, in my opinion, is one of the greatest sports movies ever.

To the players, the coaches, and the community of Odessa, Texas, Permian football was not just a Friday-night activity; it was life. At the end of the movie, everything is on the line for the team at the state championship. There isn't much time left on the clock, and there is only one more play. The Panthers need a touchdown to win. As time expires, the quarterback gets tackled on the one-yard line. The game is over and the state championship is lost. Though the ending is sad for the Panthers, it is a lesson learned. In life we should always strive for the gratification of giving our all.

In the movie, Coach Gaines repeats this line: "Be perfect." He never explains what he means by this until the end of the movie. He says that being perfect means you are able to look your brothers in the eye and know that they gave their all.

As Christians, we are to strive for perfection; we are to give our all.

*Do you feel that you are giving your all?*

*How can you strive for perfection in your Christian life, and what are some of the rewards you might reap?*

JULY 5                          WHAT IS AN AMERICAN IDOL?

*Who may ascend the hill of the LORD? Who may stand in his holy place? He who has clean hands and a pure heart, who does not lift up his soul to an idol. (Psalm 24:3-4)*

One of the most popular shows on television is *American Idol*. In a way, it's the old "rags to riches" idea. Ordinary people reach for their dream of becoming a star and having a successful singing career. The audition tapings are especially entertaining. So many people who think they can actually sing well make spectacles of themselves on national television. Then there are the ones who actually can sing well, and we find ourselves cheering them on and picking our favorites. Faithful viewers tune in each week to watch the performances and then call in their votes after the show—sometimes multiple times!

It makes me wonder: what if we got that excited about Jesus and our faith? What if Jesus truly was number one in our lives? The truth is, there are many "American idols"—things and people and activities that we give more time and attention to than we do our Lord and Savior. God wants to be number one in our lives.

*Are there any "idols" in your life? What or who are they?*

*What can you do to make God your top priority?*

JULY 6                                          THE AMAZING RACE

*"And now, compelled by the Spirit, I am going to Jerusalem, not knowing what will happen to me there. . . . However, I consider my life worth nothing to me, if only I may finish the race and complete the task the Lord Jesus has given me—the task of testifying to the gospel of God's grace." (Acts 20:22, 24)*

Reality shows are popular right now, and one that can be fun to watch is *The Amazing Race*. Teams of two race around the world performing all kinds of tasks and challenges in order to get clues that lead them to their next destination. In a recent episode, the teams had to use a variety of skills—including home repair, bobsledding, and familiarity with Russian literature—to complete that leg of the race. Sometimes teams get lost, and sometimes they get frustrated. But most teams press on anyway because they want to win the race.

The apostle Paul compared living the Christian life to running a race. He said that his goal was to "finish the race and complete the task" that Jesus had given him. That's good advice for us today in a world that often discourages us and makes us want to quit. Let's run the race well and persevere because we're promised a prize that is worth it all!

*What are some of the challenges you face as you try to live out your faith?*

*What encourages you to keep on running the race?*

JULY 7                                    BECOMING A DARK KNIGHT

*The LORD will withhold no good thing from those who do what is right. (Psalm 84:11b NLT)*

In the Batman movie *The Dark Knight,* the Joker, played by the late Heath Ledger, decides he is going to kill a person every day until Batman reveals his own true identity. Batman never shows his identity and ultimately prevails, but the citizens of Gotham still view him as a villain. In the end, the new police commissioner, James Gordon, tells his son that Batman is not a hero but a guardian angel. Batman continues to protect the city of Gotham at any cost, regardless of the way its citizens or leaders view him.

This reminds me of a lesson most of us learned back in kindergarten about doing the right thing even when no one is looking. Not only does this character trait make us feel safe at school, but it also helps us become finer citizens of a world that has seen better days. And who knows? If you continue to do the right thing even when no one is looking, you could become a hero in someone's eyes—whether you know it or not.

*What are some things you have done in your life that are considered courageous or right, and what are some rewards you have reaped from this?*

*How can you help others do the right thing no matter what?*

JULY 8                                    FIGHTING FOR OFFICE SPACE

*"Whoever has my commands and obeys them ... is the one who loves me." (John 14:21)*

One of the most hysterically funny shows on television today is the mockumentary-style show *The Office.* The thing that makes the show amusing is that you can feel the awkwardness among the characters throughout each episode. One of the most awkward relationships on the show is that between Michael, who is the boss, and Dwight, the assistant to the regional manager. Dwight continually vies for Michael's number-two-guy position and, most of all, for Michael's friendship. Dwight fights for Michael and does all the awkward and crazy things that Michael comes up with.

Why can't we "fight" for God's love in this way? If we would do all the things God asks us to do and fight for God's undying affection, regardless of the fact that we have it anyway, our lives would be more fulfilling. Fighting for God's love is simply pleasing God through our love and obedience.

***Have you ever fought for someone's love?***

***How can you fight for God's love in the same way?***

JULY 9                    CHANGING THE WORLD THROUGH
                                              BREAKING OUT

***Learn to do good; seek justice, rescue the oppressed, defend the orphan, plead for the widow. (Isaiah 1:17 NRSV)***

Another popular TV show is *Prison Break,* a show about a brother who purposely gets arrested so he can break his brother out of jail for a crime he didn't commit. The irony is that the brother who purposely goes to jail is also the designer of the prison. He knows every nook and cranny because he has the blueprints tattooed all over his body.

One theme or message of the show is the idea of justice. The kind of justice presented in the show is civil justice—bringing justice to a person wrongly accused of a crime. In the world of Christianity, the kind of justice we hear about most often is social justice.

Many of the people who are on the frontlines of the social justice battle today are teenagers, and I believe we have a voice that people will listen to. If that doesn't make you want to get involved in helping change the world, then think about this: if the world's social issues aren't bettered in our time, then our children will be the ones who are affected.

There are so many organizations to be a part of, and it doesn't require much to make a change. So I encourage you to make an effort to better the world!

**What are some injustices in the world that concern you?**

**What are some organizations you could become a part of to help make a difference?**

JULY 10 FIGHTING VOLDEMORT

*David said, "The LORD, who saved me from the paw of the lion and from the paw of the bear, will save me from the hand of this Philistine." (1 Samuel 17:37 NRSV)*

In the fourth Harry Potter movie, *Harry Potter and the Goblet of Fire*, the Triwizard Tournament comes to Hogwarts School of Witchcraft and Wizardry. Unfortunately, only "seventh years" are allowed to participate in the tournament, so Harry should not be qualfied.

However, when the school champions are chosen and announced, young Mr. Potter's name is called out despite the fact that he is only a "fourth year." This causes a great deal of controversy, but Harry has to compete regardless of his age. Harry ends up fighting against the evil Voldemort and winning the tournament, giving Hogwarts glory.

This movie is like the story of David and Goliath in many ways. David was called to complete a task that many of the greatest warriors couldn't do, and he was just a small boy. The giant Goliath laughed at his opponent, but David prevailed with his slingshot. Both stories tell us that we can be called to an enormous task at any age and, with the help of God, prevail. God has reasons to choose certain people to do certain things, and we just have to trust that God will see us through it if he calls us to it.

**When have you faced a task that seemed too big for you?**

**Do you believe God had a reason for placing this particular task in your hands?**

## JULY 11      (INSERT NAME HERE) IN REAL LIFE

*There are six things that the LORD hates, seven that are an abomination to him: haughty eyes, a lying tongue, and hands that shed innocent blood, a heart that devises wicked plans, feet that hurry to run to evil, a lying witness who testifies falsely, and one who sows discord in a family.*

*(Proverbs 6:16-19 NRSV)*

In the movie *Dan in Real Life,* Steve Carell plays the hilarious main character. Dan is a single dad whose wife has died. He has three daughters who span a wide spectrum of ages and stages of life. His oldest daughter and he are at a breaking point in their relationship because she is trying to establish her independence and Dan doesn't exactly approve. After a series of events and epiphanies, *Dan in Real Life* has a happy ending. What helps make everything OK is that Dan and his daughters bond together and finally accept who they are.

I've learned that even when your family is the root of the problem, at some point family members will be the ones to help pull you through to the other side. We tend to see our families as the problem, especially in our teen years. If we will just give our families a chance, they will be the biggest influence in our lives.

*What are some things your family has done for you over the years that you haven't thanked them for but know you should?*

*What are some other ways of showing appreciation besides just saying thank you?*

## JULY 12      NAPOLEON DANCED WITH ALL HIS MIGHT

*David, wearing a linen ephod, danced before the LORD with all his might, while he and the entire house of Israel brought up the ark of the LORD with shouts and the sound of trumpets.*

*(2 Samuel 6:14-15)*

A few years ago the comedy *Napoleon Dynamite* came out and was an instant hit. My friends and I like to quote lines from the movie. One thing I haven't learned yet, though, is the dance that Napoleon does before the entire school body on behalf of his friend Pedro, who is running for class president. Napoleon doesn't care what anyone thinks of him; he dances his heart out for the benefit of his friend, and he gets a standing ovation.

Napoleon's uninhibited dancing reminds me of King David, who danced "with all his might" before the Lord as the Ark of the Covenant was brought up. Neither David nor Napoleon cared what others thought of them as they danced; they just danced with all their might. But David, unlike Napoleon, danced for the Lord. He worshiped without restraint. He wasn't self-conscious or timid. He gave his all for God's glory. We should do the same. Whether we're worshiping in church or doing something we do well, let's give our all for God's glory!

*What are some things you do to glorify God that may seem strange or different to others?*

## JULY 13                                      A TRUE FRIEND

*A friend loves at all times, and a brother is born for adversity. (Proverbs 17:17)*

*E*dward Scissorhands is a classic comedy-drama fantasy film directed by Tim Burton and starring Johnny Depp. The movie tells the story of Edward, an unfinished "creation" who has scissors instead of hands. (The inventor dies before he is able to replace the scissors with hands.) A woman named Peg takes Edward in, and he falls in love with her teenage daughter, who is dating the neighborhood bully. At first Edward becomes popular when everyone realizes how talented he is at trimming hedges and cutting hair. But after several misunderstandings, they begin to turn against Edward and eventually chase him back to the mansion where he was created, making him an outcast. His friends are proved to be fair-weather friends. Only Peg and Kim continue to show their support for him.

All of us feel like Edward at one time or another—rejected and outcast. And all of us have been guilty of misjudging and excluding others. The Bible teaches us that a true friend loves at all times, even when times are tough and everyone else seems to have "jumped ship." If you have one or more true friends, you are blessed. And if you are a true friend to others, you are a blessing.

*Who needs your support and friendship right now?*

*What can you do to express your friendship to this person?*

## JULY 14        THE MYSTERIOUS TWILIGHT ZONE

*"You will seek me and find me when you seek me with all your heart." (Jeremiah 29:13)*

Last summer I bought a book by Earl Hamner Jr. that contained scripts of the television show *The Twilight Zone*. Every episode in the show takes place in the "twilight zone"—a mysterious place that no one can explain. Strange, inexplicable things happen there. There is an element of fear and dread to it. I think "twilight zone" should be a synonym for anything that is unknowable and a little creepy!

Though some would say that God and faith are *Twilight Zone* material, the Bible makes it clear that our God is not "twilight zone." God is knowable, certain, unchanging, and loving. It's all laid out for us in the Bible. It says that when we search for God, we will find him. When we draw near to God, he will draw near to us. We just have to look for God.

*In what ways is God mysterious to you?*

*What are some ways you can get to know God better so that he is not so mysterious?*

JULY 15                                    USING THE POWER

*We have different gifts, according to the grace given us.*
*(Romans 12:6)*

Today we are talking about the first Spider-Man movie, and you can probably tell me the lesson because it's that obvious. Uncle Ben tells Peter Parker that with great power comes great responsibility. I have found this to be very useful information because God has given us all gifts and we can use them for good or bad, much like a superhero. Some of us are gifted athletes. Are we going to use our gift by showing good sportsmanship, or by having a bad attitude when something doesn't go our way? Some of us are gifted orators. Do we use our skill of speaking to help people through their problems and to show them God, or do we use that gift to persuade people to do bad things? Whatever your gift may be, you should use it for God and for the good of others and yourself. Don't fall into the dark side! (I know that's cheesy, but I needed a *Star Wars* reference at some point during the month!)

*Have you used any of the gifts you have been given in a bad way?*

*How can you use your particular gifts to make the world a better place?*

JULY 16                                  A MASQUERADE OF SORTS

*"Let your light shine before men, that they may see your good deeds and praise your Father in heaven." (Matthew 5:16)*

In the movie *The Princess Bride,* the story line is based around a princess and a mysterious character called the Dread Pirate Roberts, although the audience knows his true identity. The princess doesn't realize who he is until later in the movie when she finds out that the Dread Pirate Roberts, who has saved her, is actually her dear farm boy Westley.

If we wait until the end of our life stories to find out who God is, it may be too late. God shouldn't be a mystery like dear Westley.

God should be someone we know greatly and make known to other people through our actions. We Christians should never hide behind a mask like the Dread Pirate Roberts, as if life is a masquerade, because then nonbelievers see our faith as a mystery. Don't let God be a mystery. Let your light shine!

*Why do we hide our faith from other people at times?*

*How do we overcome hiding our faith and help others come to know God?*

JULY 17                                   WHAT'S YOUR VOICE?

*"Fear the LORD and serve him faithfully with all your heart; consider what great things he has done for you."*
*(1 Samuel 12:24)*

In *Dead Poet's Society,* Robin Williams takes on the role of Mr. Keating, a teacher at an all-boys prep school. Mr. Keating veers away from the typical teaching tradition of the school by allowing the boys to be themselves. A lesson that Mr. Keating emphasizes is that it is important for each individual to find his or her passion and to do it for himself or herself and for no one else. In writing there is something similar called "finding your voice," and I think that term is easier to understand. One of the students takes Mr. Keating's advice and becomes an actor in the local theater rather than focusing on becoming a doctor like his father wants him to do. His father gives him a hasty lecture, dictating the boy's future. In despair over his father's demands, the boy commits suicide.

The point I want to highlight is that we should all find our own voice. God has already given it to us; we just have to find it. Oftentimes we are pigeonholed into being things we don't want to be. That should never be. God has a specific purpose for each of us, and finding our voice enables us to fulfill it.

*Have you found your voice—your passion? What is it, or what do you think it might be?*

*How can you use your voice to minister to others?*

## JULY 18                                    FAITH INTO ACTION

*Faith by itself, if it is not accompanied by action, is dead.*
*(James 2:17)*

$S$*wing Vote* is a movie about a couch potato dad named Bud who
is not interested in voting on election day. His twelve-year-old
daughter, Molly, decides to sneak into the polls and vote for him.
Because the voting machine is unplugged, the ballot is registered
but there is no decision on which candidate gets the vote. It turns
out that the entire election comes down to Bud's vote. The popular vote is the same for each candidate in Bud's state of New
Mexico, leaving Bud to decide the next president of the United
States.

   This is not a call for you to get involved in politics, though it's
important for each of us to be informed and involved. It's a call for
you to get involved in your church and put your faith into action.
You see, the church is much like a democracy in the sense that
even at your age, your voice can and should be heard. When you
put your faith into action, you can help bring about the things you
want to see happen in and through the church.

   Go out and be the change you want to see in your church, community, and world. Get involved by putting your faith into action!

*What is an issue within the church that you feel called to take*
*a stand on or get involved in?*

*How can you put your faith into action related to this issue?*

## JULY 19                                              BIG GREEN

*With such nagging [Delilah] prodded [Samson] day after day*
*until he was tired to death. So he told her everything.... "If my*
*head were shaved, my strength would leave me, and I would*
*become as weak as any other man." (Judges 16:16-17)*

$T$oday I want to focus on a character that has been featured in
both television and movies: the Incredible Hulk. The Hulk is big,

green, scary, and strong; but most of all, he is known for his strength. That's why he makes me think of a Bible character by the name of Samson. Now Samson, like the Hulk, was very strong; no one in the land was stronger. Samson had his downfall, though: a woman. This woman betrayed Samson, and he lost his strength when his enemies cut off his hair.

There are many lessons in Samson's story, but the one I want to point out is that we should know our main weakness, which can carry us away from God and God's will for our lives. We should not let anything like alcohol, sex, or drugs make us stray from God. Though God will be waiting with arms wide open to take us back, we shouldn't abuse God's grace. We need to stay close to God and keep that relationship strong.

*When have you strayed from God? What are some things that have taken you off God's path?*

*What are the things that bring you closer to God?*

## JULY 20                                                    STOOGE!

*And we, who with unveiled faces all reflect the Lord's glory, are being transformed into his likeness with ever-increasing glory, which comes from the Lord, who is the Spirit.*
*(2 Corinthians 3:18)*

When I think of American slapstick comedy, I think of the many Three Stooges movies. This kind of comedy is relatively clean, and because of that I've been watching the Stooges since I was small. You may be wondering what three guys hitting one another can teach us. Well, the Three Stooges remind me that the little victories are important no matter what.

Sometimes we struggle to be the Christians we want to be. But we have to realize that spiritual growth is a process; we shouldn't expect complete transformation all at once. Instead, we should see the little victories and steps as progress and not take them for granted. If we don't celebrate the little victories, then we begin to feel that we are not growing in our faith, which hinders our relationship with God. Just accept the little victories. You even might get a laugh out of it like the Stooges!

*What are some things you have taken for granted that could be considered little victories?*

*Why is it important to consider little victories like this as big accomplishments?*

JULY 21                        THE TRUE DAY OF INFAMY

*Christ died for sins once for all, the righteous for the unrighteous, to bring you to God. (1 Peter 3:18)*

December 7, 1941, is a day that will always live in infamy, according to Franklin D. Roosevelt. The movie that depicts this horrific day is titled simply *Pearl Harbor*. The movie illustrates the devastating bombings, the many deaths, and the relationships that were affected, as well as many other things that happened on this day. Although this was an incredibly significant day in our nation's history, the thought occurs to me that this day may be more honored or commemorated than the death of our Lord, which many consider to be the most horrific of days in all of history. We must never forget that Jesus died for our sins so that we could spend all of eternity with him in heaven.

This is a call for us to see things more clearly. Are we truly grateful for Jesus' sacrifice or do we just live our lives as if Good Friday never happened? No day should be more important than that of Jesus' death, and that day should affect the way we live our lives each and every day.

*How should Jesus' sacrifice affect the way we live our lives each day?*

JULY 22                                    A LESSON IN CHOCOLATE

*Each of you should look not only to your own interests, but also to the interests of others. (Philippians 2:4)*

In the movie *Charlie and the Chocolate Factory,* chocolate maker Willy Wonka holds a worldwide contest that brings five lucky golden ticket winners to the mysterious chocolate factory for an all-day tour. The winners are gluttonous Augustus Gloop, spoiled Veruca Salt, gum-chewing Violet Beauregarde, television-obsessed Mike Teevee, and poor Charlie Bucket—whose family is so poor that all four grandparents share the same bed. As they make their way through the factory, one after another is eliminated from the factory and the contest because of his or her vice. Charlie is the only one who does not misbehave; instead, he does the right thing.

Wonka announces that Charlie has won the entire factory and will take over the company after Wonka retires. But then he says Charlie must leave his family and come live at the factory. Charlie refuses to leave his family. He would rather sacrifice the grand prize than be wealthy apart from his family. In the end, Wonka invites Charlie's entire family to join them at the factory.

Are we like Charlie, looking to the interests of others, or are we self-centered and selfish like the other four contest winners? We are truly blessed when we think more about others than we think about ourselves.

*What unselfish thing can you do for someone else today?*

JULY 23                                    GIVE IN OR PUT OFF?

*Put off your old self, which is being corrupted by its deceitful desires.... Be made new in the attitude of your minds;...put on the new self, created to be like God in true righteousness and holiness. (Ephesians 4:22-24)*

In *Spider-Man 3,* Peter Parker faces some new villains, including a shape-shifting sandman and his friend Harry, who is seeking vengeance for his father's death. As Peter contends with these new villains, a strange alien entity from another world bonds with him and causes him a lot of turmoil as he struggles with bad behavior, revenge, and temptations. He wrestles with giving in to the alien entity, but ultimately he puts it off for good.

The alien entity that temporarily changes Spider-Man is a great representation of sin. Jealousy, anger, an unforgiving spirit, revenge, or any other sin can threaten to take us over if we allow it. Sin is dark and deadly; it is poison to the soul. Just as Peter got rid of the alien entity, we must "put off" sin—those old habits that threaten to corrupt us. The Bible says we must be made new in the "attitude of [our] minds." We have a choice. Will we give in, or will we overcome?

*What old habits or former ways do you need to put off?*

*What new attitudes do you need to put on?*

## JULY 24                  I'M NO SUPERHERO

*"Come to me, all you who are weary and burdened, and I will give you rest. Take my yoke upon you and learn from me, for I am gentle and humble in heart, and you will find rest for your souls." (Matthew 11:28-29)*

When we think of superheroes, we often think of heroes like Superman, Batman, and Spider-Man; but there is a new super-hero: Jack Bauer. Yes, the main character of the show *24* is considered somewhat of a superhero in many viewers' eyes. Jack can save the world in twenty-four hours, hence the name of the show. He gets the bad guys, flies helicopters, and still manages to kiss a beautiful girl.

Jack takes on many responsibilities in a short period of time, and many of us try to do the same. We may not be saving the world, but nonetheless we attempt to do it all. Yet none of us is a superhero—or anything close to it. We need to realize this and take moments in our lives to just breathe.

Don't try to take the world on by yourself. It's always OK to ask for help—from God and from others. It's also OK to simply say, "I can't do this right now. I have too much on my plate." You owe it to yourself to be realistic about what you can and cannot do.

*How many activities do you have going on in your life? Of those activities, are there any you don't necessarily need and can give up?*

*Are there moments in your busy day when you can stop and thank God for having an eventful life? If not, how can you make time for that?*

## JULY 25                  LIKE A BOX OF CHOCOLATES

*"I have come that they may have life, and have it to the full."*
*(John 10:10)*

One thing I've learned in my seventeen years of life is that you can't go too long without quoting *Forrest Gump*. You and I know "life is like a box of chocolates" and "we may not all be smart, but we know what love is." What else can we learn from Forrest?

Forrest lives life to the full. Jesus wants us to love others, to give to the poor, to be like him, to pray, and to do many other things we read about in the Gospels. But there is something we sometimes overlook—the part about living life to the full. Whether it's climbing Mount Everest or jumping from a plane or dancing like David in the middle of church, I believe Jesus intends those things to be just as much a part of the full or abundant life as things such as prayer. Life is not meant to be boring!

*When was the last time you dared to do something challenging or exhilarating?*

*How often do you live life to the full? What are some things you can do to make your life more fulfilling or exciting?*

JULY 26                         THE ULTIMATE TREASURE

*"Seek and you will find." (Matthew 7:7)*

In recent years the *National Treasure* movies, starring Nicolas Cage, have introduced a new twist in the popular treasure-seeking adventure. The treasure sought after in these movies is not riches but history. In the end, Nicolas Cage and his team show that knowledge of history is more important than money.

Similarly, knowledge of the Bible is far more valuable than any material treasures we might find. We should dig into our Bibles and be knowledgeable of our faith's history, and in that we will find the riches of God and the marvelous things God has done. That may seem like a cheesy analogy, but it's true. Besides, the Bible has everything a good action-adventure movie has: tender love scenes and heartbreaking betrayals; deception and cover-ups; conspiracy and murder; awesome battle sequences and heroic rescues. If we are willing to seek, we will find.

*What is one "treasure" you have found in the Bible?*

JULY 27                  FINDING FRIENDS IN ODD PLACES

*A friend loves at all times. (Proverbs 17:17)*

*"Love your neighbor as yourself." (Matthew 22:39)*

Who knew that a volleyball could be your best friend? In the movie *Cast Away,* Tom Hanks is, in fact, a castaway. Hanks's character, Chuck Noland, is the only survivor of a plane crash, and he ends up on an island all alone. However, he salvages many random things from the plane's cargo, one of which is a volleyball he names, appropriately, Wilson. This is Chuck's only friend, and he becomes very attached to the volleyball. But toward the end of the movie, Chuck accidentally kicks Wilson into the sea. He loses his friend, and it is devastating to him.

There are people all around us every day who appear to have many friends, but in reality they are very lonely. One of the hard parts of being a Christian is being outgoing and courageous enough to talk to people we wouldn't normally talk to. Everyone needs a friend; everyone needs someone he or she can go to for help. No one deserves to have a volleyball—or computer or iPod or drugs or alcohol or whatever else might be easily available—as his or her only friend.

*Who is that one person in your school who you know needs a friend? Have you ever talked to that person?*

*What kind of difference do you think you could make in that person's life if you were just friendly toward him or her?*

## JULY 28                  THE GOSPELS AS A TEEN MOVIE

*"The word of the Lord will live forever." (1 Peter 1:25 NCV)*

Today we're going to focus on the genre of teen movies. Let's stretch our imaginations and think of the gospel story as a contemporary teen movie. You have your leading star, Jesus, who is the most athletic and attractive guy in the school but who isn't as well liked as he should be because he is actually nice to people and helps them. Then you have Mary, Jesus' mom, who is an attractive young mother. You've got the twelve disciples, who are a mix of artists, athletes, theater types, and mathletes. You have Mary Magdalene, who is a snobby cheerleader with a bad reputation before she meets Jesus, and then things turn around for her and she ends up being one of Jesus' closest friends.

Jesus goes around at lunchtime to all the different clubs and talks about his mission and purpose, telling everyone about God, God's love, and how God wants them to live. However, the quarterback of the school football team, who was previously dating Mary Magdalene, doesn't like the fact that Jesus is rapidly becoming the school's most popular guy. So, in order to fix this problem, the quarterback has Jesus beaten to a pulp at the prom, and Jesus dies. However, Jesus miraculously comes back to life and continues to make an impact on the school and the community and beyond even after he returns to his true home. Just add some catchy rock and rap songs, and you have yourself a teen movie!

That may seem outrageous, but so did *Jesus Christ Superstar* in its day. The point is this: regardless of the vehicle used to tell the story, the gospel is timeless truth that changes lives from one generation to another.

*What are some creative ways our generation can communicate the truth of the gospel to a world in need?*

JULY 29                                    MY SECOND CHANCE

*Because of the LORD's great love we are not consumed, for his compassions never fail. They are new every morning; great is your faithfulness. (Lamentations 3:22-23)*

Comedian Chris Rock stars in the movie *Down to Earth*. Though the theology in the movie is bad, there is a positive message in the end. So stay with me. The story is about an aspiring comic, Lance Barton, who is killed prematurely. He then is reincarnated as a wealthy but unlikable businessman. The man whose body Lance inherits has done some bad things in his life, and many people dislike him with a passion. But Lance wins them over by doing good rather than bad with the man's money.

A positive message I got from the movie is that, although we may not do right the first time, we can learn from our mistakes, make things right, and do better than before. A second chance may be all we need to get on the right track in life.

God gives us more than a second chance. God gives us plenty of do-overs—chances to be better and do right. It's called grace. It would be crazy for us not to accept God's grace and do something good and right with our lives.

*When was the last time you got a second chance? How did you take advantage of this opportunity?*

*What are things you can do to make the second time better than the first?*

172

## JULY 30                              DISNEY AS A LIFE LESSON

*"With God all things are possible." (Matthew 19:26)*

Today we will focus on what I believe is one of the most important lessons to be learned from a movie or television show. That lesson is: follow your dreams. And I would add, your God-given dreams. We learn this lesson from practically every Disney movie ever made. Just about every Disney movie ends with the good guy winning or the handsome prince getting the beautiful princess. It really is a perfect ending.

When I went to Disney World, all my favorite characters came to life with fireworks, music, and lights. It was as if I were actually in the perfect ending. That experience helped me realize that dreams really can come true, even if sometimes they are staged. So I decided to live my life to fulfill my God-given dreams. God has given us the gift of dreams, and not to pursue them would be like spitting in God's face. Sometimes a dream seems unattainable, but as we near the goal we often find out that it is easier than we expected, so we persevere and keep going.

Reach for the impossible and strive to achieve your dreams. Never let anyone belittle you or tell you that you will never achieve your dreams. With God, all things are possible.

*How often do you give up on a task because you believe it is impossible?*

*What dream has God given you? What steps can you take to pursue this dream?*

## JULY 31                                          IT'S YOUR TURN

*Ears to hear and eyes to see—both are gifts from the LORD.*
*(Proverbs 20:12 NLT)*

I hope you have enjoyed this month as we have explored about movies and television shows and the life lessons or faith messages we can find in them. But the fun doesn't have to stop here. If only we will have eyes to see and ears to hear, we can find some kind of life application in just about everything we watch. Of course, it's important to exercise good judgment when selecting what we will watch, but a good story always has some kind of message or meaning we can apply to our lives. Perhaps this is why Jesus taught using parables. So keep on viewing and digging for those nuggets of meaning!

*What is your favorite movie or television show?*

*What message or meaning can you "uncover" in it?*

# AUGUST

# Let God's Word Change Your Life

### RACIE HELEN MILLER

AUGUST 1                            THE TRUTH

*All Scripture is God-breathed and is useful for teaching, rebuking, correcting and training in righteousness, so that the man [or woman] of God may be thoroughly equipped for every good work. (2 Timothy 3:16-17)*

That's what I want—the God-breathed book of life. It's so easy and safe to waste time trying to figure out how to become more "spiritual" or to improve my relationship with the Lord, all the while leaving that living book on the shelf to collect dust. I desperately need the uncomfortable, totally life-altering word of God. I want to read about Jesus and be challenged and inspired by his radical love and obedience to his Father. I want to read about Job, who suffered pain and loss for the sake of God but never questioned God's love for him.

It's good to be reminded, as we focus on God's word, that God chooses imperfect people to do impossible tasks, that God uses broken vessels to contain his unfailing love, and that our lives are meant to bring God glory. God's word invites us to listen to God's voice, enjoy God's presence, be immersed in God's righteousness, submit to God's love, and be transformed forever. This month I invite you to let God's word change your life.

*How can you make God's word a priority in your life?*

*What are some practical ways to incorporate Scripture into your daily life?*

## AUGUST 2 — A SACRIFICE WORTH MAKING

*But Ruth said: "Entreat me not to leave you, Or to turn back from following after you; For wherever you go, I will go; And wherever you lodge, I will lodge; Your people shall be my people, And your God, my God." (Ruth 1:16 NKJV)*

When Ruth decided to follow Naomi, she didn't try to micromanage Naomi's plans. Ruth's happiness was not guaranteed by making Naomi sign a contract. Ruth just clung to her mother-in-law and promised to be loyal to her till death. Ruth could have remained in her home country after the death of her husband, but out of devotion to Naomi she abandoned everything.

Isn't God calling us to abandon everything and follow him? Ruth could not predict the future, but she loved Naomi. Ruth considered her own hopes, dreams, and expectations worth sacrificing for Naomi. God is asking us to trust him with our lives. God is asking us to surrender our plans, our goals, and our ambitions to him. God's Son, Jesus Christ, surrendered his very life so that we could follow him and dwell with God forever. Christ's love is calling us to pick up our cross and follow him. In order for us to get a good grip on our cross, we really must let go of *everything* else we're holding on to.

*What is the biggest sacrifice you've ever made?*

*What is God calling you to let go of now?*

## AUGUST 3 — PATIENCE

*Wait for the Lord; be strong and take heart and wait for the Lord. (Psalm 27:14)*

In this culture of instant gratification, waiting seems so unnecessary and painful! Particularly as it pertains to our relationship with God, patience can be puzzling. If God is so powerful and present in every situation, as the Bible says, then why should we have to wait for God?

I think God is more concerned with the sanctification of our souls than with the meeting of our every want and desire. God is good and promises to give us the "desires of [our] hearts" when we delight in him (Psalm 37:4). But that isn't the point. Waiting for God is trusting in God. Waiting for God is really giving in to God's bigger plan and believing that God will come through for us.

We should all take comfort in knowing that our God is patient with us as we learn to be patient with him. God fully understands our circumstances and knows that we are used to getting what we want, when we want it. But God will not conform to the patterns of this world—nor will God let us.

**What is God having you wait for?**

**What was the outcome of waiting for God in the past?**

## AUGUST 4                                                    PEACE

**"Peace I leave with you, My peace I give to you; not as the world gives do I give to you. Let not your heart be troubled, neither let it be afraid." (John 14:27 NKJV)**

It was early June and I was standing in the front pasture. It was nighttime, and the stars were bright. A strong, warm breeze blew my hair back as I stood facing into the wind. In the background my friends were spinning around in circles, making themselves dizzy and falling over in laughter. All I could do was stand there and praise the Maker of it all. I have never been so filled with peace—peace from knowing that I was in the right place at the right time; peace from acknowledging a loving God who woos me with the stars and warm breezes and sounds of laughter.

Have you ever experienced one of those moments when life seems to slow down, and the moment feels almost eternal? All you can mutter is, "God is good. God is *good*."

We are blessed to be God's children. We are blessed to be filled with God's Spirit and to be vessels of God's unspeakable peace.

**Have you ever experienced God's unspeakable peace?**

**How does that peace overflow into and affect your daily life?**

AUGUST 5                                               DESIRES

*Delight yourself in the LORD and he will give you the desires of your heart. (Psalm 37:4)*

What are the desires of your heart? Do you desire to be wealthy? Do you desire to be popular? Do you desire to be beautiful? Do you desire to be respected? Do you desire to be loved? Do you desire to be satisfied?

As humans, we wrestle with discontent. Someone might say, "I thought I desired a car, but when I got one the happiness didn't seem to last"; or "I thought getting accepted into an incredible university would fulfill me, but it didn't"; or "I thought having a boyfriend would quench my need to be loved and desired, but I still feel empty and desperate."

Even when God does give me the desires of my heart, I am utterly disappointed and discouraged if my desires are not God's desires. Sometimes after the disappointment has faded, I move on to a different desire. I think, *Well, that wasn't a big deal, but this— this will really make me happy.* God has to stop me in my tracks and remind me that this longing I can't seem to get rid of is for him.

*What are your greatest desires?*

*How can you "delight yourself in the LORD" today?*

AUGUST 6                                         THE NARROW WAY

*"But small is the gate and narrow the road that leads to life, and only a few find it." (Matthew 7:14)*

I have weak ankles, and they twist very easily (not to mention that I am very clumsy). So for me, the term "narrow road" conjures up an image of me tripping off the sidewalk and twisting my ankles. Though rather amusing, my understanding of the narrow road to life that Jesus was talking about is slightly off.

The path is narrow because there isn't a plan A or a plan B; there isn't a shortcut or a bypass; there isn't a scenic-view way or a backstreet route. There is just one road to life; one very narrow but extremely dependable road. It's Christ. Christ is "the way and the truth and the life" (John 14:6). Jesus said that few people find this road. Maybe that's because, when you're used to traveling on wide highways, the little roads are easily overlooked. Don't miss the road!

Some people might say that referring to Christ as the only way to life is being narrow-minded. Well, Jesus did say the road is narrow and the gate is small.

**When have you felt restricted by the "narrowness" of God's path?**

**When has God's path proved to be the best way?**

## AUGUST 7                                          GOD IS GOOD

*Then He said, "I will make all My goodness pass before you, and I will proclaim the name of the LORD before you."*
*(Exodus 33:19a NKJV)*

Just as God promised Moses that God's goodness would indeed pass before him, God promises us the same. It is not easy to trust the Lord. It is not easy to follow God when we can't see the next step. But we must hold firm in believing that our God is *good* and will proclaim his name before us.

When we think about God's character, the attributes *just* and *holy* and *righteous* come to mind; but what about God's *goodness*? Maybe we believe that God is good, but how do we think that translates into actions—the way God governs our lives?

If we surrender to the Lord and believe that God is sovereign, then why are we so anxious and stressed out all the time? God is not out to get us. God is not out to trick us into disobeying so that God can punish us. God is completely loving and good. God's goodness extends far beyond our blurred vision, our limited understanding, and our insufficient expectations.

**How can you let God's goodness influence the way you act or think today?**

AUGUST 8                                    COURAGE

*"Have I not commanded you? Be strong and courageous. Do not be terrified; do not be discouraged, for the LORD your God will be with you wherever you go." (Joshua 1:9)*

God knew that Joshua would be afraid and intimidated. Moses had just died, and God had instructed Joshua to take over and lead the Israelites into the Promised Land. Talk about an overwhelming task! But God didn't just suggest courage in this situation; God commanded it. God reminded Joshua that he would be with him wherever he went, and God expected Joshua to obey his commands.

Have you ever been given a daunting task? Has God ever commanded you to do something that was entirely out of your comfort zone? It's not easy to follow the Lord when we know God is going to call us to do things that are intimidating and oftentimes just plain crazy! What a wonderful opportunity to realize how much we need God's presence; how much we need God to command courage in us.

Think about it: God didn't say that Joshua should not be terrified because he wouldn't encounter any danger. God said, "For the LORD your God will be with you wherever you go." What better comfort do we need?

*What daunting task is God calling you to do?*

*How can you learn to better rely on God's presence?*


AUGUST 9                                 CONTENTMENT

*I have learned the secret of being content in any and every situation, whether well fed or hungry, whether living in plenty or in want. I can do everything through him who gives me strength. (Philippians 4:12b-13)*

Wouldn't you give anything to learn the secret of being content? Contentment is priceless, isn't it?

I always found it encouraging that Paul had learned how to be content in "any and every situation." If Paul could be content, then so can we, right? But then one day, I took a closer look at verse 13 where Paul says that the secret to his contentment is that he can do all things through Christ. That threw me for a loop. I was unable to correlate our strength in Christ with contentment. I thought, *What does strength have to do with contentment?*

Lately, however, as I am learning how incredibly discontent I really am and how utterly incapable I am of achieving contentment, I understand why the "secret" to contentment is truly in Christ, and in his sufficient grace and strength. We are weak, but Christ is strong. Only he can give us lasting contentment.

*What are some areas of discontent in your life?*

*What can you do to pursue contentment in every area of your life?*

## AUGUST 10                                    LISTEN

*"But when he, the Spirit of truth, comes, he will guide you into all truth. He will not speak on his own; he will speak only what he hears, and he will tell you what is yet to come." (John 16:13)*

When most people think of the word *communication,* the speaking part seems to take center stage in their minds. But what about the listening part? What good are words if no one is listening? When I say that so-and-so isn't a good communicator, maybe what I really should ponder is whether I am a good listener.

Do we treat God as a poor communicator? God is obviously a good listener, but when it comes to talking, God often seems silent. God speaks through his word, through the Holy Spirit, through others, and through the Creation. But the question is this: Are we listening?

My life is filled with noise and distraction. Until I turn off my iPod, shut my mouth, and turn toward the loving God, I will not hear and be blessed by what he is communicating.

*What noises are drowning out God's voice?*

*How can you listen for the voice of God?*

AUGUST 11                                    UNDERSTOOD

*O LORD, You have searched me and known me. You know when I sit down and when I rise up; You understand my thought from afar. (Psalm 139:1-2 NASB)*

Have you ever been understood? You don't even have to utter a word because the person you are with just knows.

God understands. There is never a communication barrier or translation problem with the Lord because God already knows our words before we say them and our thoughts before we think them. God is completely familiar with all our ways. God knows why we do what we do, and when we're going to do it. God sees the wickedness of our hearts and the sin that stains our souls, yet loves us regardless. God sees past the visage and hears more than our habitual "I'm doing well, thanks." God knows who we are and exactly what we are going through.

We may think that we are the only ones who can understand the complexity of our own thoughts and emotions, but our God knows us better than we know ourselves. We are transparent before God's omniscient eyes. What a wild and wonderful thing it is to be loved unconditionally and to be infinitely understood by our Lord and Creator!

*How does it make you feel to know that God truly understands you?*

*How has God revealed to you that you are completely known and loved?*

AUGUST 12                                        STRENGTH

*And He said to me, "My grace is sufficient for you, for My strength is made perfect in weakness."*
*(2 Corinthians 12:9a NKJV)*

God, you know how much I need this time right now. I am so cranky and exhausted. I have nothing left to give. Listen, Lord, I need you to fill me and encourage me. Restore what has been drained out. Help me keep up the 'gusto' until Saturday. Lord, I am waiting for you. FILL ME!"

That was a prayer I prayed many times while working at a summer camp last year. By midsummer I was exhausted. Every morning the Lord brought me to my knees, reminding me that my strength just wouldn't cut it. As I cried out to Christ, he was faithful to fill me with his grace and make his strength known in my utter weakness.

In order to truly experience the power of Christ's strength, we first must experience the insufficiency of ours. So let's not become too comfortable going about the tasks we're sure we can handle. Instead, let's step out into the realm of impossible feats, knowing that as we stumble and struggle and fall short, Christ's strength is made perfect.

*Has there been a time in your life when God's strength has been displayed in your weakness? What happened?*

## AUGUST 13                                    FACE-TO-FACE

*Now we see but a poor reflection as in a mirror; then we shall see face to face. Now I know in part; then I shall know fully, even as I am fully known. (1 Corinthians 13:12)*

While trying to explain my love for Jesus to a friend, I felt almost crazy. I can't see him or touch him or hear an audible voice, or even begin to fathom what he's like. I just know that he loves me and I love him. I don't know if it's what Jesus calls faith, or if his love is just stronger than the visible objects of this world, but I trust in his reality even more than the reality of what I can touch.

There is something inside us that knows we are going to see him face-to-face someday. It seems that faith isn't required to love Christ. Rather, it's a natural result of being in a relationship with him.

Think of the moments when you've felt most aware of God's presence. Think about those times when you felt like you knew him more than ever. Now realize that someday the dynamics of this "crazy" relationship will change when we see him face-to-face and know him fully.

*What aspect of one day being in God's presence excites you the most?*

AUGUST 14                                                    LIGHT

*"You are the light of the world. A city on a hill cannot be hidden." (Matthew 5:14)*

Fluorescent lighting is very bright and very affordable. Fluorescent lights are often used to light large spaces such as gyms, cafeterias, classrooms, warehouses, malls, supermarkets, and sometimes churches. There's something about fluorescent lighting, though, that rubs me the wrong way; it gives me the opposite of "warm and cozy" feelings. Besides the fact that fluorescent lights flicker on and off, and tend to make strange buzzing noises, I don't like them because they seem artificial.

In several different places the New Testament refers to Christians as "lights to the world" or "lights in the darkness." When light is present, darkness vanishes. But what about when that light is fluorescent? What if the light is loud and clear, yet artificial and insincere? What about the Christians who talk about Jesus, sing about Jesus, wear T-shirts about Jesus, or have bumper stickers about Jesus, but who don't really live like Jesus or love like Jesus?

Perhaps the point is not that we be the brightest lights, like fluorescent lighting, but that we be the truest or most genuine form of light, like a candle or a fire.

*What kind of light are you?*

AUGUST 15                                                    NUMB

*The sacrifices of God are a broken spirit; a broken and contrite heart, O God, you will not despise. (Psalm 51:17)*

I had a cavity filled recently, and the dentist accidentally numbed both sides of my mouth. When the numbness had taken its full effect, I couldn't feel my tongue, my bottom lip, my chin, or either of my cheeks (inside and out). I could hardly even talk with any clarity. As the dentist began to drill my tooth, I thought to myself, *I'd almost rather feel the pain than leave here with this absence of feeling.*

Have you ever felt extreme guilt for a sin that you committed, and wished you could feel "numb" so you wouldn't have to deal with it? In Psalm 51, David was repenting to the Lord for his affair with Bathsheba when he realized that it was more pleasing to the Lord for him to be broken and distressed over his sin than for him to have a calloused heart.

God has blessed us with the Holy Spirit so that instead of being apathetic to our sin we can be broken over it, we can repent, and then we can be forgiven and freed from our guilt and shame. Isn't it better to be broken and healed than to be numb and in critical condition?

**When have you felt numb to your sin?**

## AUGUST 16                                    LOVE

*If I have the gift of prophecy and can fathom all mysteries and all knowledge, and if I have a faith that can move mountains, but have not love, I am nothing. (1 Corinthians 13:2)*

What unconventional words! This verse says that we can have the gift of prophecy, have an amazing faith, speak in the tongues of angels, give all we possess to the poor, and even surrender our bodies to the flame, but if we don't have love, then we are "nothing."

We can be the best evangelists out there, but if we're not sharing the gospel out of love for God and love for God's children, then we are only giving a sales pitch. This is a call to evaluate our faith and search for the substance, the love that must be the foundation.

Don't be deceived—or discouraged! This love is not something that can be mustered up or produced on our own. Jesus said that loving God and loving others are the greatest commands, but it's also true that they are the hardest. We need Christ's love to over-flow in our lives, for it's his love for us that enables us to love him and to love others.

*How can Christ's love reign in your life? Name as many practical ways as you can.*

## AUGUST 17             FREEDOM

*But now that you have been set free from sin and have become slaves to God, the benefit you reap leads to holiness, and the result is eternal life. (Romans 6:22)*

God makes it very clear that because of the gift of salvation, we are free from sin. However, in the same sentence, God points out that we are, in fact, still slaves, only now God is our Master. Our former slavery resulted in death and shame, but our slavery to God reaps holiness and eternal life.

I'd rather leave the verse at "but now... you have been set free from sin" and omit the part about us being slaves to God, but here is the beautiful thing: we have a Master who also calls us "children," "bride," "friends," "disciples," "sheep," and "beloved." Our merciful Master died for us so that we could be freed from the very slavery that condemns us. So, indeed, we are slaves to Christ! But no longer are we tripping in shackles; now we have the mark of salvation and dance to the tune of freedom.

*What old "shackles" are you still choosing to wear?*

*What would it mean for you to live in the freedom that Christ offers?*

# AUGUST 18                                    CITIZENS

*But our citizenship is in heaven. And we eagerly await a Savior from there, the Lord Jesus Christ. (Philippians 3:20)*

This isn't home. No matter how comfortable we become on this earth, no matter how many friends we acquire, no matter how much wealth we store up, no matter how great a reputation we can boast, no matter how productive we are, no matter how much we enjoy the beauty of nature, no matter how fulfilled we feel in this lifetime, we are foreigners while we roam this earth.

Time is moving fast. Even the most satisfying moments in life are only fleeting and temporary. But our destiny is not death; it is true life and citizenship in our real home.

Of course, God has us here on earth for a reason: to love and to be the hands and feet of Christ. But we would be fooling ourselves to think that this is all there is. When life is disappointing, and when joy just doesn't last long enough, we must remember that our final destination is unhindered and eternal intimacy with our Savior Jesus, which means complete joy and utter fulfillment in him. So don't be discouraged. The best is yet to come.

*Where do you feel most at home?*

*How can you live for Christ here on earth as a citizen in heaven?*

# AUGUST 19                    JESUS OUR LORD IS CRUCIFIED

*With a loud cry, Jesus breathed his last. (Mark 15:37)*

I wanted to write about Christ's resurrection, but I realized I couldn't write about Christ being risen if I didn't acknowledge the tragedy of his death. My desire to avoid writing about Christ's death reflects a desire in my heart not to dwell on the costliness of Christ's sacrifice. As a Christian, I believe that Christ, my Savior, died for me and rose from the dead; but in order to more speedily arrive at the Resurrection, I often fast-forward past the part about him dying.

God doesn't want us to fast-forward past the Crucifixion or to grow apathetic to Christ's sacrifice. God wants us to be broken as we draw near to the cross.

Do we, as Christ's followers and disciples, mourn over his death? Do we mourn because our Lord experienced the worst pain, and what's more, was separated from his Father? May we never skip Christ's death or forget when he "breathed his last."

O come and mourn with me awhile!
O come ye to the Savior's side;
O come, together let us mourn;
Jesus, our Lord, is crucified.

—Frederick W. Faber

*Has there been a time in your life when you mourned over Christ's death?*

*How did that mourning change you?*

## AUGUST 20                                    HE IS RISEN!

*"Don't be alarmed," he said, "You are looking for Jesus the Nazarene, who was crucified. He has risen! He is not here. See the place where they laid him." (Mark 16:6)*

Three days after Christ's death, Mary Magdalene and Mary the mother of James were headed to the tomb to anoint Jesus' body with burial spices. When they arrived, they found that Jesus was missing. Then an angel informed them that their Lord had risen from the dead. Imagine: your Messiah has been killed and placed in a tomb, you go to anoint him, and you find out he's missing. You think his body has been stolen. Then an angel, who you thought was a gardener, tells you your Messiah has risen! Can you think of a more overwhelming yet incredible joy?

While I was working on staff at a Christian camp one summer, one of the directors told the staff, "When you think you can't keep going, just say to yourself, 'Christ is risen.'"

Yes, our Savior was crucified, but that is not the end of the story, for Mary and Mary Magdalene found an empty tomb. This is our hope. This is our joy. This is our reason to live. Christ is risen!

*How does Christ's resurrection affect your spiritual life?*

## AUGUST 21                                        TREASURES

*"Sell your possessions and give to the poor. Provide purses for yourselves that will not wear out, a treasure in heaven that will not be exhausted, where no thief comes near and no moth destroys. For where your treasure is, there your heart will be also." (Luke 12:33-34)*

What are your treasures? Isn't it true that what you value the most is probably what most consumes your thoughts? Christ is being very blunt when he says, "Sell your possessions and give to the poor." Other than encouraging generosity, Jesus was addressing our tendency to make idols out of our "treasures."

God isn't against wealth or possessions, but if those things are going to be a hindrance to our relationship with him, it seems that God would rather us be without them, period. God wants our hearts. God is a jealous God who tells us we can't serve more than one master. We must choose to either worship God or let our hearts be captured by temporary fixes that leave us even more desperate than before. May we all learn to pray as David in Psalm 86:11b: "Give me an undivided heart, that I may fear your name."

*What possessions are keeping you from greater intimacy with Jesus?*

## AUGUST 22                                                GAZE

*Let your eyes look straight ahead, fix your gaze directly before you. (Proverbs 4:25)*

When I was learning to drive, my mom said, "Don't look at the other cars or at the white line to your right, or at people or dogs on the side of the road; just look at the yellow line, because you'll drive toward wherever you're looking."

Do you think the same is true with our faith? Can we really walk in the right direction if we're always looking somewhere else? It can be so easy to get stuck in dwelling on the past. But if my head is always settled in memories, how can I look ahead to what God has in store for the future? Or what if I am always looking to my right or to my left, observing what I could have or should have been doing if God hadn't intervened and led me in a different direction? With that distracted and wistful mentality, how can I continue walking in God's way?

Let's fix our eyes straight ahead and trust that this path we're on is leading us somewhere. Yes, we will stumble, get distracted, and lose our focus at times, but let's strive to look ahead and let Christ be our vision.

**What is your gaze fixed upon?**

## AUGUST 23                    THE SPIRIT OF FAITH

*For just as the body without the spirit is dead, so also faith without works is dead. (James 2:26 NASB)*

Faith. In Hebrews 11:1, faith is described as the "substance of things hoped for, the evidence of things not seen" (NJKV). What "evidence" or "substance" do we have to show for our faith? Yes, we have to believe in Jesus Christ in order to be saved, and that certainly requires faith; but after salvation, how does that faith play out in our lives? James says that works are the spirit of faith. That is, if action isn't the natural result of our faith in Christ, then maybe we should evaluate the faith we claim to have. Maybe it isn't faith at all.

Faith changes everything. No longer is obedience to the law something that is required to attain righteousness; rather, righteousness is earned through faith, and obeying God's commands is a manifestation of that faith. It's not about how much faith we have. It's about in whom we have faith.

So, as we put our faith in the Lord Jesus, let's not settle for a faith that is merely words. Instead, may we learn to embrace his Spirit who lives within us and who communicates a faith that expresses itself through actions and righteousness.

*How can you live out your faith today?*

## AUGUST 24                                                 BROKEN

*Grieve, mourn and wail. Change your laughter to mourning and your joy to gloom. Humble yourselves before the Lord, and he will lift you up. (James 4:9-10)*

I once heard that, as God' children, we were not created to be comfortable but to be comforted. Doesn't that say something about our God? God knows that when we get too comfortable, we forget about who he is. Throughout the Old Testament, God was in pursuit of his peoples' hearts, but only in times of crisis would they acknowledge him and seek his mercy and grace. In times of abundance and comfort they would forget God and return to self-sufficiency. So God continually afflicted them in order to win back their hearts. As David exclaimed in Psalm 119:75, "O LORD . . . in faithfulness you have afflicted me."

God does not want us to live in misery, but maybe God knows that we need his comfort more than our self-attained happiness. Maybe God knows that being "lifted up" in his loving arms and touched by his healing hands is the ultimate outcome of affliction.

So may we bow before God's throne, knowing that, as we draw near in humility, he draws near, too, with arms wide open.

*How does your view of God change in times of mourning or grief?*

## AUGUST 25                                          FORGIVENESS

*Then Peter came to Jesus and asked, "Lord, how many times shall I forgive my brother when he sins against me? Up to seven times?" Jesus answered, "I tell you, not seven times, but seventy-seven times." (Matthew 18:21-22)*

I can see myself asking Jesus the same question: "Lord, exactly how many times do I have to forgive this person before I can hold a grudge against them?"

Jesus paid the price for our sin, and he daily forgives us for our disobedience. Yet somehow when we are the ones who've been wronged, forgiveness is the farthest thing from our minds. Why is it that forgiveness is so difficult? I don't know the answer to that question, other than the fact that we are sinners. God has been so merciful and gracious to us. How can we allow that grace and mercy to overflow into our other relationships?

In the end, we must realize that we need Christ in us to help us forgive. We need to acknowledge and confess that we are proud people who desperately need our loving Savior to help us truly forgive, as he has truly forgiven us.

**How, with God's help, can you express genuine forgiveness to someone who has wronged you?**

## AUGUST 26          FRIENDS

*"You are my friends if you do what I command. I no longer call you servants, because a servant does not know his master's business. Instead, I have called you friends, for everything that I learned from my Father I have made known to you."*
*(John 15:14-15)*

The disciples passionately loved Christ and wanted nothing more than to serve him until death, but Jesus was giving them a new name. He was no longer going to call them servants, but friends.

The natural result of a relationship with our Savior is sanctification. Christ sanctifies us; that is, he makes us holy. Through sanctification Christ transforms our hearts, minds, souls, and identities. So as his beloved disciples, we are drawn near to him. We know him and his love, and that makes us want to obey him and be his servants. But he doesn't stop there. He draws us even closer, sanctifying us with an even deeper fire; he changes our identities and calls us his friends.

What a privilege! As we follow our Lord, he invites us to know him more intimately and calls us his friends.

**What are the differences between a servant and a friend?**

## AUGUST 27                                    NO EXCUSES

*"Ah, Sovereign L*ORD*," I said, "I do not know how to speak; I am only a child." But the L*ORD *said to me, "Do not say, 'I am only a child.' You must go to everyone I send you to and say whatever I command you." (Jeremiah 1:6-7)*

Jeremiah was just a teenager, but in spite of his age and inexperience, God called him to step up to the plate and be his mouthpiece to the nation of Judah. Jeremiah was to prophesy of the destruction that Babylon would bring upon the nation because of Judah's unfaithfulness to God. Jeremiah was reluctant. He reminded God that he was only a child and didn't know how he was going to deliver this awful news to the Israelites. He was afraid, but God wouldn't let him back down. Even with apprehension, Jeremiah was obedient to the Lord and served as an ardent prophet to Judah for forty years.

Jeremiah wasn't a perfect guy. He was insecure and whiney, yet God chose him to speak God's truth. God hears our excuses, but he won't let them get in the way of his plans for us.

**What "reasons" for not obeying God do you need to let go of?**

## AUGUST 28                                      SHEPHERD

*The L*ORD *is my shepherd, I shall not be in want. . . . He leads me beside quiet waters, he restores my soul. (Psalm 23:1-3a)*

Once when hiking with my brother, we came across a beautiful stream. The sight was absolutely breathtaking. The stream, which was surrounded by trees on both sides, had a long rope bridge over it. In the stream were various rocks and boulders, and the sun and clouds reflected perfectly off the clear water. Mesmerized, I skipped from rock to rock down the stream until I found a nice boulder to rest on. As I reclined against the big rock, watching the water rush gently by, all I could think of were the words, "He leads me beside quiet waters, he restores my soul."

God is so faithful. He knows what speaks to us individually, and he is persistent in communicating his love to us. Just as God knows that water reminds me of his goodness to lead and guide me as a shepherd, God also knows what touches you. Let God remind you and restore you.

**What object or place reminds you of God's hand in your life?**

## AUGUST 29 THE GOD OF RECONCILIATION

*Now all things are of God, who has reconciled us to Himself through Jesus Christ, and has given us the ministry of reconciliation. (2 Corinthians 5:18 NKJV)*

Christ took on sin that we might be made righteous before God. We have been reconciled and given the ministry of reconciliation.

This reconciliation applies not only to our relationship with God; it extends to our relationships with others as well. As human beings who sin, we hurt one another. Our relationships—some more than others—are tainted with sin and pain; but God is in the business of healing the broken and restoring the spoiled.

I have had relationships in which anger and bitterness were so deeply rooted that forgiveness and restoration seemed impossible. But God made those relationships new. God restored them, bringing reconciliation where there was hurt and resignation.

If God is capable of restoring what should be the most polarized relationship of all—our relationship with him—then we can trust him with our other relationships, too. So let's surrender our scarred relationships along with our feeble efforts to make them right. Let's surrender our discouragement to God, for he is the God of reconciliation.

*What broken relationships do you need to entrust to the Lord?*

## AUGUST 30                                          OTHERS

*But the manifestation of the Spirit is given to each one for the profit of all. (1 Corinthians 12:7 NKJV)*

When I think about the way the Lord uses me, the opportunities God has given me to speak of his name, and the gifts or talents he has bestowed upon me, it's easy to be self-centered. Why am I so inclined to think that God is concerned only with making me feel special or significant? God cares about the way I feel about myself, but it would be missing the point to assume God is thinking *only* about me!

God wants us to bless others. God's Spirit within us desires to act in a way that is for the profit of all. There have been too many times when I have chosen not to serve because I wondered, *What's in it for me?* The truth is, serving God is not about me. I must come to terms with the fact that the Spirit who lives within me desires to bless others and put them first.

So let's surrender our talents and ambitions to God and witness God transforming us into the selfless, altruistic people God wants us to be.

*What are some ways that you can put others first?*

*How can you make room for the Holy Spirit to bless others through your life?*

## AUGUST 31              THE ALL-TRANSCENDING GOD

*Before the mountains were born or you brought forth the earth and the world, from everlasting to everlasting you are God.*
*(Psalm 90:2)*

God goes beyond the limits. It's so impossible to grasp who God is that we sometimes find ourselves associating God with things. I tend to associate God with my Christian friends, nature, or church. I subconsciously categorize God, putting him in a box and giving him limits. God has been teaching me, however, that he is not limited to church or nature, and that he cannot be categorized. God was, and is, and always will be God—the God who existed before creation and who reigns over all. In Exodus 3:14, God appeared to Moses in a burning bush and gave him a message to deliver to the Israelites. When Moses asked who he should say sent him, God said, "I AM has sent me to you." This is the God we were made to praise. No, we can't praise God in complete understanding, but we can praise him in utter awe, saying, "From everlasting to everlasting you are God."

**What are the categories in which you try to place God?**

**How can you let go of these categories and increase your sense of awe and wonder in who God is?**

# SEPTEMBER

# Knowing God Leads to Action

## HOON KIM

SEPTEMBER 1            LOVE AND DISCIPLINE

*Let us also lay aside every weight, and sin which clings so closely, and let us run with endurance the race that is set before us, looking to Jesus, the founder and perfecter of our faith, who for the joy that was set before him endured the cross, despising the shame, and is seated at the right hand of the throne of God. (Hebrews 12:1-2 ESV)*

When we love a person, sport, or video game, we become incredibly disciplined in our pursuit. We'll spend money, set aside time, and plan our days accordingly. Discipline is easy when we love something.

Likewise, the secret to being spiritually disciplined is not "trying harder." Trying harder never lasts! Not only that, when one tries harder in spiritual commitments and fails, the guilt of failure becomes greater and greater. Following Jesus becomes a pain, not a joy! This is true especially when trying to resist particular sins in our lives.

Scripture never tells us to try harder. Scripture calls us to know God more. When we know God more, we fall more in love with him. When we love God more, discipline is easy. This month we will explore how we can know God more, and how knowing God more will bring discipline, growth, and action in our faith and in our lives.

*In what area(s) of your life do you find it easy to be disciplined, and why?*

*How disciplined are you when it comes to living out your faith?*

## SEPTEMBER 2                                  COURAGE

*An army with horses and chariots was all around the city. And the servant said, "Alas, my master! What shall we do?" He said, "Do not be afraid, for those who are with us are more than those who are with them." (2 Kings 6:15-16 ESV)*

One thing that holds many Christians down is fear. The remedy to fear is courage. Courage is not the absence of fear but the ability to stand when fear is present.

The servant of Elisha was scared because he saw incredible opposition. Notice what Elisha did not do. He didn't destroy the enemy. Elisha enabled his servant to the see the presence of God's greater army.

At times God may remove our "enemies" by healings and miracles. More often, however, God allows us to see the same situation through the eyes of faith. Paul writes, "What then shall we say to these things? If God is for us, who can be against us?" (Romans 8:31 ESV). In Philippians 4:7 Paul reveals that prayer enables the "peace of God, which surpasses all understanding" (ESV).

When God does not change your situation, pray for courage, and God will give you peace.

*Is there anything causing you fear right now?*

*How might the eyes of faith help you see the situation differently?*

## SEPTEMBER 3                             PLACE AND TIME

*The God who made the world and everything in it, being Lord of heaven and earth, does not live in temples made by man, nor*

*is he served by human hands, as though he needed anything,
since he himself gives to all mankind life and breath and everything. And he made from one man every nation of mankind to
live on all the face of the earth, having determined allotted peri-
ods and the boundaries of their dwelling place, that they should
seek God, in the hope that they might feel their way toward him
and find him. (Acts 17:24-27 ESV)*

Paul was teaching unbelievers the bigness of his God. God
created *all* things; nothing exists that God did not create. God
doesn't need anything—not even humankind! On the contrary, *all*
humankind needs God for life! God is not limited to a church
building. God is just as present at school as at church.

God has a purpose. God chose us to live in our specific times
and places so that we, and others through us, would find God!
Your birth date is not by chance; neither is your school, looks, talents, personality, or circumstances. God has a plan for you in your
school, church, family, and circle of friends.

**What are some ways God can "show up" through you?**

SEPTEMBER 4                                    BREATHE IN, LIVE OUT

*All Scripture is breathed out by God and profitable for teaching,
for reproof, for correction, and for training in righteousness,
that the man of God may be competent, equipped for every good
work. (2 Timothy 3:16-17 ESV)*

Have you ever gotten into trouble by listening to someone's
advice? God has made it possible for us to get perfect advice! The
One who is running the universe has written a book! This book
never changes in its content; yet through it God speaks to anyone's
unique circumstances, giving instruction, hope, correction, and
direction.

Today's passage says that Scripture is "breathed out by God."
This doesn't mean that it is always easy listening to God.
Sometimes God speaks clearly to us, and sometimes God says
things we don't like to hear. Other times what we read is so

confusing that we need others to help us understand. Regardless, God breathes his specific thoughts for our lives through his word!

So here's a question: who do you go to when you need direction? Doesn't it make sense to go to God, who is wise, good, and in control?

*When has the word of God spoken to your unique circumstances, giving instruction, correction, direction, or hope?*

## SEPTEMBER 5        LITTLE BY LITTLE, EVERY DAY

*"One who is faithful in a very little is also faithful in much, and one who is dishonest in a very little is also dishonest in much."*
*(Luke 16:10 ESV)*

No one expects a new runner to finish a marathon after training for only one week. Likewise, spiritual growth takes time, a good coach, and practice.

Jesus' followers radically changed the course of history after they saw their Lord rise from the grave. Yet their faith did not develop overnight. Jesus lived with them for about three years. During that time, Jesus taught them, loved them, and rebuked them. He sent them off on shopping errands, had meals with them, and worked miracles.

Growing in faith means learning to trust God by seeing life through his word. How does growth happen? The answer is the same today as it was then: little by little. God doesn't expect you to do more than you are capable of, but God does want you to grow!

Start by trusting God with the little things, and in time you will learn to trust him with bigger things. As you trust in God, keep your eyes fixed on the One who rose from the grave!

*What can you trust God with this week? (Praying in your cafeteria before you eat? Texting a person who needs encouragement? Applying last Sunday's message?)*

SEPTEMBER 6                                    DID YOU DO IT?

*But be doers of the word, and not hearers only, deceiving your-*
*selves. (James 1:22 ESV)*

Sometimes Christians equate knowing more with growing in
faith. But James teaches that if faith does not eventually act out,
that faith is potentially dead faith! Believers must be wary of desiring knowledge over action.

Let's pick up from yesterday's devotional. Did you do the little
that you set out to do? If not, continue that commitment today!

Compared to Christians in other parts of the world, followers of
Jesus in the United States have tons of Christian music to listen to,
books to read, churches to choose from, and pastors who desire to
teach them. Today's verse reveals that with this abundance of
knowledge comes a call to action.

As you attend Christian gatherings, small groups, or church
worship services, train yourself to be one who not only hears, but
who also actively tries to figure out how to apply what is learned!

*What is the most recent thing you have learned from God's*
*word?*

*How can you apply this learning in your life this week?*


SEPTEMBER 7                          WHEN GOD IS QUIET

*The Lord is not slow to fulfill his promise as some count slow-*
*ness, but is patient toward you, not wishing that any should*
*perish, but that all should reach repentance. (2 Peter 3:9 ESV)*

Do you ever feel that God is silent, absent, or distant? Perhaps
you see injustice, suffering, and violence, and wonder *Where is*
*God?* On a personal note, why do we keep sinning? One answer is
that we keep sinning because we haven't gotten caught!

Yet even if God is silent, that does not mean he's absent. If you
think about it, this verse is both an encouragement and a warning.

It is an encouragement because it reminds us that God will act and bring all things to good. It is also a warning because it calls us to repent and believe. This verse confronts those who reject God and also affects those who continue in sin, thinking that God's silence equals absence.

We are tempted to look outside ourselves when seeing injustice and wrong, but today's text teaches us to first take a deep look inside! God is encouraging us to be holy willingly. God sees everything. God is loving, patient, and above all, present!

***How does it make you feel to know that God is patient with you?***

SEPTEMBER 8             PRAYING THROUGH DECISION
MOMENTS

*Then the king said to me, "What are you requesting?" So I prayed to the God of heaven. And I said to the king, "If it pleases the king, and if your servant has found favor in your sight, that you send me to Judah, to the city of my fathers' graves, that I may rebuild it." (Nehemiah 2:4-5 ESV)*

Sometimes people ask you for something or ask you to do something. According to how you respond to these requests, the direction of your life will be set. There will be important decisions you have to make on the spot, and most of the time you won't even recognize these moments as "decision moments."

Nehemiah was an exiled Israelite desiring to go back to devastated Jerusalem in order to rebuild it. He served King Artaxerxes, the ruler of the time, in whom he had found favor. The king asked what Nehemiah wanted. Instead of blurting out his heart, Nehemiah prayed! Then he spoke. Nehemiah was aware that he was before King Artaxerxes, but even more he was aware that they all were before the King of Kings. Nehemiah acknowledged that God was King, and he wanted to speak from God's heart.

When in a decision moment, pause and acknowledge who is King. Pray, then answer.

***What decision do you need to make at this time?***

***How is God leading you in making this decision?***

SEPTEMBER 9                                    BIG GOD, BIG PASSION

*In the year that King Uzziah died I saw the Lord sitting upon a throne, high and lifted up; and the train of his robe filled the temple. (Isaiah 6:1 ESV)*

Some people have more power than others. Perhaps you are struggling today because someone has an influence in your life that you can't accept. Perhaps you are blessed today because someone good has good influence in your life.

Isaiah was one of God's prophets. King Uzziah had been a relatively good and successful king, and the nation thrived under his rule. When Uzziah died, there was worry in the kingdom because people had noticed a trend throughout history: good king, good times; bad king, terrible times!

In the midst of this, God blessed Isaiah with a vision that changed his life—and that can change your life as well. Kings may come and go; presidents, coaches, and bullies also may come and go. Their influence is always temporary. However, God is forever enthroned as King. He is in control of all things. He is supremely powerful and supremely good. When we, like Isaiah, lift our eyes from our circumstances and see that God alone is King, peace and endurance follow. When Isaiah recognized this, he gave his life passionately and sacrificially to God.

*How are you giving your life passionately and sacrificially to God?*

*How can you demonstrate passion and sacrifice in service to God this week?*

SEPTEMBER 10                        GRUMBLING OR STRUGGLING?

*Do all things without grumbling or questioning.*
*(Philippians 2:14 ESV)*

Everywhere we look, someone is complaining. Some complain about the economy; others complain about homework. Some complain about politicians; others complain about their parents. Yet the Bible tells us not to grumble or complain.

In the Old Testament, many people grumbled and complained to God. Some were killed and others were comforted. That should make us wonder: is there a right way to complain to God?

The answer is found in the heart. One heart grumbles and says, "God, you're really messing up here! Fix this, because I know what is better!" Another heart struggles, saying, "God, I know you are good and wise, but this is just so difficult! Give me strength!"

Do you see the difference? One attacks God while the other depends on God. One comes before God as a critic; the other comes to God as a trusting son or daughter. Which heart is yours?

*What is the difference between a grumbling heart and a struggling heart?*

*How can we share our struggles and questions with God while honoring God at the same time?*

SEPTEMBER 11    THE RESURRECTION AND THOSE
                WE CAN'T STAND

*Behold! I tell you a mystery. We shall not all sleep, but we shall all be changed, in a moment, in the twinkling of an eye, at the last trumpet. For the trumpet will sound, and the dead will be raised imperishable, and we shall be changed.*
                        *(1 Corinthians 15:51-52 ESV)*

Truth be told, I don't like everyone. I'm a pastor, so that may come as a shock. But there are some people I struggle to be patient with. Can you relate? Can God change us so that we love and even like these people?

One answer comes from God's promise of the Resurrection. One day our bodies will be raised in a new nature, and our souls will be without sin. We will be raised in the glory that now belongs to God alone. And God himself will be there. This life is short; what follows is eternal.

The Resurrection helps us see all people in their future glory now. Our words and actions are meant to help others become what they are promised one day to be. This hope is possible for all who will believe. Do your words and actions help others toward this hope?

*Who do you find it difficult to be around?*

*How could viewing this person through the lens of the Resurrection help you love this person?*

## SEPTEMBER 12        WHO'S IN CHARGE? (PART 1)

*Let every person be subject to the governing authorities. For there is no authority except from God, and those that exist have been instituted by God. Therefore whoever resists the authorities resists what God has appointed, and those who resist will incur judgment. (Romans 13:1-2 ESV)*

Today's verse makes two clear points. First, all governments and authority structures have been established and placed by God. Even moms and dads, school principals, and police officers fall under this category. Second, we are to submit to these authorities. The implication is clear: whenever we fail to submit to these authorities, we are actually rebelling against God. Underage drinking, illegal drugs, and speeding are all acts of rebellion against both God and government.

Submission to these governing authorities likewise means honoring God. Submission to these laws equals saying to the Lord, "I trust that you are good and that you are in control. To honor you, I submit to these earthly governments." When you obey those in authority over you, you are worshiping God.

*What authorities in your life do you need to submit to, and how?*

SEPTEMBER 13               WHO'S IN CHARGE? (PART 2)

*For we know him who said, "Vengeance is mine; I will repay."*
*And again, "The Lord will judge his people."*
                                        *(Hebrews 10:30 ESV)*

Read yesterday's devotion again. Any thoughtful person will ask, "What about evil and oppressive governments? Are we to submit to those authorities as well?" The short answer is yes. The Roman Christians would soon experience a season of intense persecution. Nonetheless, the teachings of Paul were still valid for them. In Romans 13:7, Paul told them to faithfully pay their taxes to this soon-to-be-oppressive government. Jesus even called his followers to pray for those who would persecute and abuse them (Luke 6:28).

Christians can take comfort in knowing that there will be a day of judgment. God will one day expose and judge all things. This includes authorities as individuals. We can take comfort in knowing, however, that on the cross Jesus took the punishment for our sins.

As Christians, we are called to wait for the Lord's judgment rather than overthrow all authorities. The present calling is to live as Christ did, who, although he was rejected, prayed for and loved his enemies.

*What enemy do you need to pray for today?*

*What would it mean for you to show God's love to this person?*

SEPTEMBER 14                    THE BLAME-SHIFTING TRAP

*The man said, "The woman whom you gave to be with me, she gave me fruit of the tree, and I ate." Then the Lᴏʀᴅ God said to the woman, "What is this that you have done?" The woman said, "The serpent deceived me, and I ate."*
                                        *(Genesis 3:12-13 ESV)*

Ever since Adam and Eve, shifting blame has been a recurring problem. It's our nature to believe that we are not fully to blame for the wrongs and sins in our lives.

If we struggle in school, we blame the teachers or the material. If we fail in a personal relationship, we blame those who have had relationships with us in the past. Parents and circumstances often take the blame for the messes that we occasionally find ourselves in.

When caught in sin, Adam blamed the woman, and the woman blamed the serpent. Adam was essentially blaming God for giving him the woman. One reason we must never blame-shift is that blame-shifting ultimately blames God!

Because God will judge all things, it is important that we take responsibility for our actions and embrace repentance. There is something freeing and liberating about coming before God and others, and fully admitting our sin and responsibility.

*When have you shifted blame?*

*What actions or sins do you need to take responsibility for now, and how can you do this?*

## SEPTEMBER 15                GOD KNOWS...TOO MUCH?

*The woman answered him, "I have no husband." Jesus said to her, "You are right in saying, 'I have no husband'; for you have had five husbands, and the one you now have is not your husband. What you have said is true." (John 4:17-18 ESV)*

When people share prayer requests, they seldom share their deepest, most intimate struggles. Yet a deep longing exists within all people to be loved and accepted despite their sins and struggles.

When people share and are rejected or judged, there is anger and shame. But when people experience intimacy and transparency followed by acceptance, peace ensues.

In this world there is at least one person who is always ready to accept us as we are: Jesus. Yet unlike others, Jesus doesn't need to be told what struggles and secrets plague our lives. He knows them all, and he is neither disgusted nor surprised. The cross of Jesus reveals the depth of our sin and the depth of God's love to cover them all.

*Why do you think we try to hide our sins, struggles, and secrets from God—who knows them anyway?*

*What sins, struggles, or secrets do you need to talk to Jesus about right now? (Remember, he accepts you unconditionally, and he paid the price for all your sins.)*

SEPTEMBER 16          MAKING THE MOST OUT OF LIFE

*What do I gain if, humanly speaking, I fought with beasts at Ephesus? If the dead are not raised, "Let us eat and drink, for tomorrow we die." (1 Corinthians 15:32 ESV)*

Christianity has always been a movement of people who love God and live this love out sacrificially. What compels Christians of any age to live life so radically? The answer, historically, is the Resurrection. It is the Resurrection that transformed those who followed Jesus to live radical lives. Prior to the Resurrection, they were actually a timid and fleeing bunch!

In today's verse, Paul acknowledges that without the Resurrection, living for Jesus is absolute nonsense. But he says that because the Resurrection happened, fighting beasts (or being shipwrecked and beaten) in order to tell others of God's love is the only logical way to live!

Jesus promises that the blessings and rewards in the next life are incomparable next to the temporary problems of this life. Similarly, C. S. Lewis wrote, "Aim at heaven and you will get earth thrown in. Aim at earth and you get neither."

If you struggle with expressing God's love sacrificially, have you stopped to consider what the Resurrection means in your life today?

*How should knowing that the Resurrection is real change the way you live your life each day?*

*What if every sacrifice is actually an investment in eternity?*

## SEPTEMBER 17   SPEECH THAT CREATES GOOD

*And God said, "Let there be light," and there was light.*
*(Genesis 1:3 ESV)*

God, from the beginning, is a God who speaks and creates. In Genesis 1, God speaks and creates by the power of his word. Then God looks over his creation and declares, "Good!" God's word not only creates; it also sustains. Hebrews 1:3 claims that all of creation is held in its place at this very moment by the "word of [God's] power" (ESV). Your book, your hand, your eyes are all in place because God is sustaining at this very moment. Without God, these would dissolve into nothingness!

The nature of God's words and speech is that God always desires to create "good" and to restore broken things to "good." Jesus, the incarnation of God's word, always spoke truth, even when it was difficult to hear. On the cross, instead of cursing those who were crucifying him, he uttered, "Father, forgive them, for they know not what they do" (Luke 23:34 ESV).

God calls us, his children, to imitate him so that our words—as we keep our eyes fixed on the cross of Jesus Christ—will always be for good.

*How can our words create good?*

*How would imitating Jesus, keeping your eyes fixed on his example, change the way that you speak?*

## SEPTEMBER 18   DIFFICULT CONVERSATIONS

*Rather, speaking the truth in love, we are to grow up in every way into him who is the head, into Christ, from whom the whole body, joined and held together by every joint with which it is equipped, when each part is working properly, makes the body grow so that it builds itself up in love.*
*(Ephesians 4:15-16 ESV)*

Sin lures and deceives. Scripture makes it clear that sin entangles us like flies in a spiderweb. Once we're caught, it's very hard to be freed. Over time, even our own minds can begin to rationalize and make arguments about why sin is OK. Because sin deceives us, we need others to point sin out.

In today's verses, Paul teaches us three things. First, we are to speak the truth. In other words, we need to point sin out. Second, we must do so with love. After all, being confronted about sin is painful! Third, speaking the truth about sin in love is everyone's responsibility because everyone sins! The promise is that as we do this, the body of Christ will be built up in love.

Ask God to send someone to speak the truth to you in love whenever sin deceives you. And be willing to be God's mouthpiece if there is someone who needs to hear the truth in love. Just remember that your words must always be loving, so that they build up rather than tear down.

**When has someone spoken the truth to you in love? What happened?**

SEPTEMBER 19                                THOUGHT LIFE

*We destroy arguments and every lofty opinion raised against the knowledge of God, and take every thought captive to obey Christ. (2 Corinthians 10:5 ESV)*

God is omniscient; he knows all things. This means he knows our thoughts. Worshiping God, therefore, means that even our thoughts are brought before God's eyes and made to be worshipful.

Paul is instructing the believers in Corinth to bring their thought life under the lordship of Christ. There are a number of reasons this is important. One is that our thoughts, when entertained long enough, will birth actions, whether good or bad. In order to obey Christ, it is crucial to bring thoughts, arguments, and opinions that are in opposition to God under his control through prayer.

Develop an awareness of God and continuously ask, "God, are these thoughts pleasing to you?" When they are not, ask God to renew your mind so that you may be transformed (Romans 12:2).

**What can you do when your mind drifts toward things that are not pleasing to God?**

## SEPTEMBER 20              FORGIVENESS

*Be kind to one another, tenderhearted, forgiving one another, as God in Christ forgave you. (Ephesians 4:32 ESV)*

Because of human sinfulness, we will wrong others and be wronged ourselves countless times throughout our lives. Sometimes the pain we experience in these moments may be unbearable; other times, it may be us inflicting the suffering on others!

In Paul's mind, the question is not whether these moments will come, but how we will respond when they do. In today's verse, Paul instructs believers to forgive one another not according to how much hurt was caused or how serious the transgression was. Rather, Paul instructs believers to forgive based on God's forgiveness through Jesus. Although humanity committed the ultimate crime against God, God forgave us through the sacrifice of his innocent Son. God became the victim and paid the penalty for our sin! Likewise, when we are the victims of wrong, we are called to imitate God and absorb the penalty—rather than retaliate. Sometimes this penalty may be a dollar amount; at other times it may be emotional pain.

In a world where true forgiveness is rare, God calls us to model the infinite forgiveness he displayed toward us.

*How did you respond the last time someone wronged you?*

*Is there someone you need to forgive? How can you demonstrate forgiveness through your actions?*

## SEPTEMBER 21              "INSIDE OUT"

*Religion that is pure and undefiled before God, the Father, is this: to visit orphans and widows in their affliction, and to keep oneself unstained from the world. (James 1:27 ESV)*

God's heart is "inside out." In other words, all of the goodness, beauty, and blessings that are part of God are displayed outwardly in the universe. This display began during creation and continued after the fall of humanity in Genesis 3. God ultimately displayed all his goodness by coming in the person of Jesus. During his earthly ministry, Jesus continually displayed his heart by going after those who needed him and sharing his love. Jesus was "inside out"!

What about you? Are you living "inside out"? Do you use your time, talents, money, treasures, and prayers to bless those who have less? James writes that the religion that pleases God is not the kind in which believers forever stay within their circles, sing songs, and memorize Scripture. These good activities must ultimately produce a life that is "inside out," where orphans, widows, and the hurting are blessed. This is Christianity that pleases God!

*How does an "inside-out" Christian live?*

*How can you bless those who are hurting and in need?*

SEPTEMBER 22                                             UNITY

*"I do not ask for these only, but also for those who will believe in me through their word, that they may all be one, just as you, Father, are in me, and I in you, that they also may be in us, so that the world may believe that you have sent me."*
*(John 17:20-21 ESV)*

God is a triune God. God is three persons in one: Father, Son, and Holy Spirit. Within God, there is absolute harmony, love, communication, agreement, and understanding. There is a distinct difference within the three persons of God, but there is also a oneness among them.

Contrast this with the world. There hasn't been any significant period of time throughout history when war hasn't torn people and lives apart. These conflicts are everywhere—within marriages, families, churches, and communities.

Before his crucifixion, Jesus prayed for unity. Jesus desired oneness, harmony, and peace for his people. The incredible statement in Jesus' prayer is that when this unity is actually displayed by believers, Jesus will become believable to a world that is always in conflict. In other words, forgiving others, loving others, and sacrificing our lives for those in need is powerful evangelism. Therefore, the question that each of us needs to ask is, *Where can I bring unity?*

*Where and how can God use you to bring unity?*

## SEPTEMBER 23        HOW BADLY DO YOU WANT IT?

*When Jesus saw him lying there and knew that he had already been there a long time, he said to him, "Do you want to be healed?" (John 5:6 ESV)*

God desires to bless you. Do you want to be blessed?

Jesus asked a man who had been paralyzed for thirty-eight years whether he wanted to be healed. Why would Jesus ask that question? The answer is not as obvious as you may think. You might say, "Of course he wants to be healed, Jesus! What are you waiting for?" The simple answer is that Jesus wanted him to answer!

Suppose Jesus asked you, "Do you want to be healed?" What would that mean for you? What thing, condition, or situation would have to be changed or eliminated? What would you have to lose in your life in order to become spiritually healthy? Are you ready to be parted from that? In other words, do you *want* to be healed?

Is having a right relationship with God and others more valuable than whatever may be holding you down? This text teaches that sometimes the most difficult thing to do is not restoring wholeness, but wanting wholeness above all.

*What kind of healing do you need right now?*

*Is there something you need to lose—to part from—in order to realize this healing? Are you ready to let go?*

SEPTEMBER 24                              COUNTERFEIT SAVIOR

*The sick man answered him, "Sir, I have no one to put me into the pool when the water is stirred up, and while I am going another steps down before me." (John 5:7 ESV)*

When things get tough, what do you do? Do you drink? Do you hide? Do you find comfort in a person? Whatever your answer may be, only God can change things. Getting advice is important. Finding time to think and heal is necessary. But only God is Lord.

Notice this man's response to Jesus' question, "Do you want to be healed?" He shared how difficult it was to get into the pool. The pool was believed to have miraculous healing powers; when the water mysteriously moved, the first to get into the pool would be healed. Just imagine the scene!

The pool held a promise of healing for the invalid. He was tied to the pool with invisible chains of false hope. He was paralyzed physically and spiritually.

Perhaps you are stuck today because of someone or something that promises you freedom. Yet this promise has never been fulfilled. And you wait. This text teaches us to give up false saviors and come to God instead.

*Is there a false savior in your life—something other than God that promises you freedom, healing, or deliverance?*

*What is God calling you to do?*


SEPTEMBER 25                              MEETING REGULARLY

*And let us consider how to stir up one another to love and good works, not neglecting to meet together, as is the habit of some, but encouraging one another, and all the more as you see the Day drawing near. (Hebrews 10:24-25 ESV)*

Unlike God, we are limited beings. We have limited money and other resources, limited physical abilities, and limited length of days. Because of our limited days, God calls us to be wise in the way we live.

The author of Hebrews reminds us of our calling to stir others up to acts of love and good works. Some will stir while others will be stirred. This is encouraging to all because it acknowledges that some are more spiritually ready or mature than others, and this is normal.

The author is quick to point out that regardless of our maturity, our attendance is extremely important. We need to be in the presence of other believers in order to grow. It is impossible to love and to be loved if we're not around. Therefore, we must commit ourselves to faithful participation in worship and study with other believers.

*Why is it important to meet together with other Christians?*

*Are you involved in regular worship and Bible study? If not, find a group or church you can try this week.*

## SEPTEMBER 26          NOTHING SHORT OF EVERYTHING

*"I know your works: you are neither cold nor hot. Would that you were either cold or hot! So, because you are lukewarm, and neither hot nor cold, I will spit you out of my mouth. For you say, I am rich, I have prospered, and I need nothing, not realizing that you are wretched, pitiable, poor, blind, and naked."*
*(Revelation 3:15-17 ESV)*

The message here is clear: the Lord desires our love and passion for himself alone. The Laodiceans were once hot, but they became lukewarm because what they valued changed. Money, health, and comfort became more valuable than God.

When popularity, grades, or friends become something worth pursuing more than God himself, we risk the same fate as that of the Laodiceans.

It makes total sense. Think about it. If God is God, doesn't it make sense that God would react so dramatically to lukewarm faith? God is utterly sure that he truly is awesome, worthy, and glorious. Therefore, anything short of passionate love for him must be repulsive! That is an awesome picture of God.

*Is there anything or anyone you are pursuing more passionately than God?*

*How can you become more passionate and devoted in your pursuit of God?*

SEPTEMBER 27                              GOD'S LOVE IN TIME

*The L*ORD* appeared to him from far away. I have loved you with an everlasting love; therefore I have continued my faithfulness to you. (Jeremiah 31:3 ESV)*

I have a friend who was a stand-in in a famous Mel Gibson movie. Funny thing is that she talked about her four-tenths-of-a-second movie appearance as if she were the protagonist of the two-hour blockbuster!

In a similar fashion, we do the same thing with God's story. From beginning to end, Scripture is the account of God's creation, fall, and restoration. God is the director, and Jesus is the protagonist. In the context of eternity, our earthly lives are a microsecond in God's story. Yet unlike my stand-in friend, we have an important and strange role: to be loved by God!

Ephesians 1:3-14 tells us that God loved us before our own existence. God knew us eternally and chose to love us and forgive us in Christ, regardless of our sins, spiritual track record, and failed attempts. God's grace is center stage. When we place our own opinions above God's word, our sense of guilt above God's grace, or our comfort above others' needs, we're trying to steal the show. We are meant to live our lives in such as way that others will applaud Jesus.

*How would you explain or define your role or purpose in life?*

*Are you living your life so that others will applaud you or Jesus?*

## SEPTEMBER 28        THE EYES OF THE HEART

*Remembering you in my prayers, that the God of our Lord Jesus Christ, the Father of glory, may give you a spirit of wisdom and of revelation in the knowledge of him, having the eyes of your hearts enlightened. (Ephesians 1:16-18a ESV)*

A popular hit television show follows police units as they patrol neighborhoods and respond to different situations. Some situations involve domestic violence; others revolve around disorderly conduct; and a few document the conflict and capture of lawbreakers.

Watching the show from a living room and getting pulled over by a police officer are two completely different experiences. From a couch, the show may be interesting, but behind the wheel, with flashing lights in the rearview mirror, the experience is nerve-wracking!

Similarly, there is a difference between knowing about God and knowing God. Did you ever notice in a worship service how some people seem to be listening politely to a sermon and learning about God while others seem to be meeting him?

Prayer is essential for having a personal encounter with God. It opens the eyes of the heart. We must pray for one another—and ourselves. Many things about God cannot be learned by observation; they are learned through prayer, which opens our eyes to God.

*Do you know people who know about God but who don't know God? Begin today to pray God into their reality!*

## SEPTEMBER 29        UNENDING LOVE

*To comprehend with all the saints what is the breadth and length and height and depth, and to know the love of Christ that surpasses knowledge. (Ephesians 3:17-19 ESV)*

Whenever we receive a gift or favor, we have the urge to pay the person back. Why can't we just accept favors for free? What causes this compulsion to repay? Is it because we don't like "owing" people? Is it that we want to be polite?

How we respond to earthly gifts gives us insight into how we respond to God's grace. God gave us the infinite gift of love and forgiveness through the cross of Jesus. All our sin debts are paid off; nothing else is owed. What do we do with such a gift?

The answer is nothing—and everything. In one sense, we can't pay God back. There is nothing for us to pay back. In another sense, God wants us to completely marvel at his love, savor his grace, and love his forgiveness. This is an act of worship. And when we worship, everything changes!

*How do you tend to respond when someone gives you a gift or does you a favor?*

*Why should worship be our response to God's grace and forgiveness?*

SEPTEMBER 30                                        FUEL FOR ACTION

*We love because he first loved us. (1 John 4:19 ESV)*

Have you ever wondered how God could use you? If so, you're not alone. The truth is there are countless ways we can serve God, but we tend to pick and choose ways that don't require much risk or sacrifice on our end. After all, who wants to look weird, be rejected, or sacrifice without a guarantee of success?

The greatest miracle in history, the forgiveness and reconciliation of man with God, came at a terrible cost. Jesus was scourged and crucified! Why would Jesus choose to do this? Jesus' choice is impossible to understand unless we figure out what fueled him on during his suffering. Hebrews 12:2 teaches us that Jesus found the necessary strength in his love for us. What gave him the incredible strength to endure the cross? You! Jesus saw you, and his love for you fueled him on.

Is there anything you know God wants you to do but the cost of doing it seems too high? This is the fuel for being used by God: we love because God first loved us (1 John 4:19).

*Is there something you know God wants you to do yet you are reluctant to do it? Why?*

*Meditate on God's incredible love for you and ask God to use this love to fuel you into action.*

# OCTOBER

# Decisions, Decisions

## TEGA EWEFADA

OCTOBER 1 GOD'S WORD: OUR FINAL ANSWER

*Do not be wise in your own eyes; fear the LORD and shun evil. This will bring health to your body and nourishment to your bones. (Proverbs 3:7-8)*

As teenagers, we often find ourselves reminiscing about the "good old days" when responsibilities were few and life was carefree. Every day we are faced with decisions that will establish the kind of persons we will become. Will we choose to run our mouths upon hearing a juicy rumor, or will we practice self-discipline? Will we lower our standards to hang out with the group everyone wants be friends with, or will we choose to stand alone on our morals? Some decisions are harder than others.

Our lives are the outcome of the choices we make. Sometimes the problems we face don't have a simple solution. Sometimes a situation feels like a trick question; sometimes it feels like perhaps there should be an exception. Nevertheless, when it comes down to it, God's word needs to be our "final answer" when making every decision. It's only when we refer to God that we can be sure we are making the right decision. When we put God's word before what our emotions may dictate, we become healthier in every way.

This month we will explore how God's word can help us make good decisions—in our teen years and throughout our entire lives.

*What emotion-based decisions have you made that should have been made in accordance with God's word?*

## OCTOBER 2        PUTTING YOUR MIND IN CHECK

*Finally, brothers, whatever is true, whatever is noble, whatever is right, whatever is pure, whatever is lovely, whatever is admirable—if anything is excellent or praiseworthy—think about such things. (Philippians 4:8)*

Every day we must fight against evil thoughts, because if we don't they will slowly tear our lives apart. Negative thoughts are like termites. Once termites grab hold of something, they slowly eat away at it until it's destroyed. What once seemed to be a minor problem soon develops into a major catastrophe. Negative thoughts can be the same way. They pop into our heads, and though we know we should get rid of them immediately, we let them take their course. Given the chance to do so, negative thoughts will grow into feelings and actions.

Instead of giving negative thoughts a chance to evolve into bad behaviors, we must nip them in the bud. Train your mind to think only good things. It may be hard to find a positive outlook on certain people or things, but it is a decision worth making. We must consciously put our minds in check. We must always remember that all emotions—even the most passionate ones such as hate—start with one negative thought.

*Can you think of any serious problems or bad habits (procrastination, lying, and such) that you have formed because of just one negative thought?*

## OCTOBER 3        GOD'S MASTERPIECE

*Thank you for making me so wonderfully complex! Your workmanship is marvelous—how well I know it.*
*(Psalm 139:14 NLT)*

With the billions of people who populate the world—or maybe with just the hundreds or thousands of people who populate your high school—we sometimes lose sight of who we are. Instead of thanking God for the talents and blessings that we have, we become jealous of others. We ask God, "Why can't I have that?" We try to live our lives according to someone else's standards, and in doing so we disappoint our Creator.

We all were created with treasures inside us. Some have a caring heart; some have a knack for numbers; and some have a musical gift. We all have something. The only one with the key to that treasure is God. It is only when we choose to seek wholeheartedly after God that we will find our treasure. It may be hard to wait patiently for God's timing; but instead of trying to be a cheap knock-off of someone else, choose to see the big picture. Imagine all the things that God, who knows you better than anyone, has in store for you.

*Have you ever, instead of choosing to search for God's plan for your life, tried to "wing it"? What happened?*

## OCTOBER 4                                   BAGGAGE CLAIM

*Cast all your anxiety on him because he cares for you.*
*(1 Peter 5:7)*

Life can be so stressful that we make really dumb decisions— decisions that include trying to solve our problems on our own. Knowing full well we have a Father in heaven who waits for us to give him our burdens, we sometimes struggle through life convinced we can figure it out on our own.

We may live in a world filled with pain and problems, but we were never meant to carry the burden alone. When Jesus lived on this earth, he experienced everything we are going through. God understands our pain and has the perfect remedy. Instead of going through life with all that weight on our shoulders, we need to give it to God. In the Bible, Peter advises us to cast our burdens. He doesn't say to set them aside or to push them to the back of our minds, but to *cast* them. Throw them! We are to fling our burdens out of our minds and into the hands of the One who will give us peace. Once we have given them to God, we are not to take them back. We're not to start worrying about them again. God will take care of it.

*What baggage do you have in your life that you need to give to God?*

223

OCTOBER 5                                          HAVE NO FEAR!

*For God has not given us a sprit of fear, but of power and of love and of a sound mind. (2 Timothy 1:7 NKJV)*

Remember when we were younger and almost everything scared us? Now that we are older, we look back and realize how ridiculous we acted. The older we get and the more educated we become, the fewer things we fear. The same goes for the fears we face as teenagers. Once we realize that we don't have to be afraid because God will always take care of us, the world becomes a less scary place in which to live.

After we watch the news and become up-to-date on all the murders and kidnappings, suddenly the world seems like a darker place. We can decide either to live in fear or to resist fear with the word of God.

Fear is easy; it comes naturally to us. When something bad happens, we instinctively begin to worry. But we must equip ourselves with God's word and rise above our fears. Instead of being defeated by the enemy's sneaky tactics, we need to tap into God's reservoir of power, love, and soundness of mind.

*What would your life be like if you always went to God for comfort when you were afraid?*

*What fears do you need to give to God now?*

OCTOBER 6                                          R-E-S-P-E-C-T

*Be devoted to one another in brotherly love. Honor one another above yourselves. (Romans 12:10)*

Teenagers are constantly being associated with words like *rebellious* and *disrespectful*. Although these words may describe some teenagers, they are not true for all of us. Having such stereotypes isn't completely bad, because it challenges us to break them.

It goes without saying that we should respect our teachers. We've known that since preschool. But why not take it one step further? As

Christians, we should always respect those who are in authority over us—not just when we are at school, but even when it's not expected from us. Unfortunately, respecting others—especially those we don't agree with—can be very hard. It is hard because in order to respect someone else, we have to humble ourselves.

Throughout our lives we will always have someone in authority over us. God doesn't tell us to try to be respectful, but to *devote* ourselves to being so. This devotion, in turn, will strengthen our devotion to God, and we will be blessed for it.

**What authority figure in your life do you need to respect?**

## OCTOBER 7          NOT JUST HAPPY, JOYFUL

*Yet I will rejoice in the LORD, I will be joyful in God my Savior.*
*(Habakkuk 3:18)*

When good things happen to us, we're happy. However, what if "happy" isn't good enough? What do you do when everything that could possibly go wrong does go wrong? It's in times like those that we need joy, because happiness just isn't going to cut it.

Happiness is dependent on our circumstances. The word *hap* means "chance, fortune." It's the root word of *happy* and *happens*. Things that happen are based on chance. Likewise, what makes one person happy may not necessarily make another person happy. However, one thing that is sure to lift anyone's spirit is the joy of the Lord.

In Habakkuk 3, Habakkuk is praying to God. His life is falling apart, but still he chooses to remain strong in his faith and to praise God. He knows his Savior will always see him through. Even when we are going through a disaster, we need to pull ourselves up by our bootstraps and emulate Habakkuk. God will give us joy and strength that aren't dependent on our circumstances.

**What are you going through?**

**In what ways do you need God's supernatural joy?**

OCTOBER 8                                    HEART TRANSPLANT

*No one has ever seen God; but if we love one another, God lives in us and his love is made complete in us. (1 John 4:12)*

When Jesus left this earth to be with his Father, he told his disciples that although he would no longer be around, he would leave a helper, the Holy Spirit. With the help of the Holy Spirit we are able to finish where Jesus left off. One thing that Jesus was very passionate about was loving others.

Jesus loved with his whole heart and treated others' pain as his own, so we must do the same. When he saw someone hurting, he didn't just overlook the person; his heart broke. He gave the biggest sacrifice of all by choosing to die a painful death because he didn't want to see us hurt.

Sometimes we get so caught up with our lives that we forget those who are desperately in need of God's love. This is why we need our Helper. If we choose to allow it, the Holy Spirit can transplant God's perfect heart in place of our imperfect one. This way we can love like Jesus did.

*Do you know anyone who desperately needs the love we have graciously received from God?*

*How might you share God's love with this person?*

OCTOBER 9                                    THE SCORE IS ZERO

*[Love] is not rude, it is not self-seeking, it is not easily angered, it keeps no record of wrongs. (1 Corinthians 13:5)*

I remember one day at school in the first grade. After we had taken our bathroom break and had returned to our seats, I found mine already occupied by another little girl. So I made a decision, which seemed completely justified at the moment, to push the girl out of the chair. As you can imagine, I got in a lot of trouble. I don't remember what punishment I received, but I still remember that incident. For weeks I refused to forgive her or allow her to be my friend—which I'm sure she probably never actually noticed. I was only hurting myself.

We've all done silly things like this before. As Christians, we need to set higher standards for ourselves. To everyone else, simple forgiveness may be good enough; but God wants us to wipe the slate clean. He knows that an unforgiving spirit impairs us physically, spiritually, and emotionally. God wants us to forgive and to forget. Like in the game of tennis, when you have "love," the score is always zero.

*Is there someone you need to forgive?*

*How can you express forgiveness to this person?*

## OCTOBER 10          LISTEN TO WHAT YOU ARE SAYING

*"Is it not the task of the ear to discriminate between [wise and unwise] words, just as the mouth distinguishes [between desirable and undesirable] food?" (Job 12:11 AMP)*

Our words can be like a pot of soup. The more water you add to a pot of soup, the less flavorful the soup is. Likewise, sometimes the more words we speak, the less meaning our words have. When we speak, we need to choose our words carefully and use diplomacy. It's better to speak just a few wise words than to ramble in an effort to make yourself seem smart. Spewing out words doesn't benefit anyone.

Because it is human nature to be self-seeking, oftentimes all we care about is what we have to say. But there is a reason that God gave us two ears and only one mouth! When we take the time to actually listen to what people are telling us, we understand what they are feeling.

Everyone wants to be heard, but sometimes it takes self-discipline to just listen. As ones who follow Christ, we need to be selfless and listen more than we speak.

*How can the Holy Spirit help you filter out "worthless talk"?*

OCTOBER 11                                                         JEKYLL AND HYDE

*"So, because you are lukewarm—neither hot nor cold—I am about to spit you out of my mouth."*
*(Revelation 3:16)*

It's really entertaining to watch movie characters with split personalities. One second they're good, and the next they have turned to the dark side. Although it may be exciting to watch the Hulk morph in the blink of an eye from an average Joe into a monster, having a split personality regarding our faith is no laughing matter.
    The fact that God says he will spit us out of his mouth shows how important it is that we not play around with our faith. God isn't a tyrannical ruler; he will not force us to do anything we don't want to do. This verse is so strongly worded because God knows that if we obey his commandments and seek after him with all we have, he will do his part. God's part is more than just a ticket to heaven; it is deliverance, prosperity, joy, wholeness, and so much more! Kick the evil Mr. Hyde to the curb and choose to live God's way.

*How would you describe a lukewarm Christian?*

*What would it mean for you to seek after God with all you have?*

OCTOBER 12                                                         THE MAGIC WORDS

*Words kill, words give life; they're either poison or fruit—you choose. (Proverbs 18:21 THE MESSAGE)*

The average person speaks thousands of words a day. Whether we realize it, each one of those words carries a lot of power. Every time we say something, whether negative or positive, it's as if we are throwing out a rope that attaches itself to something in our future. Each time we speak about a certain thing, we gradually pull it into existence. A small percentage of the things that happen in our lives are out of our control; the rest are things that we cause to happen. The life we are living today is the result of the words we spoke yesterday, the day before, and so forth.

Instead of pondering the negative, choose to speak only positive words. Speak positive words to the people who surround you— and even to yourself! God's words are powerful; the Bible says they are alive and active. When we quote God's words aloud, they unleash power.

Remember, spoken words can make you or break you.

*Are you poisoning yourself with the words you speak? (Listen carefully to the words you speak for one day. Are your words positive or negative?)*

## OCTOBER 13                                    GOOD FRUIT

*"By their fruit you will recognize them. Do people pick grapes from thornbushes, or figs from thistles? Likewise every good tree bears good fruit, but a bad tree bears bad fruit."*
*(Matthew 7:16-17)*

Your reputation is like a shadow on a sunny day. No matter how hard you try, you can't get rid of it. Since actions speak louder than words, no matter what kind of person you claim to be, your actions are the deciding factor.

Before Jesus left this earth, he commanded us to "go into all the world and preach the gospel" (Mark 16:15 NKJV). Unfortunately, as badly as we may want to share the gospel with others, some- times they just refuse to listen. This is where your reputation comes in.

Our actions are a direct reflection of our hearts. Once people begin to notice your character, they will soon realize that it comes from somewhere deeper. They will begin to wonder, *What does he or she have that I don't?*

Sometimes too many words can drive people away from God. We can't shove the Bible down other peoples' throats, but we can show them a life overflowing with peace and joy that isn't dependent on anything physical. Our actions may lead them to salvation.

*How can you witness to others by letting Christ's light shine through you?*

OCTOBER 14                    SPREADING WORDS OF LIFE

*Do not let any unwholesome talk come out of your mouths, but only what is helpful for building others up according to their needs, that it may benefit those who listen. (Ephesians 4:29)*

We can let God's love shine through us when we donate money to the poor or help build churches in third-world countries. Yet one of the simplest ways we can let God's love shine through us is by uplifting others with our words.

People do not like to be constantly reminded of their downfalls. It only makes them feel worse. Sometimes we even do this to ourselves. We demean ourselves with phrases like "I'm not good enough" or "I'll never be able to do this."

As Christians, we know this is worthless talk. We know that God has created us to do amazing things. But there are plenty of people in this world who never realize their self-worth. If you spot someone digging his or her own ditch with this kind of talk, speak words of life over the person instead. When we take the time to tell others the potential we see in them or what we love about them, we help them see the masterpiece God created them to be.

*How can you build others up with your words?*

*Who needs your encouraging words today?*

OCTOBER 15                                        GENEROSITY

*"Give to the one who asks you, and do not turn away from the one who wants to borrow from you." (Matthew 5:42)*

May I have some? Everyone seems to have one of those friends who are always asking for something. Those who act destitute may become bothersome; however, those who are generous will be blessed.

All children need to be taught how to share, and as we grow older we sometimes need to be reminded. In case you've forgotten, here's a rule of thumb: be as willing to give as you are willing to receive. Don't be that friend who is always asking, with an out-stretched hand, "May I have I some?" and then has a closed fist once the tables are turned.

Generosity is more than just good etiquette. Jesus gave as often as he could. He washed his disciples' feet, fed a multitude of five thousand, spent days on end preaching, and eventually gave his life. Giving to others brings God's love full circle. God's love is not meant to be hoarded. It's meant to be shared!

*Why do you think God asks us to share the things we have?*


OCTOBER 16 THE WOLVES, THE SNAKE, AND THE DOVE

*"I am sending you out like sheep among wolves. Therefore be as shrewd as snakes and as innocent as doves." (Matthew 10:16)*

When we accept Jesus into our hearts, we accept the responsibility to fulfill the Great Commission. In the Great Commission, Jesus tells us to go into the world and preach the gospel. He realizes this isn't always an easy task. So before he gives us a gentle nudge "out of the nest," he advises us to use wisdom and to maintain innocence.

There are plenty of things that will hinder us from spreading God's word, and God tells us to watch out for these things. Oftentimes snakes have a negative connotation in the Bible—but not in this case. Jesus wants his disciples to be on their guard, like snakes. He wants us to identify the moments when we need to tame our tongues and guard our hearts. He wants us to realize that we can't live life with one foot in and one foot out. We have to carefully choose our words and actions. We also have to make sure that the things we do are honorable.

*In what situations did Jesus take on the characteristics of a shrewd snake or an innocent dove?*

OCTOBER 17                                    KEEPING THE PEACE

*"Blessed are the peacemakers, for they will be called sons [and daughters] of God." (Matthew 5:9)*

Peace—it's more than just a 1960s fad. Peace signs look cool on T-shirts and backpacks. People sing about peace all the time. Beauty pageant contestants often say all they want is "peace on earth." We seem to be all about peace; but are we really?

Being a peacemaker means more than just holding up two fingers in a v. It is a decision to surrender yourself—sinful nature and all—to God. Having Jesus in your heart is the ultimate peace; no one knows peace better than Jesus does. This is why he calls those who choose to be peacemakers "sons [and daughters] of God." Children are made in the likeness of their parents. Likewise, peacemakers live in the likeness of their heavenly Father.

Peacemakers, like Jesus, aren't only peaceful or calm; they are constantly loving others and working to create togetherness. The peace we have on the inside of us should manifest itself in the way we act, talk, see the world, and view others.

*What are three ways that you can be a peacemaker?*


OCTOBER 18                            AT THE TOP OF YOUR LIST

*"For where your treasure is, there your heart will be also".*
*(Matthew 6:21)*

Jesus taught his disciples that if they really loved their heavenly Father as they said they did, they would be willing to trust that what God has to offer is better than anything else. It's not that God doesn't want us to have nice things or to live a comfortable life. God has been around since before the beginning of time and has seen it all. God knows houses burn down, cars break down, fashions change, and people come and go. Through it all, God is the one who always has been and always will be with us.

When we became Christians, we asked Jesus to be our Lord, not our wingman. Simply put, his way is always better than ours. Life is already hard, so why make it harder? Why would you put your trust in anything besides our everlasting, all-knowing God?

Just like the disciples, if we truly treasure God as we say we do, we will give him all of our heart.

**What things have you placed before God on your list of priorities?**

OCTOBER 19                              ZIP IT, LOCK IT, PUT IT
                                        IN YOUR POCKET

*"Do not rebuke a mocker or he will hate you; rebuke a wise man and he will love you." (Proverbs 9:8)*

Working a part-time job at a day care has taught me plenty of things. I expected to learn a lot because it is one of my first jobs, but I didn't expect to learn the finer points of communication from a group of preschoolers.

Preschoolers do what they want, when they want. Sometimes getting them to listen can be a difficult task. If I say, "Don't climb on the table, you might fall," they scream back, "No, I won't!" Actually, it's no different with us.

Someone advises you to consider hanging out with a different group of friends. You roll your eyes, mutter a retort, and soon enough you have become some kind of evil clone of yourself. If you had just taken time to consider the constructive criticism that you were given, you would have saved yourself the time and pain it took to get yourself back on track.

The Bible tells us that if we are wise, we will learn to accept constructive criticism. Instead of refusing direction, next time just "zip it, lock it, put it in your pocket."

**Do you sometimes have trouble accepting constructive criticism?**

**What was the last constructive criticism you were given and how might it benefit you?**

OCTOBER 20                                            PLUGGED IN

*These commandments that I give you today are to be upon your hearts. (Deuteronomy 6:6)*

Reading the Bible every day is like being plugged into our source of power. As strange as it sounds, human beings are like cell phones that need to be charged every day. Without our source of power (God's word), we lose the strength that keeps us going.

The book of Deuteronomy is filled with instructions for the Israelites. During the forty years that they were aimlessly wandering around the desert, they could have used all the advice they could have gotten!

Moses instructed them to keep God's word close to their hearts. He told them to impress it on their children—to talk about it when they were at home, when they were out and about, when they woke up, and when they went to bed. He even went as far as to tell them to write it on their hands, tie it to their foreheads, and put it on the doorposts of their homes!

Simply put, we need the Bible. Without it we might as well be wandering around a desert.

*How is the Bible our "source of power"?*

*What can you do to keep God's word close to your heart?*

OCTOBER 21                                       GIVING GOD GLORY

*But, "Let him who boasts boast in the Lord."*
*(2 Corinthians 10:17)*

It's elementary, my dear Watson! If you want to get anywhere in life, always remember to give credit where credit is due. We all know the story about the world's first case of sibling rivalry, but in case you forgot, here's a quick rundown. Abel gave honor to God in everything he did, but Cain refused to do the same. God honored Abel but not Cain.

When we give God the glory for the things he has blessed us

with, it shows that we really believe that God is the source of our blessings. You may already be a good basketball player, but with God's blessings you can become amazing. It's easy to take the glory when good things happen to us, but we have to remember where our blessings come from. God loves to bless his children with great things. Like any parent, God is more willing to bless you when you take the time to say thank you. In fact, don't just say thank you; tell others of the incredible God you serve!

*For what things can you give God the glory, and how will you do it?*

## OCTOBER 22                              ONE SIZE FITS ALL

*Therefore confess your sins to each other and pray for each other so that you may be healed. The prayer of a righteousness man is powerful and effective. (James 5:16)*

Prayer is our "one size fits all" cure. God is indeed omnipotent and knows exactly what's going in everyone's life, but we still need to pray. Prayer isn't the preparation for God to bring change; it is what brings change.

The encompassing advice that James gives to a body of Christians going through horrible persecution is to pray. He tells them that despite what they may be feeling (sickness, happiness, or sorrow), they need to pray. Because we have the righteousness of God described in this verse, this message applies to us also. Our prayer is powerful and effective. This power does not come from the number of times we utter our prayer or the amount of fervency we express; it is the power of God that brings the solution.

When we pray, we must remember to pray as Jesus did: with faith (without doubt) and selflessly. You don't have to let life knock you down when you are the child of the One who holds the earth in the palm of his hands!

*When have you seen or experienced the power and effectiveness of prayer?*

*What things do you need to bring to God in prayer today?*

OCTOBER 23                                              MORAL SCALE

*For He will render to every man according to his works [justly, as his deeds deserve]. (Romans 2:6 AMP)*

Don't cheat yourself out of blessings by choosing to do bad things. When you take your driver's test, do you expect to be able to complete the test halfway and still pass? Do you think entering only half of the parking space or stopping at only some of the stop signs will bode well with the tester? Then why do we sometimes do bad things and expect God to bless them?

God says that with every action we make, he will *render* something in return. The meaning of *render* implies a debt. The things that happen to you in life are indebted to you. If you continue to live life in a godly manner, you are indebted blessings. If you choose not to live life in a godly manner, you are indebted misfortune. The scale evens out.

*In what ways have you seen the moral scale affect your life?*

OCTOBER 24                                        GOD'S HEART OF GOLD

*"And if you spend yourselves in behalf of the hungry and satisfy the needs of the oppressed, then your light will rise in the darkness, and your night will become like noonday."*
*(Isaiah 58:10)*

The Bible is clear about the fact that God wants us to give to the poor. Numerous times the Bible mentions feeding the hungry, taking care of widows, and so forth. God cares about the poor and wants us to help those who are unable to help themselves. If we are followers of Christ, we will pay heed to his request.

Unlike Old Testament days, there are no laws forcing us to give to the poor or to help those in need. In the books of Exodus, Leviticus, and Deuteronomy, there are plenty of laws regarding caring for widows, orphans, and aliens. God cares so much for the less fortunate that he attaches a blessing and a curse to this commandment. He promises blessings to those who selflessly give of themselves to others. Likewise, God says that those who simply look the other way will be cursed.

This is just another example of the heart of God. As Christians, we should strive to have a heart like God's—full of compassion.

*What can you do to help the less fortunate?*


OCTOBER 25                                          SOBER UP

*As obedient children, do not conform to the evil desires you had when you lived in ignorance. (1 Peter 1:14)*

Why do people drink alcohol or do drugs? Basically, they do it to have fun, to forget their problems, or to relax. In the First Letter of Peter, Simon Peter is encouraging Christians to live a fulfilled life. He says in order to do this we have to be in full control of our speech and actions. In other words, sober up!

Purposeful ignorance is a drug because it is disabling. We need to take hold of an energetic life in Christ. Instead of running away from life's problems and slapping duct tape on them, we should face them full-force. Settling for anything but God's best only leads to sloppy living. When you choose to be ignorant, you miss out on God's reward for a faithful commitment to him.

Jesus died on the cross to steer us clear of that dead-end road we called life. We are called to holiness: a life with special purpose and discipline. Living life to the fullest is walking in holiness, reverencing God, and loving others—no intoxication needed.

*What can help you stay committed to holiness and keep focused on what God has in store for you?*


OCTOBER 26                          A FULL UNDERSTANDING

*I pray that you may be active in sharing your faith, so that you will have a full understanding of every good thing we have in Christ. (Philemon 1:6)*

Imagine that you are stranded in the middle of a desert. You are tired, hungry, and thirsty. Conveniently enough, within arm's reach is a big buffet with all your favorite foods. Wide-eyed and drooling, you look at all the food. You count the number of pieces of fried chicken in the bucket and imagine how refreshing the lemonade will taste, but you don't budge an inch. You can imagine every aspect of that meal, but you won't get the full effect until you eat it.

The Letter to Philemon is one that Paul wrote to his friend Philemon concerning Philemon's runaway slave, Onesimus. Paul advises Philemon not to be angry but to forgive Onesimus. Philemon was a godly man, so he knew exactly what forgiveness was; but until he showed forgiveness, he didn't have full understanding.

Reading the Bible cover to cover is useless unless you apply what you read. Love, forgiveness, mercy—these are all things that we need to put into practice so that we can fully understand what it means to be a Christian.

**What truths or lessons in the Bible do you need to apply in your life?**

OCTOBER 27                    YOUR MENTAL COLANDER

*Discretion will protect you, and understanding will guard you. Wisdom will save you from the ways of wicked men, from men whose words are perverse. (Proverbs 2:11-12)*

Every day we are faced with opportunities to pick and choose what we allow ourselves to believe. If we didn't protect our minds, they would be corrupted. Thankfully, God's word is always true. This is why we need God's wisdom, not just biblical knowledge.

Instead of just reading God's word and stopping there, we need to try to understand it and make it useful. The Bible is filled with Old Testament stories and New Testament parables that often seem irrelevant to our lives. Instead of just skimming through, ask the Holy Spirit to help you apply God's word to your life.

When we are filled with God's word, it's as if we gain a mental colander that separates the lies we hear from the truth. We should equip ourselves with God's word so that when we are faced with a difficult situation we can ask ourselves, *What does the Bible say about that?*

**What Bible verse can you apply to a problem you're having now or have had recently?**

## OCTOBER 28 WHO FRAMES YOUR THINKING?

*"Leave your country, your people and your father's household and go to the land I will show you." (Genesis 12:1)*

Abraham was blessed without measure because of his willingness to obey God. In today's verse, we see that God told him to leave his friends, family, and home; and in verse 4 of the same chapter, he did it. Four verses are all it took to sum up Abraham's obedience.

It must have been hard for Abraham to leave everyone he loved and everything he was accustomed to, but he knew he had to do it. He may not have known exactly what the future held for him, but he knew that God had something amazing planned.

The Bible makes it very clear how much friends can influence our lives. The people we call our friends help shape the decisions we make and help frame our thinking. We can hinder God's blessings with the decisions we make, which are influenced by our friends.

God may not ask you to pack up and leave home, but he may ask you to distance yourself from ungodly people. Abraham's life did a complete 180 once he decided to pack up and follow God. Yours could do the same.

**Do you need to rethink some of your friendships?**

**How is God calling you to obedience at this time in your life?**

OCTOBER 29          KEEP YOUR EYE ON THE PRIZE

*If you fully obey the LORD your God and carefully follow all his commands I give you today, the LORD your God will set you high above all the nations on earth. (Deuteronomy 28:1)*

It's pretty simple: if we obey God, we'll be blessed. The book of Deuteronomy is filled with blessings that God wants to give us. God will bless our families and everything to which we put our hands. God will even fight off our enemies for us. It's pretty obvious that God has our backs, but first we need to fully obey him—not partially, not when we feel like it or when it's convenient, but *fully*.

The next verse doesn't just say that God will sprinkle our lives with blessings. No, the blessings will overtake us. The stereotypical definition of *blessings* is "things and money," but God's blessings aren't limited to material objects. God's blessings will empower us to succeed. Wealth is merely the by-product.

Every aspect of our lives will be overflowing with God's blessings. But here comes the hard part: obedience. God calls the path of righteousness long and narrow. Carefully following God's commandments is no easy task, but we need to keep our eye on the prize because it's worth it!

*Are you missing God's blessings because of disobedience?*

*What would it mean for you to fully obey the Lord right now?*

OCTOBER 30          KRYPTONITE

*I will praise the LORD at all times. I will constantly speak his praises. (Psalm 34:1 NLT)*

Praise affects the enemy the same way kryptonite affects Superman: it weakens his power. We need to praise God at all times, not only in good times.

When we need to memorize a speech, we repeat it several times until it sticks. Praising God, even in negative circumstances, is not only humbling; it reminds us of God's blessings and stirs up our faith. Praising God keeps our minds off our problems and focused on the amazing God we serve.

If we praise God and ignore the enemy's attempts to distract us from God, we will foil the enemy's plans. Even doctors have said that there is healing power in a joyful spirit. The enemy knows that God has amazing plans for your life. The enemy also knows that if he can keep you depressed and away from God, you will never amount to much. Don't allow yourself to be defeated. Use praise as kryptonite!

*When have you observed or experienced the power of praise?*

*What can you praise God for today?*

OCTOBER 31                    WHO ARE WE TO JUDGE?

*"Do not judge others, and you will not be judged."*
*(Matthew 7:1 NLT)*

It takes only a few seconds to build a brick wall. When we judge others, this is what happens. "She didn't smile at me. She must not like me." "His family is really rich. He must be stuck-up." Some judgments are less petty than these, but they all are just as ridiculous.

When we build a brick wall by judging others, we close ourselves off from them. This would be fine if the world revolved around us, but it doesn't. As Christians, we need to love everyone, especially the "difficult people." Showing God's love opens us up to a world of possibilities. We can learn so much from those around us. Besides not being Christlike, judging others is also useless. Unfairly judging people only gives others permission to judge you.

It may seem humanly impossible to love those who irritate us, but choose to put on God's supernatural love and believe the best in others. Instead of spending time nit-picking at peoples' flaws, think about which things you can change about yourself.

*Instead of judging others, what personal flaws can you work on?*

# NOVEMBER

# Staying on the Right Path

## ANJELYKA SHAW

NOVEMBER 1                                    DON'T GIVE UP

*The LORD is my shepherd, I shall not be in want. (Psalm 23:1)*

God is top priority for me because he is always there when I need him. I don't have to worry because I know he will always guide my path. God is my shepherd.

My family moves a lot, and most of the time I have to start over, which means new schools, teachers, and friends. I remember when I had to move to Florida at the end of one school year. It was really hard for me to meet new people. Everyone already had friends, and it was difficult for me to make the transition. When I found the right church, the young people made me feel welcome. Some even went to my school. I knew that if I did not give up on God, did not worry, and stayed strong in my faith, God would always be there for me, guiding my way.

No matter how hard things are going, always keep praying and don't give up. The things you're waiting for might be only a prayer away.

It's hard to stay on the right path, but God will help and guide us. This month we will look at how we can stay on that right path with God's help.

*Was there a time when you did not give up on God and eventually found what you were looking for?*

*How does your faith help you stay on the right path?*

NOVEMBER 2                    TRUST THE LORD TO DO
                                  THE RIGHT THING

*Trust in the Lord and do good; dwell in the land and enjoy safe pasture. (Psalm 37:3)*

Why do so many people think it is wrong to do the right thing? From this scripture and from my experiences, I know that not doing good and not trusting in the Lord will lead you nowhere. It is hard at times to do the right thing, but if you trust the Lord, you will be able to do the right thing.

We all have times when someone tries to get us to do something that we know is wrong. But it is up to us to choose the path we want to take. You don't want to regret later making the wrong decision. Trust in the Lord with all your heart, and he will guide you.

There are moments when nothing is going the way you want it to, and making the wrong choice seems like the best thing, but you really should think about how your choices will affect you later.

*Describe a situation when you had to choose to do the right thing. How did you feel after making your choice?*


NOVEMBER 3          GOD IS WITH YOU IN EVERYTHING

*I lift up my eyes to the hills—where does my help come from? My help comes from the Lord, the Maker of heaven and earth.*
*(Psalm 121:1-2)*

My help is from the Lord, and I know the Lord is involved in my life. At this moment in time, the economy is not in great shape and many people are having financial issues. Even if at this very moment you are in a bad situation, think of what you do have. Think of every single good thing that has happened to you today. No matter how small it is, know that it is from God. Also know that he will always be there. God made this earth, and he shows us miracles every day.

When things seem really bad, you may start to go through your days without noticing the good things. You may stop seeing God's grace. But he is there, no matter what. Just don't give up on him, and never stop looking for the work of God. Think of the things that remind you of opening your heart to experience God's grace, and know that God is there.

*How is God involved in your life right now?*

*What are the things that remind you of God?*

## NOVEMBER 4          GOD WILL FIGHT FOR YOU

*"Do not be terrified; do not be afraid of them. The LORD your God, who is going before you, will fight for you."*
*(Deuteronomy 1:29-30)*

At school and at many other places, you will meet different people and encounter different situations. God will be with you and fight for you during each of those times. You have to know that.

I remember when I had just moved to a different school and people made fun of me. It hurt. That was a very difficult time for me. Even though people didn't accept me the way I was, I found ways to stay strong. I found a friend who understood me. I also stayed after school to help teachers instead of dealing with the people who didn't want to make me feel welcome. God was with me the whole time.

I had to deal with that situation, and I now use it as knowledge to help me. I've learned not to care what people think of me or my faith or the things I do. I don't hold back, and now I have friends who like me for being myself. I'm not afraid, because I know God will fight for me.

*When has God fought for you?*

*How did he do so?*

NOVEMBER 5                                THE STRENGTH TO LIVE
                                                    DAY TO DAY

*"The LORD is my strength and my song; he has become my salvation." (Exodus 15:2)*

God protects me. There are so many bad things in this world, so many dark places where I could be this very moment. But I'm not there. I'm here and I'm safe. Every day when I wake up, I thank God for this life and for another day to live and to be the best person I can be. Living in the United States is a blessing in itself. I'm thankful that I don't live in a place where I have to practice my faith in secret. God gives me the strength to live day to day. He is there, and he lets me know that.

I can't give up, because God made me for a reason. And I am here to tell everyone that God is truly real. He is my Savior. God gives me the strength I need to be the person he wants me to be. He is my strength, my song, and my salvation. He is that for you, too! There is no one higher than God. There is no one who can replace him.

*How is God your strength? Your song? Your salvation?*

*Who is God to you?*

NOVEMBER 6                                GOD SHOWS ME THE WAY

*I have put my trust in you. Show me the way I should go.*
                                                    *(Psalm 143:8b)*

Trusting God is a huge part of my life. As a Christian teenager, I follow God and do what he asks because I know in my mind and my heart that he is right.

I deal with a lot at school. Maybe it makes it harder for me at school because I stand up for what I believe in. People may not like it, but that's too bad, because nothing is going to change my mind about God. God shows me the way. He lays it out for me. Yet

I get choices in life. If I want to continue in my faith, then I must make the right decisions. It is my choice.

I have learned that God is always there and helps me with the hardest problems. That is why I choose God's way. I know that God is there with me! I feel God's grace every day. I'm always improving in every aspect of my life because I learn things every day—sometimes in the most unexpected ways.

*How do you show that you trust God?*

*How do you see God?*

## NOVEMBER 7                    THE BIBLE HELPS

*Your word is a lamp to my feet and a light for my path.*
*(Psalm 119:105)*

The Bible contains all of God's teachings. His book is powerful and amazing in every way. Whenever I have had a bad day—when things just seem like they are out to ruin me—I read the Bible. The Bible truly does help me carry on. It gives me what I need to be who I am. It reminds me that God is there, watching over me.

One day I was in the lunchroom at school and I really didn't think I could go though the rest of the day. Every minute, there was bad news of people being hurt or people hurting others. I opened my Bible, which I carry around with me, and the first words I saw helped me tremendously. They calmed me completely. I knew I was going to be OK. I didn't have to worry any longer because I knew God would guide me through my day. He would show me the good parts of the day, even if I couldn't see them right then.

God has his way of working in our lives. The Bible helps me know that.

*What does the Bible mean to you?*

NOVEMBER 8                                    THE WAY I LIVE MY LIFE

*"Man looks at the outward appearance, but the LORD looks at the heart." (1 Samuel 16:7)*

So many people, mostly girls, care way too much about what they wear. It's all about who looks the best and who has the best design-er clothes. No one seems to really care who the nicest or the most caring person is.

This is one reason I choose to dedicate my life to God. I dedi-cate my life to him because he is so much more important than what people think about how you should look or what you should have in your makeup kit.

I refuse to dedicate my life to striving after what others think I should look like. God sees you for who you honestly are. When we all die, who wore the best clothes or makeup is not going to mat-ter. What will matter is how we lived our lives.

I take care of myself and try to be as healthy as possible, but I wear what I want to wear and don't try to look a certain way. I just am who I am. I live a life dedicated to God because his judgment matters the most.

*What matters most to you?*

*Why do you choose to be dedicated to God?*

NOVEMBER 9                                    LIVING WITH PEOPLE
                                              YOU DON'T LIKE

*"Love your enemies and pray for those who persecute you."*
*(Matthew 5:44)*

I do not always get along with everyone I come in contact with, and everyone does not always get along with me. I am able to accept that. This verse reminds me, though, not to hate others but to love them—no matter what. I also need to pray for those who might be choosing the wrong path to walk on.

I once met this girl who would try everything in her power to get me down. I knew I had to do the right thing, which was not to be mean to her but to show her that no matter what, she was not going to get me down. I prayed to God many times, asking him to give me the strength to be wise and to contain my anger. The girl and I never became friends, but we learned how to live with each other. I thank God for giving me the strength to do that.

*What are some ways that you show love to your enemies or people you simply don't like?*

*When has God helped you contain your anger?*

NOVEMBER 10                    WALK IN BETTER COUNSEL

*Blessed is the man who does not walk in the counsel of the wicked or stand in the way of sinners or sit in the seat of mockers. (Psalm 1:1)*

Being "in the counsel of the wicked" is not walking in the path of God. When you make the wrong choices, it affects not only you but also the people around you. When transitioning your life, you will be able to feel the difference from inside—from your emotions. When I turned my life around and became a Christian, everything was different. Because of this, I now handle situations differently. I also see things in a new light. My views have changed, and I care about things I never cared about before.

I am still learning from other Christians. They are a better counsel to walk in because I know that I want my life to be successful. I know that if I follow God's word and do what he has asked, my life will be all he has planned it to be.

*How do you know what is wrong and what is right?*

*How do you feel when you are around people who make the right choices?*

NOVEMBER 11          FORGIVING AND COMPASSIONATE

*You are a forgiving God, gracious and compassionate, slow to anger and abounding in love. (Nehemiah 9:17)*

I am not a perfect person; I make mistakes. I sin and am willing to admit it. God understands that I am human and will make mistakes. God is compassionate and forgiving. He forgives me because he knows I try to be the best Christian that I can be. He knows that I am not a perfect person. This is yet another reason I love God. He is slow to anger and gives his love to everyone.

I had a friend who had been to a church a few times. She had come to me because she had tried so many times to be a Christian. She told me that she would always feel ashamed for sinning. She did not feel worthy of God's love. I told her that he is forgiving and understanding, and I explained how his love is forever. I told her that she just needed to ask for forgiveness and truly mean it. I believe I opened her eyes to how God does forgive her and is compassionate.

God is compassionate toward you, too!

*How have you experienced God's love and forgiveness?*

*Have you told anyone else about God's abounding love and forgiveness? Explain.*

NOVEMBER 12          WHAT YOU DO NOW MATTERS

*I will be careful to lead a blameless life. (Psalm 101:2)*

As a teenager, I am trying to make the right decisions because the things I do now will affect me when I get older. You might not think so, but just think about this: if you were to start hanging out with a bad crowd—meaning people who skip class, curse, and so forth—you are going to start getting into habits. You could end up not leading the rest of your life as a Christian. Instead, you could be caught up in worldly things. But if you start to hang out with a good group and follow God's words, when you are older you are most likely going to be living the same way.

What you do now has so much impact on what happens in the future. Don't do something now that you will regret later. Choose wisely now. Be careful, because it is so easy to fall into a trap.

*What are some decisions you are making now that might influence your life in a bad way?*

*What decisions can you make now so that you will lead a good life—now and in the future?*

NOVEMBER 13            WALK THE GOOD WAY
AND REST YOUR SOUL

*"Ask where the good way is, and walk in it, and you will find rest for your souls." (Jeremiah 6:16a)*

Finding the "good way" requires reading the most reliable source first, which is the Bible. Reading it will help you understand what God did for us. It also will help you understand what God promised and what he asks from us. If you have a question about what you read, ask your parents or your pastor or youth leader to clear things up for you. Once you know what it means to walk in the good way, follow what God says and do it!

Today's scripture verse says that you will find rest for your soul if you walk in the good way. In other words, if you do the right thing, you will be at peace with who you are. The way I walk in the good way is by not giving in to peer pressure—not doing what other people tell me is cool. I just don't care about what is cool if it doesn't allow me to be true to myself and what I know is right. I also keep myself busy. The more I keep myself busy and active in my church, the less upset and stressed I am.

I find that my soul is rested when I walk in the good way.

*What are some healthy activities that can help you focus on what's good?*

NOVEMBER 14                               WE ALL NEED ADVICE

*Make plans by seeking advice. (Proverbs 20:18)*

Making plans—such as what you might want to do in life and how you will continue to live as a Christian and spread the word of God—is a good idea. A good reason for having plans is so things will go smoothly. Another good idea is getting advice from an adult you can talk to and trust.

When I have questions or when I am looking for help, I talk to my mom first. I mainly just ask her if she's busy and if she would mind if we talked. I wait for times when other people aren't around, like when we are cleaning up after dinner, or when I'm about to go to my room before bed. I also can talk to some people at my church.

It is a good idea for you to ask for advice from someone you feel comfortable with and respect. But do ask someone! We should always ask for advice, because we don't know everything. There's a lot we don't know, so we need to ask someone older, who has more experience, to answer our questions. He or she can advise us better than we can advise ourselves—better than even our friends—because he or she has more knowledge.

*Who is someone you can go to for advice?*

NOVEMBER 15                               WATCH AND LEARN

*"Observe what the Lord your God requires: Walk in his ways, and keep his decrees and commands, his laws and requirements." (1 Kings 2:3)*

You can learn a lot by observing people who are more mature and older than you. When you are at church, watch and see how the adults talk to one another as well how they show their respect to one another. Watching them is a good way to see how they walk in the Lord's way and how they handle different life situations. The more a little child learning to talk watches and listens to the people around her, the more she picks up and learns to speak. The same is true of us when we're learning how to follow Jesus.

I have noticed that when the people at my church greet one another, they shake hands and make eye contact. I also see them trying to learn and remember names. Both of these things are signs of respect. My grandmother also taught me how to be respectful of others. She explained and showed me how to take in other people's opinions and feelings. When she taught me new lessons in life, I was smart enough to actually listen and take in the knowledge she was giving me.

**What is one thing you have learned from someone who is older than you—perhaps someone at church?**

**Who is someone you can observe to learn how to follow Jesus better?**

## NOVEMBER 16                    THE REALITY OF LOVING ONE ANOTHER

*"Love one another. As I have loved you, so you must love one another." (John 13:34)*

God loved us so much that he gave his only Son to die on the cross for our sins. God also left us this command to follow and obey, even though it might be hard for us at times.

I had to learn how to love others. It was difficult at first because there are so many different types of people. People have different ways of expressing themselves. I know that I'm not going to agree with everyone on everything, but I know I can still love each person with my heart.

At the beginning of the school year, I always get assigned a new teacher and have to be in classes with people I do not know. I always ask the Lord to give me the strength to be understanding and very slow to anger. This verse helps me know that God is with me and not to give up on people or myself. I can and I must keep pursuing love, no matter how hard it seems.

**How do you live out this important command that Jesus left us?**

NOVEMBER 17                                    WHAT I KNOW IS TRUE

*I trust in God's unfailing love for ever and ever. (Psalm 52:8b)*

God's love is the only true thing you can count on. As one teen to another, I promise you that you can always trust in him. He will always keep his love for you, and he will always stand by you. God's love is a never-ending promise.

When I was younger and first decided that I wanted to dedicate my life to being a Christian, I felt overwhelming love and hope for my soul. I knew that God would always love me. I knew that his love for me was not going to go away no matter what problem, challenge, or obstacle I might have to go though.

When life gets hard for me, God is there to help. He carries me though. He shines the light on my path. I can say God's love is unfailing because I know his love is true!

*How do you see God's love as unfailing in your everyday life?*


NOVEMBER 18                                    WHEN I CHOOSE
                                               THE WRONG THING

*The LORD is good, a refuge in times of trouble. He cares for those who trust in him. (Nahum 1:7)*

There are times when we must choose to do either the right thing or the wrong thing. I hope we all know which way to choose, even in a difficult situation. The Lord is a refuge in those times of need.

After I make a wrong decision, I ask God for his forgiveness and for help in fixing the mistake that I made. At times, though, I cannot fix what I have done. That's when I learn the most from what I've done. I also learn things from other people when they tell me their past mistakes as well as their right choices.

Every day in school and in all the places I go, I face new things. In all this, I know that God is there to help me be the person he asks me to be. I trust him, especially in the hard situations. Then it's up to me to walk in faith and make the right decisions.

*Remember a time when you made a bad decision. How did you get through that time?*

*How is God your refuge?*

## NOVEMBER 19                              GOD IS GRACIOUS

*Return to the LORD your God, for he is gracious and compassionate, slow to anger and abounding in love. (Joel 2:13)*

When you make a mistake it is OK to come back to the Lord. He will be there for you to help you because he is gracious. God gave us free will, and that alone shows me he is gracious and compassionate. Free will means that we can choose to be with God, and it is so wonderful to know that we can choose to walk with God. Not everyone does.

I remember once I made the wrong decision not to tell the whole truth one day at school. I ended up telling a huge lie. Then, in the end, I told the truth. It would have been much easier if I had been honest from the beginning. I asked God to forgive me, and I had to learn from what I did; and I felt like God knew that.

Learning things every day and making mistakes is part of being human, but consciously deciding to do the right thing is exercising free will. It's up to us. With God's help, it is much easier.

*Describe the first time you were aware that God was showing you abounding love.*

*When has God forgiven you for something that you did? How did it make you feel?*

## NOVEMBER 20                              PRAY EVERY DAY

*"Evening, and morning, and at noon, will I pray . . . and [God] shall hear my voice." (Psalm 55:17 KJV)*

Every day the first thing I do when I get up is pray, because I want to thank God for allowing me to live another day on the earth, to serve him, and to spread his word among everyone I meet. I also pray many times throughout the day. I know that throughout the day I can go to God in prayer to help me with problems, big or small. I pray to God before a test, asking him to help me. I also pray that I can influence other people in a positive way with my actions. I have no idea what it would feel like to go one day without the Lord by my side, giving me the strength to move on and make the right choices.

God helps me see the world with a positive outlook. God helps me see where people need help, and I reach out to them. I try to show them that God is worth everything and more. God has truly changed my life. "Because of this, I believe we should pray every day and give thanks for every single thing, big or small."

**When are times you pray to God?**

## NOVEMBER 21                      WHO I TRUST FIRST

*Some trust in chariots and some in horses, but we trust in the name of the LORD our God. (Psalm 20:7)*

There are many materialistic things in this world, and it is very easy to become attached to things that entertain us. But when the world comes to an end, none of these earthly things we interact with every day are going to matter. That is why it is very important to be aware of how much feeling you're putting into something that is materialistic, something you can touch. We are to trust in and rely on God, not material things.

Whenever I'm playing a video game or just listening to music, I still try to remember the importance of God. Music cannot save me; only God can. That is why I try my best not to let anything become the thing I turn to when I'm upset or feeling down. I go to God first; then I might try to cool down by listening to music or playing some video games. I trust in God and rely on God, turning to God first.

**What do you turn to first when you need comfort or help?**

**Explain a time when God was there for you. At that moment, how did you feel?**

NOVEMBER 22          WHEN YOU ARE MISTREATED

*If your enemy is hungry, give him food to eat; if he is thirsty, give him water to drink. In doing this, you will heap burning coals on his head, and the LORD will reward you.*
*(Proverbs 25:21-22)*

When you have an enemy, someone you dislike for any reason, no matter what it is, you should not be mean or hurtful toward that person. God wants you to be nice and kind to that person. If he or she needs something, give it. Don't just turn away. It can be difficult at times to be giving or kind to someone you dislike or to someone who has mistreated you, but God has asked us to do this. I see this as a test of faith.

There was a time when I met someone I did not get along with. This person did some hateful things to me. But there came a day when she needed my help in school for a community service project. I took the opportunity to show her that I was not going to have a negative reaction toward her. In the end, it felt good knowing that I had done what God had asked of me.

*When was a time you followed this command from God?*


NOVEMBER 23          WHAT'S YOUR ATTITUDE?

*A happy heart makes the face cheerful, but heartache crushes the spirit. (Proverbs 15:13)*

The type of attitude a person has can make a huge impact on how their day goes. I have learned to think positively and to see the good things that God has shown me and given me. It might be hard at times to think positively when your day seems like it's not going the way you planned. No matter what has been happening, you should look for even the smallest blessing that God is giving you.

I had a really awful day a while back. I prayed to God and asked him to open my eyes to the good of my situation. I realized at that moment that the world was not coming to an end for me and that there will always be a tomorrow.

As a practice, I don't get mad at other people or God because I know there are going to be days when things just don't work out. We all have to check our attitude about how we deal with problems in our lives. We can choose to face them with hope and optimism.

**What attitude do you have when dealing with your problems?**

**How does God help you in these times?**

NOVEMBER 24                    UNDERSTANDING GOD'S WAY

*"Walk in the way of understanding." (Proverbs 9:6)*

Walking "in the way of understanding" is walking in the right way—the way that God is showing us to follow. When you are following God's words and actually doing what he has asked, things will seem to come to a better understanding.

There was a time when I was not a Christian and things did not make much sense to me. Hearing and reading God's words from the Bible has helped me understand what I was put on this earth to do. I hear God's word when I am at church and when I talk with other Christians I respect. I also read God's word myself. Through these things, the way of understanding becomes clearer. In school I face obstacles every day, but I choose to do the right thing based on God's word.

**What are some things that you do to make sure you are making the right choice?**

**How do know that you are making the right choice?**

NOVEMBER 25                    LEARNING TO BE FAITHFUL

*For the LORD God is a sun and a shield; the LORD bestows favor and honor; no good things does he withhold from those whose walk is blameless. (Psalm 84:11)*

When I first became a Christian, I had to learn many things. One of those things was to have the right mind-set and to listen to my elders and others who are wise and have experience. I had to learn how to go though my day being strong and faithful, not giving in to doing wrong deeds. It was hard for me, but God helped me though it. He was by me every step of the way. At times I felt like there was no way I could go through the day. With prayer and devotion, I learned to stay on a right path, striving to be the best that I could be with God's help. After my struggle, I learned to walk with God and I started seeing every blessing that was given to me.

This verse is saying how God does not keep good things from coming to those who truly follow his word. God is faithful to his word.

*Do you see the blessings of each day? What are your blessings today?*

*What are some things that remind you of God's teachings?*

## NOVEMBER 26                               PRAYING DAILY

*"Ask and it will be given to you; seek and you will find; knock and the door will be opened to you." (Luke 11:9)*

I love this verse because it has proved true to me time and time again. I ask and God always provides. I seek and God reveals himself to me. I knock and I know which way to go. At times it may not be the way I expect, so I also have to be patient. That doesn't change the fact that I do know God will give me the things I truly need. And God will do the same for you.

My most common daily prayer is asking God to give me strength to follow him and to make the right choices. Daily I trust in God and know that he will provide me with what I need.

*What are some things that you ask God for?*

*Have you ever asked God for something and didn't get what you asked for, but later you found out why?*

NOVEMBER 27                    MY SONG AND MY SALVATION

*The LORD is my strength and my shield; my heart trusts in him, and I am helped. My heart leaps for joy and I will give thanks to him in song. (Psalm 28:7)*

The Lord is my strength because he provides me with all the things I need—and more—to be the person he has asked me to be. Some days seem so long, but when I am having a rough time I know that God is there to give me strength. I know that God is with me no matter what happens. It is amazing what a person can accomplish with the help of God!

The songs that are sung at my church go though my head every day. They remind me of God, and that reminds me that he will be there when I need help. There are many other signs on this earth that show us God is here with us to help and guide us in the right direction.

God is your strength. God does not give up. God is always there with you.

*What are some ways that God has guided you in the right direction?*

*How does God give you strength?*

NOVEMBER 28                              SEEKING GOOD FOR
                                        ME AND OTHERS

*Seek good, not evil, that you may live. Then the LORD God Almighty will be with you, just as you say he is. (Amos 5:14)*

Those who seek evil don't see God's grace and mercy for all his children. God asks us not to seek evil so that we can live with him.

There are many teens in my school who have no idea about God and his teachings, so that is where I come in as a Christian. I try my best to open up to different people all around my school to show them how God loves us all. I think of many different ideas to try to get the word out to other people and still be respectful. The littlest things that I do can help open the eyes of people who have not found God yet. The things that help me to keep from seeking evil are reading God's word every day and following the commands of God.

God has left us with wisdom beyond what we can comprehend, and it is there for us so that we may seek good as God has said.

*What are some ways you seek good?*

*How do you show others to seek good?*

NOVEMBER 29                      FINDING GOD WITH YOUR
                                          WHOLE HEART

*"You will seek me and find me when you seek me with all your heart." (Jeremiah 29:13)*

To truly find God, you need to put your whole heart into it. Knowing with every part of your soul that God is there will help you see the truth and become the person God wants you to be. There are so many things in this world that will tempt you to fall away from God. Seeking God with all your heart and having faith in God will help you know how to ignore evil ways. Keeping yourself involved in church and around people who you know make right choices will influence you to put your whole heart into seeking God.

One option for me is going to my church's youth group. There I feel more comfortable knowing that I will be under less pressure to do the wrong things. Another option is trying my best to make the right choices every day by reading the Bible daily. This is how as a teen I seek God and find God.

*Is your whole heart seeking after God? Why or why not?*

*What helps you find God with your whole heart?*

NOVEMBER 30                    PRAISING THE LORD TODAY

*"Praise be to the name of God for ever and ever." (Daniel 2:20)*

God is amazing in every way. I see this in the things I go through each day. Even when I'm at school, I am praising God and how he loves everyone so much that he gave his only Son to die on the cross. I praise God for giving everyone another chance. I praise God because he gave us the option to follow him, and he told us of the consequences if we don't. God asks us to praise his name forever and ever, and that is something that is not hard to do.

I happily praise the Lord throughout the day just by saying thank you for all the blessings that he gives to me. Even if the day does not seem to be going well, I still thank God for letting me be alive and letting me have new experiences every day. Praising God is something that makes me glad.

*What are some ways that you can praise God throughout the day?*

*What are some things you can praise God for?*

# DECEMBER

# From the Manger to the Cross

## BRIAN COATS

DECEMBER 1                                      BEGINNING

*In the beginning was the Word, and the Word was with God,*
*and the Word was God. He was with God in the beginning.*
*(John 1:1-2)*

Beginnings are exciting. Think of the energy and anticipation
that surrounds the first day of school, for instance, or the rush of
adrenaline baseball players feel when the umpire says, "Play ball!"

Today, we begin a new month with John's profound announce-
ment: Jesus (the Word) was with God in the beginning. Some of
John's other writings contain this idea (Jesus "is, and...was,
and...is to come"; he is "the Alpha and the Omega"), but only
John's Gospel begins—excitedly—with this truth.

For the next thirty days, we will spend time with the book of
John. It is fitting during this season of Advent, as we journey to the
manger, to read John, given his stated purpose: "that you may
believe that Jesus is the Christ, the Son of God, and that by believing you may have life in his name" (20:31). This will be a different
kind of Advent experience, for we will focus on the cross and
Jesus' sacrifice. May we remember that Bethlehem ended at
Calvary, and may we remember that the same brow that rested on
straw would one day be pierced by thorns—all for you.

*What does it mean to have life in Jesus' name? How are you*
*experiencing this life?*

## DECEMBER 2             SIN

*The next day John saw Jesus coming toward him and said, "Look, the Lamb of God, who takes away the sin of the world!" (John 1:29)*

Think back to the season of Lent—the forty days before Easter. Did you give up something for Lent—soda, perhaps, or maybe chocolate? Many people take on a Lenten discipline of sacrificing something as a way to focus on and remember the ultimate sacrifice—Jesus' death on the cross.

Jesus sacrificed himself so we could be freed from sin and freed from the wages of sin, which is death. John the Baptist has a bit of a reputation for being eccentric (having locusts and wild honey as the main staples of your diet will do that for you), but when you consider what it means for sin to be forgiven, perhaps we all should be so bold as we praise God.

*Have you ever given up something for Lent? If so, how did your sacrifice help you remember Jesus' sacrifice? Give up something today and remember Jesus' sacrifice.*

*How can remembering Jesus' sacrifice enrich our preparation for the celebration of his birth?*

## DECEMBER 3             TRANSFORMATION

*Jesus said to the servants, "Fill the jars with water"; so they filled them to the brim. Then he told them, "Now draw some out and take it to the master of the banquet." They did so, and the master of the banquet tasted the water that had been turned into wine. (John 2:7-9a)*

The weddings of two thousand years ago were festive celebrations that could often last a week or more. In our culture, the wedding and wedding reception usually do not last that long, but they too are celebrations. Recall a recent wedding and wedding reception you attended. Undoubtedly it was marked with hope, love, and good cheer.

Jesus appreciated and attended such celebration. As the wine ran out at one wedding he attended, he used his divine power to keep the wine flowing: he turned water into wine. John tells us in verse 11 that this was the first of Jesus' "miraculous signs."

Water is not the only thing capable of transformation through the touch of Jesus. The same One who changed water into wine has the power to change tear-stained desperation and loneliness into hope-filled community and friendship. Jesus can change water into wine. He also can change us. He can turn bitterness into peace, anger into joy, and hatred into love.

*What things in your life need to be changed?*

*What can you do to more fully trust Jesus to bring about that change?*

## DECEMBER 4                      BORN AGAIN

*Now there was a man of the Pharisees named Nicodemus, a member of the Jewish ruling council. He came to Jesus at night and said, "Rabbi, we know you are a teacher who has come from God. For no one could perform the miraculous signs you are doing if God were not with him." In reply Jesus declared, "I tell you the truth, no one can see the kingdom of God unless he is born again." "How can a man be born when he is old?" Nicodemus asked. "Surely he cannot enter a second time into his mother's womb to be born!" (John 3:1-4)*

Several years ago, I baptized a young lady who was about fourteen years old. A couple of years later, she shared with me that she had been doing a lot of partying. She said, "I thought I wasn't supposed to mess up anymore after I was baptized."

Immediately, I thought of the phrase "born again," which Jesus said to Nicodemus. Another way to translate the original Greek phrase is "born from above."

To be saved—to be born "again" or "from above"—is to place trust and hope in Jesus Christ as Lord and Savior, and that is not a one-time event. We fall down and we get up, all the while looking to "from above" for the strength, grace, and faith we need to keep getting up—again and again and again. Then perhaps, if we're paying attention, one day we look up and realize we're falling down a little bit less than we used to.

**Recall a time when you were given a second chance. How did that feel like a second birth?**

## DECEMBER 5                                                    LOVE

**"For God so loved the world that he gave his one and only Son, that whoever believes in him shall not perish but have eternal life." (John 3:16)**

Today's scripture is well known, of course. We see it on plaques, signs, and banners in many places. One of the quarterbacks in the 2008 Bowl Championship Series National Championship game actually had it written on the black marks under his eyes!

This scripture can summarize almost everything we are reflecting on this month. It is the main point of the Gospel of John. It *is* the gospel.

I love the word *so* in this scripture. God does not just love the world; God *so* loves the world—much like you might say, "I am *so* looking forward to Christmas!" or "I *so* can't wait until school is out for Christmas break!"

All these usages denote emphasis and importance. When you say "so," you do not just mean it, you *so* mean it. So does God.

**How do you know God loves you?**

**How have you experienced God's love?**

## DECEMBER 6                                                    WATER

**Jesus answered, "Everyone who drinks this water will be thirsty again, but whoever drinks the water I give him will never thirst. Indeed, the water I give him will become in him a spring of water welling up to eternal life." (John 4:13-14)**

Last summer our youth group finished a hard day of mission work with a trip to a spring-fed pool. It was beautiful, refreshing, and very cold. The water stays a constant sixty-eight degrees all year, as it comes straight up from the ground. Nevertheless, we all jumped in, splashed, swam, and generally had a great afternoon.

In a conversation beside a well with a Samaritan woman, Jesus talked about a spring—not a spring of cold water (although the water in that well was probably chilly too), but a spring of living water. Describing the spring, Jesus said the water would well up to eternal life. The phrase "welling up" implies force and vigor, with a meaning like "leaping up." The "water" (life) Jesus offers is more than refreshing and more than quenching. It is abundant.

*Recall a hot summer day in which you were refreshed with water. How is life in Jesus like water?*

## DECEMBER 7                                    MAGIC?

*Now there is in Jerusalem near the Sheep Gate a pool.... Here a great number of disabled people used to lie—the blind, the lame, the paralyzed. One who was there had been an invalid for thirty-eight years. When Jesus saw him lying there and learned that he had been in this condition for a long time, he asked him, "Do you want to get well?" (John 5:2-6)*

As long as there have been human beings, there have been superstitions. I'm guilty myself. In college, I had a tradition that whenever my school lost a football game, I would never wear the shirt I had worn to that game to any other game again. I ran out of shirts a long time ago, unfortunately. In John 5, people who were disabled and hurt hung out at the pool of Bethesda because they believed it had magical properties. After the water bubbled, there would be a mad rush. Can you see these people fighting, clawing, and scraping to get in the water first? And who probably won? Well, certainly not the people who needed the healing the most. The winners were probably suffering from chapped lips or hangnails.

Maybe we don't sit around waiting for bubbles and fighting others off, thinking we'll be the only ones healed; but many of us are still looking for the lucky magic charm that will lead to life eternal. However, the ultimate source of healing, hope, and salvation is found not in magic water but in the grace of God through faith in Jesus Christ. After thirty-eight years of trying, the man in John's story finally was healed. Did you notice how? It was through the touch of Jesus.

**Do you have a lucky charm or superstition?**

**What can you do to depend more on God?**

## DECEMBER 8                                    ACCESS

*When Jesus looked up and saw a great crowd coming toward him, he said to Philip, "Where shall we buy bread for these people to eat?" He asked this only to test him, for he already had in mind what he was going to do. (John 6:5-6)*

The story of the feeding of the five thousand (the actual number was probably between ten thousand and fifteen thousand!) is a familiar one. I think, though, that this story is as much about access as it is about feeding.

Think about the last time you tried to call a big company, such as your cell phone carrier, for instance. Undoubtedly that phone call began with a connection to an "interactive voice response system"—a friendly but dispassionate computer-generated voice asking you to press or say necessary numbers. In 2002 alone, companies spent around $7.4 billion to beef up their IVR systems, placing more and more layers of menus and information between themselves and their customers.

Even though Jesus saw a "great crowd" coming toward him, he made sure the people had access to him and to his power. We do not have to wade through a maze of menus in order to have access to Jesus himself. We bring our needs directly through prayer ("Ask...seek...knock"), and the CEO of the universe makes the connection with us. And as John's story makes clear, he knows what we need even before we do.

*Do you feel that you have a direct connection with Jesus? Why or why not?*

## DECEMBER 9                                        COURAGE

*When they had rowed three or three and a half miles, they saw Jesus approaching the boat, walking on the water; and they were terrified. But he said to them, "It is I; don't be afraid."*
*(John 6:19-20)*

Recently, my five-year-old daughter began moving with relative ease across suspended bars at playgrounds. This was a big deal, as she had been working on this skill for several months.

Every time I am with her, I always walk underneath her and spot her as she grabs each bar and swings to the next one. She expects that if she misses a bar, I will catch her. She knows I will never let her fall.

During the night the disciples saw Jesus walking on water, they probably thought they were seeing a ghost. But if they had thought about all they had already seen Jesus do, they could have accepted this miracle. Faith is a mind-set that expects God to act. We know God will always catch us. When we act on this expectation, we can overcome our fears.

*What is causing fear in your life right now? Take a minute to pray, asking God to give you courage to overcome your fear.*

## DECEMBER 10                                          SHINE

*When Jesus spoke again to the people, he said, "I am the light of the world. Whoever follows me will never walk in darkness, but will have the light of life." (John 8:12)*

I began a relationship with Jesus Christ in 1988. Having been a Christian for more than twenty years now, I have had plenty of opportunities to see "the light of the world" in action. Jesus' love has been a light to my path through everything life has thrown at me.

Having been a youth minister for thirteen years, I also have had plenty of opportunities to see teenagers shine their light as well. In John, Jesus says, "I am the light of the world"; but in the Sermon on the Mount, which Luke and Matthew record, Jesus encourages his followers to "let your light shine...that [people] may...praise your Father in heaven" (Matthew 5:16). On mission trips, while leading worship at church, and in unexpected acts of kindness I have witnessed teens shining their light; and it has strengthened my faith immensely.

**When have you seen the light of Jesus?**

**When have you let your light shine?**

DECEMBER 11                                                          SIGHT

*Having said this, he spit on the ground, made some mud with the saliva, and put it on the man's eyes. "Go," he told him, "wash in the Pool of Siloam" (this word means Sent). So the man went and washed, and came home seeing. (John 9:6-7)*

Life in Jesus means that people who were lost are found and people who were blind can see. That is what John Newton eventually discovered.

Newton was a slave trader from England in the eighteenth century. Late in life, he had a series of religious experiences that ultimately led to his conversion. He renounced his former profession and became an Anglican minister. Newton became a prolific hymn writer, and in 1779 he wrote "Amazing Grace." He had experienced firsthand the grace that saved "a wretch like me."

Ironically, the movie *Amazing Grace* (2007) was about William Wilberforce, the English politician who led the charge to abolish the slave trade; the character of Newton had a supporting role. In the movie, Newton tells Wilberforce, "I am a great sinner, but Christ is a great Savior."

None of us were ever slave traders, but Newton's words are ones we all can echo. If you have not seen *Amazing Grace*, take time this week to watch it.

*Have you had a "was blind, but now I see" experience? If so, have you ever told someone about it?*

## DECEMBER 12                                                     NAME

*"The watchman opens the gate for him, and the sheep listen to his voice. He calls his own sheep by name and leads them out."*
*(John 10:3)*

A name is so important. Both times that my wife was pregnant, we gave great thought and prayer to what we would name the new life growing inside of her. We spent countless hours on websites such as www.babynames.com, going through almost every female name in the English language! We took this responsibility very seriously.

In John 10, we learn that the God of the universe calls us by name. God loves you deeply, and God loves you personally. God knew you before you were born, and God knows you so well that he counts the number of your hairs on your head. At the end of the day, the story of Christ is the story of a God who desires to be in a personal relationship with each one of us. It is the story of a God who knows our name.

This must have left an impression on John, because he ends one of his letters by encouraging the believers to greet one another by name (3 John 14).

This week, seek out someone who might need an encouraging word, and remind this person that he or she is named and loved. No telling where the conversation will go after that!

*What does your name mean?*

*Is there a story associated with your naming?*

## DECEMBER 13                                                   WEEPING

*When Jesus saw her weeping, and the Jews who had come along with her also weeping, he was deeply moved in spirit and*

272 More Meditations for Teens

*troubled. "Where have you laid him?" he asked. "Come and see, Lord," they replied. Jesus wept. Then the Jews said, "See how he loved him!" (John 11:33-36)*

As the noise of an increasingly busy world gets louder, so do the cries. But do we hear them? And if we do hear them, how do we respond? Do we respond as Jesus did, by weeping? When you survey the scene of human need and despair—poverty, corruption, disease, natural disaster, lack of sanitation, lack of education— what emotions, if any, well up inside you?

Like Jesus, the church—Christ's body—can and should be God's instrument on earth that proclaims resurrection. The church can be God's instrument that works to unbind the grave clothes and proclaim life.

**What does it take to be the sort of church that hears, weeps, and responds?**

**Is your church that kind of church?**

## DECEMBER 14                                          POWER

*When he had said this, Jesus called in a loud voice, "Lazarus, come out!" The dead man came out, his hands and feet wrapped with strips of linen, and a cloth around his face.*
*(John 11:43-44)*

The story of the raising of Lazarus is the final and most spectacular of the seven most fully described public miracles or "signs" Jesus performs in John's Gospel. Remember the others? They were: turning water into wine, the healing of the official's son, the healing of the paralyzed man by the pool, feeding of the five thousand, walking on water, and the healing of the man born blind.

In John, the miracles are always performed in public and are done so that nonbelievers will believe in Jesus. The miracles serve to publicly make Jesus' identity as the Son of God apparent to all. Perhaps that is why John—like Matthew, Mark, and Luke—is sometimes called "the evangelizer."

**Are you an "evangelizer"?**

*What do you say or do to make Jesus' identity as the Son of God apparent?*

## DECEMBER 15                                EXPECTATION

*The next day the great crowd that had come for the Feast heard that Jesus was on his way to Jerusalem. They took palm branches and went out to meet him, shouting, "Hosanna!" "Blessed is he who comes in the name of the Lord!"*
*(John 12:12-13b)*

In varying degrees, there is something in all of us that loves competition. This is especially true on the playing fields and courts, but we also want to be the best in the classroom and on the job. This drive is not in and of itself a harmful thing, except that we are not too good at controlling it. It spins out of control to excesses that lead to poor sportsmanship at minimum and hatred, anger, and violence at most. In either case, our competitive nature ignites our sinful nature.

On Jesus' triumphal entry into Jerusalem, the crowd was interested in being better. They wanted a better king. They wanted a better life. In Jesus, they saw the possibility of both. So they treated him like a king as he entered the city. So much of what is happening here is tied to expectation. The people expected victory—the victory that would come when the Messiah led them to freedom and salvation. But the freedom and salvation Jesus would indeed bring to those who believed came not through a sword, but through a sacrifice.

*Are you a competitive person? What brings out your competitive spirit the most?*

## DECEMBER 16                                  HEARTACHE

*"Now my heart is troubled, and what shall I say? 'Father, save me from this hour'? No, it was for this very reason I came to this hour. Father, glorify your name!" (John 12:27-28a)*

Unlike Matthew, Mark, and Luke, John does not record Jesus' prayer in the garden of Gethsemane. However, the same agony and sorrow that the other Gospel writers describe in Gethsemane, John describes here as Jesus speaks about his death at an earlier time.

Jesus could have prayed that God would save him from what was to come. He did not. Instead, he prayed that God would be glorified. In the other Gospels, he prayed, "Not my will, but yours be done."

I hope that you will not experience the depth of despair that Jesus was feeling, but there is much to learn from his prayer. Even though he did not completely understand, he chose to trust his Father. He was obedient and faithful to the very end.

***Do you trust God that much? If not, what is keeping you from trusting God more?***

## DECEMBER 17                                    PRIDE

*So he got up from the meal, took off his outer clothing, and wrapped a towel around his waist. After that, he poured water into a basin and began to wash his disciples' feet, drying them with the towel that was wrapped around him. (John 13:4-5)*

I was watching ESPN recently, and the sportscasters were talking about a football player who always desires the spotlight. They were saying that many of his actions seem to indicate he is more interested in personal success than team success. According to these commentators, this player is "all about me."

That player may have a reputation for it, but in truth we are all prideful. Pride is the root of sin because from pride come all other sins. The fact is that we center on ourselves a whole lot more than we center on others. We are great at pointing out how great we are.

Jesus challenges us to be different and to do differently, but he does more than that. He shows us the way. He shows us the way to live a life that is about the other, not about us.

***Is there a difference between being proud and being prideful?***

*How can you be proud of something, like good grades or nailing a musical solo, without becoming prideful?*

## DECEMBER 18                                            BETRAYAL

*After he had said this, Jesus was troubled in spirit and testified, "I tell you the truth, one of you is going to betray me."*
*(John 13:21)*

Survivor, *Dancing with the Stars, The Apprentice, The Bachelor, The Amazing Race,* and *American Idol*—no need to explain that list. At last count, there have been 214 reality television shows aired on network and cable television in the last eight years.

On-camera commentaries are major parts of almost all of these shows. Contestants take a break from the "reality" and remark about some of the things happening on the show. Some of these shows will frequently feature alliances, so often the commentary is about feeling betrayed after someone has broken the alliance.

Much of reality television drama is, in fact, staged—it is hardly reality. Jesus' betrayal, however, was all too real. Judas's act of betrayal set in motion a chain of events that would ultimately lead to Jesus' crucifixion. If Judas could have looked into the camera after he saw what Jesus was undergoing because of this betrayal, one wonders what Judas might have said.

*Why do you think Judas betrayed Jesus?*

*When have you felt betrayed?*

## DECEMBER 19                                            THE TRUTH

*Jesus answered, "I am the way and the truth and the life. No one comes to the Father except through me." (John 14:6)*

Early in his career, the late, great Christian singer-songwriter Rich Mullins composed a song entitled "Alrightokuhhuhamen." Mullins did not concoct a crazy new word when he titled his song. It is actually four words: *alright, OK, uh huh,* and *amen* meshed togeth-er. The song reminds us of all the great things God has done for us, and it reminds us that all we need to do is say yes (or "alright," "uh huh," and so on) to these things. "You can argue with your Maker, but you know that you just can't win," Mullins sings.

Jesus called himself "the truth." In Paul's letter to the Philippians, Paul writes that someday every knee will bow to that truth. And when that happens, everything will be "alrightokuh-huhamen."

*Would your friends and family—those who know you best—say you live your life in such a way that your knees bow before Jesus?*

## DECEMBER 20                                              REMAIN

*"As the Father has loved me, so have I loved you. Now remain in my love. If you obey my commands, you will remain in my love, just as I have obeyed my Father's commands and remain in his love." (John 15:9-10)*

If your Bible uses red letters for Jesus' words, you will notice that most of John 13–17 is red. These chapters record Jesus' last night with his disciples. During the night, he taught and prayed with his close followers whom he called "friends," and, thankfully, John recorded much of his teaching and praying.

At one point, he told a story about vines and branches. He said that we are to "remain in [his] love." Other translations use the word *abide* instead of *remain.* As I have sought to teach my young daughter what it means to remain in Christ's love, we have devel-oped a bedtime habit of examining our day and pointing out what we are thankful for. My hope is that she will come to see that God is moving and working at all times, all around her, through her and with her. I pray she will discover that all ground is holy, and that, as pastor and author Rob Bell says, "Everything is spiritual"; and as a result, I pray she will continually and constantly "remain" in the loving arms of Jesus.

*How do you remain in Christ's love?*

*Reexamining the past twenty-four hours, where have you seen God moving and working in your life?*

## DECEMBER 21                                    SACRIFICE

*"My command is this: Love each other as I have loved you. Greater love has no one than this, that he lay down his life for his friends." (John 15:12-13)*

Several years ago the youth group at the church where I was serving was preparing for a ski trip. At a pretrip meeting, I told the group that we needed one high school girl to room with the middle school girls in their condo. That was just how the numbers worked out.

One young lady did not hesitate. She raised her hand enthusiastically and said, "I will." I knew, though, that was definitely not her first choice, but she sacrificed a little for the good of the group and it was uplifting to see a young person do that.

Jesus said sacrifice is the greatest love. Jesus chose to die on a cross. He sacrificed himself for you and for me. He loves you—deeply, passionately, and intimately—and he stretched out his arms to show you that love.

*Recall a time when someone sacrificed for you. How did it make you feel?*

## DECEMBER 22                                    FRIENDS

*"I no longer call you servants, because a servant does not know his master's business. Instead, I have called you friends, for everything that I learned from my Father I have made known to you." (John 15:15)*

This is perhaps one of the most personally encouraging passages in all of Scripture. That Jesus calls his followers "friends"—the fact that Jesus calls *me* "friend"—has profound implications. It was through friendship that I first experienced the deep, life-changing love of Christ.

The summer after my sophomore year in high school, a close friend invited me to a church camp. At that camp, I was introduced to a level of love and a depth of friendship that, until then, I did not know existed. During that week, I realized the love I was experiencing was the love of Christ. I have never been the same since. It changed my life. I am now a Christian and a minister largely because of that week at church camp—the week where I saw Christ's love firsthand.

**What difference does it make to you that Jesus calls you "friend"?**

**Where have you experienced Christ's love?**

DECEMBER 23                                         PROTECTION

*"My prayer is not that you take them out of the world but that you protect them from the evil one." (John 17:15)*

A couple of years ago I spoke at a church camp. The leaders had come up with a creative and fun theme: "Department of Faithland Security" (based on the above scripture). We spent the week talking about our "weapons of faith"—things like Bible study, prayer, and Christian community. The last day, however, I told them that ultimately our "defense" is limited because we are sinful. That led into a conversation about Christ and how, at the cross, he redeemed us and saved us.

One of the consistent images John gives us of Jesus is his deep compassion. He weeps over us. He prays for us. He dies for us. And his sacrifice is the best security system from the wages of sin, which is death, ever.

**Why do we need the protection that Jesus prayed for?**

## DECEMBER 24                    INCARNATE (PART 1)

*The Word became flesh and made his dwelling among us. We have seen his glory, the glory of the One and Only, who came from the Father, full of grace and truth. (John 1:14)*

It is Christmas Eve, and today and tomorrow we will look back to earlier chapters in the book of John. Today's scripture captures the heart of what really happened in a manger behind a Bethlehem Inn. We are moving toward Christ's death and resurrection, but that journey begins with Christ's birth; that journey begins in the incarnation.

I love that Jesus chose to "dwell among us" as a baby. A baby is humble, innocent, and precious. A baby is a gift. When both of my daughters were born, it was overwhelming. It felt like God's grace was "incarnate," like God's grace was made real. God's hope, peace, joy, and love took on skin, and I have never been the same.

*When has God's love been made real to you? On this Christmas Eve—and for the rest of this month—look for the ways God's grace is being made incarnate in your life.*

## DECEMBER 25                    INCARNATE (PART 2)

*The royal official said, "Sir, come down before my child dies." Jesus replied, "You may go. Your son will live." The man took Jesus at his word and departed. (John 4:49-50)*

Merry Christmas! Perhaps you found a new Xbox or Wii under the tree this morning. When you turn on that Xbox or Wii console and begin Guitar Hero World Tour, you trust that there will be power coming out of the wall outlet and that it will be a matter of only seconds before you are mashing the green, blue, red, and yellow buttons as fast as you can.

We can put our trust in something like electricity, but sometimes we struggle to put our trust in God. Perhaps that is why the story of the royal official's son is encouraging: he trusted Jesus to heal his son, and *then* he saw a miraculous sign. Many people in

Jesus' time—and many of us—want the sign first. But Jesus consistently lifted up as a model of faith those who believed without seeing.

*Do you trust God or do you wait for a sign from God to come before you put your full faith in God?*

## DECEMBER 26                                              CRUCIFIED

*Carrying his own cross, he went out to the place of the Skull (which in Aramaic is called Golgotha). Here they crucified him, and with him two others—one on each side and Jesus in the middle. (John 19:17-18)*

Mel Gibson caused quite a stir several years ago with his film *The Passion of the Christ*. The gore and the blood were over the top, critics said. Those critics must not have been familiar with the ancient Roman practice of crucifixion, as it was one of the most horrible and torturous methods of execution in human history. Gibson's film powerfully brought to life the pain Jesus experienced. On *The Passion of the Christ* website, Gibson says that he wanted to depict Jesus' courage and sacrifice as realistically as he could.

As we celebrate Christ's birth, it is important to remember that the manger led ultimately to the cross. To help you shift your focus from the manger to the cross, you might rent *The Passion of the Christ* and watch it in a spirit of prayer and a spirit of worship.

*When you see a cross, what does it mean to you?*

## DECEMBER 27                                              DARKNESS

*Later, Joseph of Arimathea asked Pilate for the body of Jesus. Now Joseph was a disciple of Jesus, but secretly because he feared the Jews.... He was accompanied by Nicodemus, the man who earlier had visited Jesus at night. (John 19:38-39)*

During and after the Crucifixion, all of Jesus' closest followers ran away or went into hiding. His burial was left to two men who, up until Jesus' death, had followed him and learned from him only behind closed doors or under the cloak of night.

On the day between Jesus' crucifixion and his resurrection, there was so much darkness, so many secrets. Fear, uncertainty, and doubt were everywhere. Yet John tells us at the very beginning of his Gospel that a light shines in the darkness (1:5). That light is the light of Christ, and all of the darkness in the world cannot extinguish it.

*Why do you think Joseph took the time to care for Jesus' body?*

*Why was a proper burial important?*

## DECEMBER 28                                                      LIFE

*On the evening of the first day of the week, when the disciples were together, with the doors locked for fear of the Jews, Jesus came and stood among them and said, "Peace be with you!" After he said this, he showed them his hands and side. The disciples were overjoyed when they saw the Lord. (John 20:19-20)*

One of the key themes of John's Gospel is "life." In John (and only in John), Jesus calls himself the "bread of life" (6:35) and says that he has come so those who believe in him can "have life, and have it to the full" (10:10). Also, he tells Martha that he is "the resurrection and the life" and that whoever believes in him will live (11:25). The power of Jesus' victory over the grave is that these are not just words; they are truth.

Jesus disciples' were overjoyed when they saw him. They knew that everything he had said was true. The peace he spoke of was real. The life he gave was also real.

Christ the Lord is risen! Hallelujah! Today, celebrate the peace and life his resurrection means.

*Who have you told recently about the life you have found in Jesus?*

DECEMBER 29                                    PRAYER

*Jesus came and stood among them and said, "Peace be with you!" Then he said to Thomas, "Put your finger here; see my hands. Reach out your hand and put it into my side. Stop doubting and believe." Thomas said to him, "My Lord and my God!" Then Jesus told him, "Because you have seen me, you have believed; blessed are those who have not seen and yet have believed." (John 20:26b-29)*

Poor Thomas. He is the one with the reputation. He is the one forever marked, the one people are referring to when they say someone is a "doubting Thomas."

We all are doubting Thomases at some point or another. Jesus calls us to believe without seeing—to trust and have faith—but that is really hard work. Jesus knew that, though. In another story, a man who wishes for Jesus to heal his son cries out, "Help me overcome my unbelief!" Jesus then heals his son.

Jesus desires for our faith to be strong and for our faith to grow, but he helps us on that journey. Our job is to pray and go. By and by, the trust will come and the doubt will diminish.

*What causes you to doubt God? Say a prayer now that God will help you overcome that doubt.*


DECEMBER 30                                    COMMITMENT

*When they had finished eating, Jesus said to Simon Peter, "Simon son of John, do you truly love me more than these?" "Yes, Lord," he said, "you know that I love you." Jesus said, "Feed my lambs." (John 21:15)*

It is one thing to believe in Jesus; it is altogether another to serve him. Your love of Jesus is revealed in the way you love others.

During Jesus' arrest and crucifixion, Peter disowned Jesus three times. Now Jesus asks Peter three times if he loves him. Three times, Peter says he does. But Jesus' answer reveals that Peter must now demonstrate that love and commitment by serving others—by feeding Jesus' lambs.

How do you demonstrate your love and commitment to Christ? Perhaps your youth group or a friend's youth group is going on a mission trip next summer. Mission trips are excellent ways to share in and experience the love of Christ, and they are excellent ways to serve.

*Have you committed your life to Christ with your words and actions? How have you lived out that commitment with service?*

## DECEMBER 31                                      SENT

*Again Jesus said, "Peace be with you! As the Father has sent me, I am sending you." And with that he breathed on them and said, "Receive the Holy Spirit." (John 20:21-22)*

Tomorrow we turn the calendar to a new year. Undoubtedly, there will be many resolutions made. What if, in addition to the usual resolutions—eating better, making better grades, and so forth—you resolve to be "sent"?

Throughout the Bible, God sends messengers and heralds to proclaim his redemptive grace and love. He sent Moses, Jeremiah, Mary, and Peter. Most important, he sent his Son Jesus to redeem the world through love and sacrifice. Now God is sending you into a new year full of new opportunities to share the story of that redemptive love and grace. As you are sent, know that you are not going alone. The Holy Spirit is with you, guiding and directing you to reach out to a troubled world with the greatest news of all time—news that John summarized so well: "For God so loved the world that he gave his one and only Son, that whoever believes in him shall not perish but have eternal life" (3:16). Happy New Year!

*Looking back over the previous year, where did God "send" you?*

*Where do you think God may be sending you in the New Year to tell the story of his love?*